101
DISNEYLAND
TIPS

An insider guide full of time-saving
advice and lesser-known,
can't-miss experiences

Cam Bowman

101
DISNEYLAND
TIPS

An insider guide full of time-saving
advice and lesser-known,
can't-miss experiences

Cam Bowman

Edited by Roxanne Piskel
Foreword by Dawn Cullo
Contributions by Dennis Beckner

First edition
Published by Cam Bowman
Designed by Douglas Bowman

© Copyright 2013 by Cam Bowman

ISBN 978-1-49-360914-7

Printed in the United States of America

For Emma and Addison.
Never stop dreaming.

"All our dreams can come true, if we have the courage
to pursue them."
—Walt Disney

CONTENTS

WELCOME TO DISNEYLAND!.. XIII

1 BEFORE YOU GO... I

2 WHERE TO STAY II

3 PARK OVERVIEW 15

4 STRATEGY 29

5 DINING 49

6 LESSER-KNOWN EXPERIENCES 65

7 CHARACTERS 73

8 ENTERTAINMENT 81

9 MEMORABILIA 93

10 CHILDREN 103

11 ADULTS 115

12 CAUTIONS 121

13 SPECIAL NEEDS... 127

ABOUT THE AUTHOR 133

THANKS... 135

DISCLAIMER AND TRADEMARKS... 137

INDEX 139

FOREWORD

When Walt Disney's daughters were young, he took them to the Griffith Park Merry-Go-Round on Saturdays for Daddy's Day. Walt would sit on a bench, eat peanuts, and watch his daughters giggle with delight as they went around and around. It was here that the idea for Disneyland was born. He wanted an amusement park where families could have fun together. He dreamed of a park that was clean, friendly, and fun for the entire family.

Walt traveled to many other amusement parks through the years. But he never found what he was looking for, until he discovered Tivoli Gardens in Copenhagen. The park there was clean, the staff was friendly, and he could clearly see families having fun together. This was the type of amusement park Walt Disney wanted to build.

In 1948, Walt outlined his vision for Mickey Mouse Park. He wanted to build it next to his Burbank Movie Studio. He envisioned a place for people to come for studio tours. And he wanted his employees and their families to share in the joy of the park on the weekends. Walt planned to have pony rides, a train, a horse-drawn streetcar, shops, a restaurant, a town hall, fire and police stations, and a park for relaxation.

Walt's dream eventually grew too big for the small eight-acre plot of land. So he began a search for a larger piece of land. In 1953, Walt found 160 acres for purchase in the orange groves of Anaheim, California.

Construction began in July of 1954. The initial investment that Walt and his brother and business partner, Roy, secured didn't last long. Building Disneyland was an expensive project, costing $17 million to complete. Walt never gave up on his dream, even when faced with the possibility of running out of money. His passion for his project was infectious; anyone he talked to about the project became passionate about it too. Disneyland opened twelve months after construction began.

One of my favorite Walt Disney quotes is, "If you can dream it, you can do it." Walt knew how to dream big and make it happen. He believed in himself and in Disneyland with so much passion that others also believed in him. Where would we be today if we didn't have Disneyland? It's such a magical place; I can't imagine my life without it. I thank Walt each time I enter the park for having the courage to follow his dream.

Disneyland is a family tradition for many people. They come to Disneyland to celebrate birthdays, anniversaries, graduations, and just about anything else they can think of. Disneyland means something different to everyone.

For me, Disneyland is a place where I go to walk in Walt's footsteps; it's rich with Disney history. There are many aspects of Disneyland that offer us a glimpse into this history. One of my favorites is Walt's apartment above the Firehouse. Whenever I walk into Disneyland, I glance over to Walt's apartment and thank him for having the courage to follow his dream. I love seeing the numerous names painted on the windows on Main Street.

As I walk down Main Street, the names of men and women remind me of all who helped bring Disneyland to life. They each believed in Walt and his dream.

It doesn't matter if you've been to Disneyland thirty times or just once. There's something new to experience every time you visit. In this book, you'll find many tips that will make your Disneyland vacation magical. Her book is fantastic for all Disneyland guests—whether you're a guru or a first-timer, Cam has tips here to enlighten everyone.

She covers everything from the best times to ride the rides, where to find the best snacks, some lesser-known experiences, and the ins and outs of Character Dining. She even reveals a seldom-used, conveniently located restroom. I've already found her tips to be invaluable, and will be making use of them on many future trips to Disneyland.

This book functions somewhat like a checklist, because planning a Disneyland vacation can be overwhelming. Once you step foot in the park, the day goes by so fast. There is so much to do here, and this book will help keep you on track.

I hope that you'll dream about your next trip to Disneyland while reading her book. While you do, I'll be plotting out my next trip to The Happiest Place on Earth.

See you real soon.

Dawn Cullo
iamadisneynerd.com

WELCOME TO DISNEYLAND!

I remember my first trip to Disneyland like it was yesterday. I was twelve years old and it was summertime. It was blistering hot, and I probably had hair stuck to the back of my sweaty neck. The park was crowded. But I didn't notice. I was just happy to be there. I remember the magical feeling of being there the most—I never wanted it to end. Little did I know back then, it would be years before I would walk through the Disneyland turnstiles again.

Disneyland's Main Street Station has welcomed visitors since 1955.

Through most of my adult years, I only went back to the park a few scattered times. It wasn't until I married and had children that my love of Disney really ignited.

Family trips to Disneyland have been fantastic adventures for our family, and they're helping create many amazing memories. Watching our oldest spot Princess Belle for the first time was priceless. Hearing our youngest squeal with delight as she flew around in circles on Dumbo was worth all the effort it took getting her to Southern California in the first place.

Disneyland is a special place where everyone can be a kid. That kid side just comes out—the park lures it out of you. Experiencing Disney's magic again through the eyes of our children has been one of the best gifts we've been given. Over many visits and stays at the Disneyland Resort, I've learned what works and what doesn't, how to make the most of our time, and what not to miss.

Whether you've never been to Disneyland and you're planning your first trip, or you return to the park frequently, this book is for you. I've assembled a set of tips on these pages that openly share the knowledge and experience our family has accumulated over many repeat visits. I hope you'll gain valuable ideas and insight, and that your next visit to Disneyland (and every visit after) will be filled with as much magic and wonder as possible.

If you have a special Disneyland tip or two of your own that you'd be willing to share, send them to *tips@growingupgoofy.com*. I may incorporate them into a future edition, or a similar type of book. You can also subscribe to my newsletter at *GrowingUpGoofy.com* for more tips and semi-regular updates.

1

BEFORE YOU GO

If you only have one day

I get asked the same question over and over: What if we only have one day to spend at Disneyland? My short answer is, stick with the classic: spend your one day at Disneyland. Don't try to park-hop back and forth between Disneyland and California Adventure. You'll spend too much time going back and forth, exiting and re-entering, and in general, you'll walk a lot more.

Make sure you get to the park early. Arrive just before it opens, and don't try to run in different directions. Plan ahead for the areas you want to experience most and start there. If you're traveling with smaller kids, head straight to Fantasyland and hit *It's a Small World* and Toontown shortly after. Families with older kids should head toward Adventureland or Tomorrowland.

Mickey and his magical map entertain in Fantasyland.

Not everyone in your group will have the same agenda. Decide early what's important. Whether it be riding key rides, shopping for a souvenir, visiting with Characters, or getting a perfect spot for the parade. Plan to see a show where you can be entertained and get some time off your feet. *The Enchanted Tiki Room* and *Mickey and the Magical Map* are perfect for breaks. Eating can take a lot of time, and the hours of your single day are precious. So plan your meals in advance. Consider whether you want to have a sit down meal, or if quick counter service will work for your group. Just like the attractions, many dining areas have wait times too.

Most importantly, have fun, and try not to be too stressed about your day in the park. Disneyland has so much to offer your whole family. You will rarely be able to see and do everything in one day. If you find yourself low on energy, stop and grab a Dole Whip or Mickey-shaped ice cream bar, then sit and watch all the people. Quick rests are underrated at Disneyland, but they help you enjoy all the fun an activity even more.

No matter how long or short your trip is, remember... you're at The Happiest Place on Earth. Make a few precious memories, and enjoy it as much as you can.

Building the excitement

One way to get the kids, especially preschoolers, excited before a trip to Disneyland is to read them some of the classic Disney stories. There are so many great attractions based on these stories that it's a fun way to prepare for your trip. One of my favorites is *Walt Disney's*

Classic Storybook. This book has stories like Dumbo, Peter Pan, Alice in Wonderland, Snow White, and Sleeping Beauty. These are all stories that come to life throughout Fantasyland.

Should you buy an annual pass?

We live in Northern California, about a six-hour drive to Disneyland. For us, it was an easy decision to buy annual passes to Disneyland. After two trips, and spending three days in the park for each, our passes were paid for. You might be wondering if annual passes are right for you, and if you would save in the long run.

If you know you're already going to Disneyland once, and you'll be in Southern California again within twelve months, ask yourself if a trip to Disneyland that second time is a possibility. In general, the lower-cost annual passes pay for themselves with two three-day visits. If the cost will be more for individual trips, consider the annual pass option.

There are also discounts that go along with your passes. Your annual pass will get you discounts on hotels, tours, food, and merchandise. The discount range is typically 10%-20% depending on which pass you choose.

We've been buying annual passes for the last two years now. It didn't take us long to recover the up-front costs involved with the passes. Passes were easily worth it for our family of four since we end up going at least three times each year. Once our oldest daughter is in school, we may reconsider the annual pass cost, because we may not get to go as often.

Annual passes range from $269-$849, depending on whether you live near Disneyland, and what kind of blackout dates you're willing to accept. For now, children under three years of age are free, and children ages three-nine get a discounted pass. Because our first daughter's park admission was free until she turned three, we felt like we were really getting the best value for our visit.

Note that you can also opt to start with a basic park ticket (like a three-day park hopper). If you decide while you're there at the park that an annual pass makes sense for you, Disney will let you apply the cost of your park hopper ticket toward an annual pass. You just need to do the conversion before your park hopper ticket expires.

For more information about annual passes, and to see which pass might be right for you, visit Disney's website.

Make dining reservations in advance

On our earlier visits, we didn't think of making dining reservations. We were staying at a Good Neighbor hotel, and decided we wanted to eat at Goofy's Kitchen in the Disneyland Hotel. This wasn't too far away, but it was a long walk with a toddler. Our daughter was only 18 months old at the time, so we knew we needed to be there early. We arrived at the Disneyland Hotel around 5:00pm. We thought that would give us plenty of time to check in and wait. Wow, were we wrong.

Without reservations, the wait time for a table was over two hours. But once we were there, we couldn't leave. We could see Goofy hanging out, getting photos taken with other kids, and dancing to the Macarena. We waited for those two hours, but learned that we would never make this mistake again. It was a hard lesson to learn.

If you plan on doing any dining at Disneyland, especially a Character meal, plan ahead. You can make reservations up to 60 days in advance of your visit. Even if you aren't sure of your plans, make the reservation anyway. You can always change it or cancel once you get there. Otherwise, you may be facing an epic, hunger-driven meltdown at The Happiest Place on Earth.

Buy souvenirs at home

A great way to cut the cost of your Disneyland trip is to buy souvenirs at home before you go. It took us a lot of time and money before we figured this one out. We no longer spend our time and money shopping for perfect souvenirs at the park. Instead, I take time before our trip to find special souvenirs along the way. We keep them hidden from our kids until we're at the resort, where a grand unveiling makes them feel special and associated with that visit.

For instance, I found some Disney magic towels at a dollar store. They had so many Disney Princesses, Cars, and Tinker Bell Characters to choose from. At night, I'd put a new towel on our daughter's pillow so she'd discover a new one each day. Most recently, I was able to get a Tinker Bell nightshirt at the Disney Store for only $4.99!

It's helpful to keep your souvenirs small (and thus, easy to pack in your suitcase) and something your child will love. Cut down on your shopping time and save it for more fun in the park!

Know what "Day" it is

When you're planning your trip to Disneyland, check the park calendar before you go. Disneyland has many days throughout the year that are designated to individual groups and organizations.

Disney "Days" include Dapper Day, Homeschooling Day, Star Wars Day, and Gay Days. On any of these given days, both parks will have higher crowds than normal. Last year, Gay Days brought in an additional 30,000 people over one weekend.

Not only will this affect Disneyland attendance. It will also impact the price and availability of hotels, parking, and wait times. If you can avoid visiting during these high-crowd periods, you can end up saving a time and money.

Celebrating your special day

Many of us travel to Disneyland to celebrate a special occasion. Whether it be for a birthday, an anniversary, or even if this is just your first visit to Disneyland, Disney wants to celebrate with you.

We've been celebrating birthdays at Disneyland for a few years now. Both my husband and daughter have been lucky to get a few extra treats from Cast Members because they were wearing a special birthday button.

If you're at Disneyland to celebrate something special, one of the first things you should do is head to City Hall and pick up a celebration button from Guest Relations. Throughout the day, you'll hear Cast Members and park guests wishing you a happy birthday or congratulating you on your special day. Our daughter was thrilled when a surprise cupcake was brought to the table for her third birthday. Who knew the Mad Hatter could sing "Happy Birthday" so well?

Cast Members will create a celebration button for you at City Hall.

On our last trip, my husband was very happy he left his birthday button on. We ordered beignets from the Mint Julep Bar, and were pleasantly surprised to find a few extra treats of powdery goodness in our bag. You just never know who might notice and decide to do something special for you. A little extra pixie dust goes a long way!

Download maps from home

Before you leave home for Disneyland, print a couple maps from the Disney website. Having maps in hand before you go lets you get a head start on planning and familiarization with the parks. You can get a feel for dining, entertainment, restroom locations, and the overall layout of the park before you arrive. If you have special needs, the map will also give you information on what guest services are available and where to find them.

Even though we've been to the park several times, we still take a look at the park maps before we go. As our daughters get older, their needs and wants change. We let them look at the map, and show us what they want to do. It's a fun way to build the excitement before we go. Each park has a separate map in PDF form, available from Disneyland.com.

Smartphone apps

Rather than downloading and reviewing all the Disney apps that are out there, I'll focus on two I've used and why I like them. *DL Waits* (short for *Disneyland Wait Times*) and *MouseWait* are both good, each for separate reasons. Their design leaves a little to be desired, but they both offer good utility.

Use DL Waits when you want the most important information: how long are the lines at your favorite rides? You can even check this app before you head to the park to know what you're in for. They track all of the rides in Disneyland and California Adventure.

MouseWait is another app I love that's a bit more detailed than DL Waits. MouseWait's front page tells you which annual passes can be used that particular day. Depending on whether you have an annual pass or not, and what type you have, this information may or may not be valuable to you.

Also, be sure to check out MouseWait tabs at the bottom of the screen. My favorite is the resources tab for tips, secrets, and available discounts. Both apps tell you which rides are closed, which is always helpful to know in advance.

Bottom line: if you want just the simple facts, use DL Waits. If you want a lot more information, use MouseWait. Both are currently available for iOS and Android.

2

WHERE TO STAY

Disneyland Resort hotels

Disneyland has three hotels on-site: The Grand Californian, The Disneyland Hotel, and Paradise Pier Hotel. If your budget allows, I highly recommend staying at one of these three hotels. Although each hotel has a different feel and level of quality, the basic amenities are similar. The biggest differences are the decor and ambiance, and the relative cost of each.

The biggest perk to staying at one of the Disneyland hotels is the proximity to both parks. You'll be able to walk back to your hotel in just a few minutes. Or the monorail can whisk you from Tomorrowland to within steps of all three Disney Hotels. On-site hotel guests have a private park entrance to California Adventure from the Grand Californian, and they receive early entry into both parks on select days.

We've been to Disneyland enough times to try different hotel experiences. We've stayed at Good Neighbor hotels nearby, and we've stayed at Disneyland Resort hotels. I propose that it's very worthwhile to spend a little extra to stay on-site, and for several reasons. Our children are still at an age where they need to take a mid-day nap. Staying on-site allows us to get back for nap time quickly, without spending too much in transit to the hotel. Even if we skip nap time, it's still nice to have a place to take a mid-day break and regroup.

Staying on-site also makes it easier to get around. You don't need to take a lot of things with you to the park if you know all your possessions are just a few minutes away when needed. Other perks to staying at the Disney resort are the pools, dining options, and additional entertainment at Downtown Disney. These are all pieces of the experience that folks often miss when they don't stay on-site.

Good Neighbor hotels

If a Disneyland hotel is not available, there are several Good Neighbor hotels to choose from. Disney partnered up with several hotels around the Anaheim area to make sure your stay is memorable. These hotels are approved by Disney. Most are within walking distance to the Disneyland. Several hotels have their own shuttle service. The Anaheim Resort Transportation (ART) service is also available to make travel back and forth as easy as possible.

Many Good Neighbor hotels offer complimentary shuttle service, free wifi, parking, and sometimes, a free breakfast. If you're traveling with a larger party, some of these hotels have suites available. With so many Good Neighbor hotels to choose from, these are all amenities to consider when booking your vacation.

We've stayed at several of the Good Neighbor hotels. Some were over a mile away, and some were just a few blocks away. Take into consideration what is most important to your family and decide from there. With so many options, you'll find a Good Neighbor hotel perfect for you if on-site hotels are booked up, or are too pricey for your budget.

3

PARK OVERVIEW

Early entry to Main Street

If you're waiting to get into Disneyland before it opens, expect a fluid opening time. We've learned over the years that Disneyland has a loose and varied opening procedure for the park that changes from day to day. Some days, everyone waits outside the Main Gate and gets let in right at normal opening time. Other days, the front gates open thirty minutes early, but the crowd gets held back at the end of Main Street. Magic Mornings opens the park one hour earlier for those staying on-site at a Disney Hotel. The rope at the end of Main Street prevents everyone else entering the rest of the park until normal opening time.

Mickey and Minnie mugs line the shelves of a Disneyland store.

If you get lucky, and are let into the park early, but you can only go as far as the end of Main Street, take your time and look through the shops. They open when the Main Gate opens. Grab coffee, buy sunscreen, get a PhotoPass card, or use the restroom during this waiting period. Once the rope is dropped at the end of Main Street, you're free to go anywhere you want. Beware that the crowd waiting on Main Street turns into a small stampede as most walk (and others run) to be the first in line for rides that have just opened.

Lines, lines everywhere

A few days each year, Disneyland reaches capacity. We saw this happen over New Years a couple years ago. Cast Members at the front gate eventually had to turn away visitors because the park was full. If you're inside the park on one of these days, lines will form everywhere. But you can still have a great time. You just need to be smart about it.

Make no mistake; most lines will be very long. Use this time to take advantage of rides that can hold more people. Pirates of the Caribbean, Space Mountain, Jungle Cruise, and Indiana Jones tend to have faster moving lines because of the high frequency at which they can move people through each ride. Another option is to see any of the great shows you may not have seen yet. This is a great way to see *Presenting Great Moments with Mr. Lincoln*, *the Enchanted Tiki Room*, or *Mickey and the Magical Map*. These shows may not have been on your radar, but they are not to be missed.

If you must endure a long line, consider something to make the wait time seem shorter. Start the alphabet game with your kids where they must spot each letter, one at a time, in order, on someone's clothing or something they're carrying. Or buy some portable food to bring with you, and start eating it while you're in line. And always be on the lookout for hidden Mickeys. Think of anything that might distract you and your little ones. When you do this, even the longest lines can feel a bit shorter.

Try using the Railroad to get around. You might see a huge line at the station, but the train holds a lot of people at once. Trains are scheduled at each of the four stops every 5-10 minutes, so you won't be waiting long.

Guided tours

Walk through the Main Gate, under the railroad bridge, and into the Town Square, and you'll find yourself near the Guided Tour Gardens, just to the left of City Hall.

If you're going to be in the park for several days, I recommend taking one of several tours Disney offers. These tours are an additional cost beyond your park admission, and last anywhere from 2-3 hours. If you've ever wanted to know more about what Walt was thinking when creating Disneyland, *Walk in Walt's Disneyland Footsteps* is the perfect tour for you. Not only do you get a private glimpse into Walt's apartment. You'll also get to go into the lobby of the exclusive, members-only, Club 33.

Children and tweens tend to love *Discover the Magic*. They'll experience the tour through a fun, interactive treasure hunt throughout the park. During the holidays,

Disneyland offers two additional guided tours. *Disney's Happiest Haunts* is offered during the Halloween season, and *Holiday Times at Disneyland* is offered during Christmas festivities. Most tours are complemented with a collectible souvenir pin and a tasty treat.

If you think a tour might be a good idea for your family, make sure you call ahead and reserve a spot. Reservations can be made up to thirty days in advance of your arrival. These tours are popular, so don't wait to book your reservation!

What attractions are closed?

Last year, we made a critical mistake. Our daughter finally hit 40-inches tall, and we couldn't wait to take her on Big Thunder Mountain Railroad. After talking about it for weeks, we arrived at Frontierland to find it closed for an extended renovation that would last almost two years. It might as well have been an eternity. Because that's what it felt like at that moment, and we all walked away greatly disappointed.

Had we checked the Disneyland calendar before we left home, we'd have known the ride was closed for renovations. You can see any planned closures on the Disneyland or DCA calendar. And if you're staying at a Disney hotel, the Cast Member checking you in will generally give you an update on any expected park issues. Renovation closures are also printed on the weekly itinerary available at the park entrances.

Check before you go. Do this ahead of time to save everyone unforeseen disappointment. You may want to avoid any affected areas entirely.

Hidden Mickeys

Years ago, many Disney employees believed that images and shapes representing Mickey Mouse should only exist in very specific and very obvious locations. However, many of Disney's Imagineers didn't agree. So they decided to hide Mickey Mouse shapes throughout the parks as "Easter eggs." So we now have the fun of looking for the shape of a round head and two large ears everywhere we go. Where are they? You can find hundreds of hidden Mickeys everywhere throughout the resort, both inside and outside the parks.

As you walk down Main Street, U.S.A., wait for a ride, or stand in line for the elevator at one of the Disneyland Hotels, don't forget to look for Mickeys that are probably staring right at you. Next time you're looking at decorative window writing, see if you can spot Mickey's silhouette looking back at you. A perfect example: The Disneyland Casting Door located on Main Street, U.S.A. There are two Hidden Mickeys on the door. Over at Toontown there's another obvious Hidden Mickey. The Toontown public telephones have Mickeys hidden in the center of the rotary dial.

There have been several books written about Hidden Mickeys and all their clever hiding locations. Next time you're in the park, make a game out of how many each of you can find on your own. Once you start looking for them, you'll begin to realize that those little Mickeys are everywhere.

Main Street windows

One of the things that makes Disney stand out is its attention to detail. Main Street, U.S.A. is the perfect example. When you walk down Main Street, be sure to take in the details all around you. Main Street was modeled after the small town of Marceline, Missouri, where Walt Disney grew up.

Notable Disney names grace the windows on Main Street, U.S.A.

Something you'll likely notice is the set of names on windows above each storefront. These aren't just made-up names. In fact, they're names of some really cool people. The names on display are people who have had a great impact on the Disney brand at some point in time.

For example: above Carnation Café, you'll see *Golden Vaudeville Routines - Wally Boag - Prop. In honor of the great works of Wally Boag*. Above Main Street Confectioners, you'll see, *If We Can Dream It - We Can Do It! - Roy O. Disney - Dreamers & Doers Development Co.*

Whenever there is a change in the window names, Disney holds a public dedication ceremony commemorating the event. Occasionally, you can stumble upon a ceremony without even knowing it. Next time you're walking down Main Street, take a look around and see if you recognize any famous names.

Ride the railroad

Riding the railroad is a long-standing tradition at Disneyland. Walt was a huge train enthusiast. He even created a small-scale version of the railroad that stands today.

The Disneyland Railroad has been a favorite for park visitors ever since the opening in 1955. If you're visiting Disneyland for the first time, this is an excellent way to get an overview of the park from its perimeter. Hop on the train at the Main Street, U.S.A. station and take the ride around the park. You'll make stops at New Orleans Square, Tomorrowland, Mickey's Toontown, and then eventually loop back to where you started, at Main Street, U.S.A.

If you're a veteran Disneyland visitor, don't forget to utilize the train. This may seem obvious to most, but we've been guilty of running from one side of the park to another. We could have avoided the crowds and enjoyed a relaxing ride around the park at the same time.

There are typically three trains running, with an arrival about every 5-10 minutes. The ride around the entire park takes about 20 minutes.

Lilly Belle

If you're lucky, you might get a chance to see Lilly Belle on the train tracks. Lilly Belle is a special train car named after Walt Disney's wife. Some visitors get to take a ride in this beautiful train car. Lilly Belle was used as a private train car to entertain VIPs. Decorated in red velvet, stained glass, and detailed woodwork throughout, she was designed to match Walt's apartment above the Firehouse. Lilly Belle isn't always on the tracks, but she has been known to be out and ready for the first ride of the day around the park.

Taking a ride on Lilly Belle is still a well-kept secret. If you want to take your chances, which I highly recommend doing at least once, be at the train platform when the park opens. If Lilly Belle is going to be out, chances are, it will be for the first ride of the day. Always ask the Conductor if, and when, she'll be out. He or she might be able to give you an exact time to come back to ride. If you don't see the Conductor, you can also stop in at City Hall, just to the side of the train station. A Cast Member there can call the train platform for you to get the schedule for the day.

Entrance of the rarely seen, luxurious Lilly Belle train car.

Note that even if Lilly Belle is out on the track, Cast Members will not allow anyone to ride inside the car on especially hot days for safety reasons.

Mickey's Toontown

Toontown is a phenomenal little area of the park. It was designed as a three-dimensional little town for our favorite animated Characters. This interactive area is perfect for little explorers, as Toontown was made for little hands to touch everything. Since Toontown was made with younger children in mind, make sure you open, close, pull, push, look, and listen to everything around you. You never know what might be behind the next door you open.

Although Toontown is perfect for smaller children, Roger Rabbit's Car Toon Spin brings in children of all ages. Grab a Fastpass for the ride and enjoy the rest of Toontown while you wait. The Roger Rabbit Fastpass machine isn't connected to the main system, meaning you can get a pass even if you are already holding one for another ride. Be warned though; the Roger Rabbit attraction is dark and a little rough. It might not be suitable if you have sensitive little ones.

The welcoming entrance to Mickey's Toontown.

Toontown opens one hour after the park opens, and closes one hour before the park. This makes it easy to be one of the first families to experience the fun at Toontown before it gets too crowded. I recommend riding Gadget's Go Coaster early in the day, as this is one of only two rides inside Toontown, and the line gets long fast. My daughter typically begs us to ride it again and again until a line starts to build up; that's our cue to move on.

Critter Country and Tigger Tails

While I was growing up, one of my favorite shows at Disneyland was the Country Bear Jamboree. Sadly, it closed in 2001. I still get a little sad walking through that area of the park, knowing I won't ever get to see that show again. However, Disney kept with the bear theme, and introduced Critter Country with Pooh and Friends in the same location.

Bring your autograph book. Because you'll see Pooh, Tigger, and Eeyore at scheduled times throughout the day. Look for them just outside the exit of The Many Adventures of Winnie the Pooh ride.

Tigger Tails and chocolate/caramel-dipped marshmallow wands.

I also like this spot for a different reason. Just as you exit the Winnie the Pooh ride, you can walk right into Pooh's Corner. It's a small and often uncrowded gift and sweet shop where you can find the infamous Tigger Tails, or its close sibling, the chocolate and caramel-dipped marshmallow wand. This is one of my favorites and a must have on every visit. You can also see various treats being made here. A big picture window lets you get an up-close look at Cast Members making chocolates, candies, cookies, and other favorites. Stop by anytime, and they'll be making a variety of treats for the park.

Downtown Disney

Downtown Disney is a stretch of outdoor shopping, dining, and entertainment, that runs between the park entrance plaza and each of the Disneyland hotels. Downtown Disney provides a fun, lively place for a much needed break in the middle or at the end of long days. Whether you just need to regroup, escape the frenetic energy of the park, or find a place a slightly different kind of place to eat, Downtown Disney can be a great go-to spot. At a minimum, don't miss a casual stroll through Downtown Disney, possibly while enjoying an ice cream cone or a soft pretzel.

During the day, hoards of people walk to and from the hotels and parks, so Downtown Disney can sometimes get a bit crowded. However, if you already have park tickets or passes in hand, you can use the special entrance in Downtown Disney near the Disneyland Hotel, and take the monorail directly into Tomorrowland.

At night, Downtown Disney transforms and really comes to life. I love to walk around Downtown Disney because of the open space and continuous live entertainment. You'll find local artists and musicians lining the walkways entertaining young and old. Downtown Disney isn't just for the Disney resort, it's open to the public and can get very busy. If you're looking to eat dinner here, just like eating inside the park, making reservations in advance will save you time.

4

STRATEGY

Best time to go

Our two favorite times to go to Disneyland are December and April. Both months, we're typically able to walk off a few moderately popular rides and get right back on because the lines are so short. And the weather is sunny but cool. According to some Disney sites, September and May are the best months to visit. I think the logic must be that kids are either just starting school, or are still finishing school, so families are less likely to choose those months for a Disneyland vacation.

Despite the advantage of smaller crowds and shorter lines, there are a few downsides to going during off-peak months. During these times, park hours are shorter, and the weather might not be as agreeable. Rain dampens any trip to Disneyland, and hot weather can make The Happiest Place on Earth hard to bare. Off-peak times seem to be the best times to close rides for renovation, so you may not get to experience an attraction you were really eager to ride. We've been going to Disneyland the second week in December when we want to avoid the crowds. We know the park hours are shorter, but so are the lines. There is still so much to do, and we'll be waiting in lines less often. So the shorter hours don't bother us. If you're flexible with your travel times, this shouldn't stop you from going.

Keep in mind that every Saturday will be busy, regardless of time of year. Sundays are the second busiest day of the week. Summer months and holiday weekends will draw even larger crowds. Historical crowd records show that the best times to venture into the park are in

January and February (after New Years), just after Labor Day, and the few weeks between Thanksgiving and Christmas breaks.

Hit the parks early

This might seem like a no-brainer, but you'd be surprised at how many people like to sleep in while they're on vacation. Even when they're vacationing at a Disney resort.

One of the key tips to having a great experience is to get in the park early. If you have "Magic Mornings" with your passes, take advantage of that extra hour in the park. We've been able to enjoy a few more rides with the extra hour passes and avoid the lines.

On the mornings we don't have the extra hour, we plan our day to ride the more popular attractions first. If the wait is already long, we get a Fastpass. The park tends to get busy about an hour after it opens. Getting there early will help maximize your day.

If you need to purchase tickets, ticket booths open half an hour prior to the park opening. If you're driving and you get to the park early, you'll also get the best available parking spots.

Prioritize your rides

You'll be amazed at how fast the time goes by when you're inside the park. Before you know it, it's time to go and you've missed one of the most important rides on your list. Whether you're in the park for one day or multiple days, make sure you prioritize the attractions you want to ride. Basically, always ride the most important rides early in the day. Possibly even ride them first when you can. This way, you won't miss out and leave disappointed. If time permits, you'll be able to go back and ride those important rides a second or third time. But at least you won't end your visit with zero times on your most important rides.

By riding your important rides earlier in the day, you'll get them knocked off the list before the crowds get larger and the lines get much longer. Alleviating the pressure of riding your most important rides early each day, you'll also get to be choosier as the day goes on.

If your schedule doesn't allow you to ride your important rides first, take advantage of Disney's Fastpass system. Use Fastpasses as a way of ensuring you get a time to ride something later in the day, and a way to dramatically shorten your wait time in line. Obtain your Fastpasses in order, and you can plan your day without missing out on what's most important to you or your group.

Use lockers to lighten your load

The first few times we visited Disneyland, I loved having our huge stroller in the park with us. This allowed me to pack everything under the sun in the large basket under the stroller. Now that we're using a much smaller umbrella stroller, I can't do that anymore. And what about the souvenirs and gifts for family members that you might acquire throughout the day?

Fortunately, Disney provides lockers for rent. But they only exist in a few key locations, so plan accordingly.

Locker bays are located outside the Disneyland Main Gate, and another set halfway down Main Street inside Disneyland. California Adventure has a set of lockers located across from Guest Relations.

Multiple-size lockers, available via an automated payment kiosk.

Several sizes of lockers are available, and they range in cost from $7-$15 for the whole day. Use them as long as you need, and access them at any point without having to pay again. You may remember much cheaper lockers that used the old key system? Those lockers may have only been fifty cents. But you had to pay each time you wanted to open and re-lock the locker.

If you're inside DCA, and only need to store something for a short period of time, look for lockers near Grizzly River Run. These lockers are free to use for up to two hours.

Just don't forget to claim your belongings at the end of a long day at the park. Lockers are cleared out each night, and the contents are turned over to Lost and Found.

Determining ride times

Depending on what time of year you hit the park, the most popular attractions will have very long wait times. Some wait times can surpass the hour mark. There are several things you can do to avoid these long lines and get in a few more rides than usual.

A great way to avoid the busy times is to go when the majority of people are doing other things. Think about getting in line while most people are watching the parade. If you are going to be in the park a few days, you really only need to see the parade once. You can spend the rest of your time taking advantage of fewer people in line.

The lines also seem shorter during meal times, especially around the lunch hour. Plan your meals a little earlier, or later, so you can ride during the lunch rush. This will free up ride space and get you on faster.

During peak hours, ride the rides that can hold more people. Pirates, Jungle Cruise, and Indiana Jones can fit more than two at a time per ride. This will also speed up your wait time.

Located on Main Street, just to the left of the Jolly Holiday Bakery, you'll find a message board with ride times. A Cast Member provides information and keeps up to date information on ride times for the bigger attractions. This will help you find the shortest wait times and avoid hour-long (or longer) wait times.

There is a ride board in DCA as well. You can find the board across the street from Carthay Circle. These locations will always have a Cast Member available for up to date information on ride closures as well.

The Disneyland ride board provides updated ride and show times.

There are several smartphone apps you can download too. However, ride board times are updated regularly by the Cast Member and have the most current information available.

When to eat, when to ride

Many of us are accustomed to eating three meals a day, and around the same time each day. It shouldn't be much of a surprise that those meal times generally hit at the same time for most people inside the park. Over time, we've learned two things about eating at Disneyland. First, we can't eat at the same time as everyone else. This takes up more time. Two, during peak eating times, we should be riding the rides.

Most people will eat lunch between 11:30am and 1:30pm each day. If you have flexibility in your schedule, eat a little earlier or later. Since most people will be enjoying their lunch, you'll get a slight advantage on bigger attractions via shorter lines. This won't always work, especially in the summer months. But any advantage will help with popular rides. And if you're eating during off-peak meal times, you'll get to take advantage of a faster experience there too.

If you're thinking of eating at a sit-down restaurant, try to make reservations in advance, even if you need to do so the same day. Some restaurants book up in busy months, but many will still have availability right up to your preferred time. Same rules apply; make a reservation earlier or later than peak eating times to avoid the crowds. Also, chose a dining location close to the attractions you want to ride next. There are so many dining options, and so many lines to wait in, that you can really save time by planning out your next moves a bit in advance.

Optimize your time with Fastpass

If you plan on riding many rides at Disneyland, you need to understand and take advantage of Disney's Fastpass service. They're free, and anyone with an activated park ticket can get one. A Fastpass will let you skip most of the long wait for popular rides, and you'll end up much closer to the front of the line.

The person collecting Fastpasses for your group must have one activated park ticket for each Fastpass they wish to obtain. Each person must have their own Fastpass.

Use your park ticket to obtain Fastpasses from automated machines.

Pay attention to the "return" times on the pass. This window of time is when your Fastpass will be honored. Most Cast Members now strictly enforce both start and end times.

Consider grabbing Fastpasses as you're walking past a popular ride if you think you might ride it later. But note that once you obtain a Fastpass, you can't get another pass until two hours later, or until the start time of the pass you just obtained, whichever is sooner. Disneyland

and DCA are on two separate Fastpass systems. So you can get a pass for a ride in one park, and walk right over to the other park and immediately get a Fastpass for another ride there.

If you have a people in your group who may not want to (or be able to) ride certain rides, consider using a portion of your park tickets to get Fastpasses for one ride, and use the other portion to immediately get Fastpasses for another ride.

Fastpasses for Radiator Springs Racers

Radiator Springs Racers is currently the most popular ride at Disney's California Adventure. Rightly so; it's over four minutes of indoor cruising and fast outdoor racing in a six-person track car. And it's one of the most expensive attractions Disney has ever built.

The popularity of this ride draws long lines. At the shortest, you'll wait about an hour, but up to two hours at peak times of the day. To cut down Racers wait time, get a Fastpass, and get it early in the morning, immediately after park opening. Have someone in your group take all the park tickets and wait in line to get Fastpasses; send the others go to get coffee. Fastpass distribution for the Racers often concludes by mid-morning. Once that ends, there are no more Fastpasses for that day.

You won't have much choice in your return time to ride since Racers passes get distributed so quickly. If you get an early return time, but can't ride until later, try swapping with someone else coming out of the Fastpass distribution line. Most folks are eager to ride as soon as possible, and will gladly switch passes with you.

Racers Fastpasses are currently disconnected from the rest of the Fastpass system. Remember this, because you can get a Fastpass for another attraction at DCA immediately after getting one for Racers, without the normal two-hour delay.

Single-rider lines

If you have your heart set on a ride, like Radiator Springs Racers, but you failed to get a Fastpass early in the day, you might consider the single-rider line. These lines were created for people who are either truly riding alone, or who don't mind splitting up from their group to ride solo. The idea behind the single-rider line is to fill up each seat of a ride using people who are willing to fill those open slots by splitting off as a single rider. These lines are typically shorter than the regular lines and they move faster.

In Disneyland, single-rider lines are available on the bigger attractions such as Indiana Jones, Splash Mountain, and the Matterhorn. And in California Adventure, on Radiator Springs Racers, California Screamin', Goofy's Sky School, Grizzly River Run, and Soarin' Over California.

Single-rider lines can work well for parents traveling with small children. One parent can stay with the kids (or even go back to the hotel with them) while the other parent cruises through the single-rider lines. This way, at least one parent gets to experience the bigger thrill rides without the full wait-time of the normal lines.

Rider switch passes

The rider switch pass is one of the best-kept secrets around. Once you figure out how it works, it's great. One of the challenges of traveling with young kids is when one of them might be too short to ride certain rides, and one parent gets left out. A rider switch pass lets each parent enjoy the attraction with the child who is tall enough, while one stays behind with a child who can't ride. All without doubling your wait time.

Find a Cast Member once you get to the front of the line. Tell them you'd like to get a "rider switch pass" so that one parent and child can ride, while the other parent waits behind with a child who can't ride. When the first parent and child are done riding the ride, the second parent who was watching the child gets to ride without waiting in line again.

Rider switch passes are only offered on larger attractions. It's offered at both Disneyland and Walt Disney World. Take advantage of the fact that they can be used anytime on the day they are issued. We've taken advantage of the switch passes now for a while, I don't think we'd be able to enjoy ourselves as much without them. I love that you can use them anytime throughout the day. Just don't forget to use your pass if you've obtained one!

Best seats for Soarin' Over California

Soarin' is one of the best attractions at Disney's California Adventure. The ride glides you through California's treasured beaches, forests, and several major landmarks. Even though there really is not a bad seat on this ride, there are seats that will give you the best experience possible.

The seats on Soarin' are divided into three sections: A, B, and C. Each section has three rows: 1, 2, and 3. Soarin' uses a lift mechanism to suspend riders in the air, facing a giant movie screen. Section B riders are seated in the middle of the screen. The screen is curved, so riders in Sections A or C have a slightly sharper viewing angle. Row 1 gets elevated to the highest point and becomes the top row. Seats in rows 2 and 3 will have slightly obstructed views with the dangling feet from higher rows.

If wait time is not a problem, you should request Section B, Row 1 for the best view of this amazing journey that soars over California.

Mickey's Fun Wheel

Mickey's Fun Wheel offers a twist to the classic Ferris wheel. This ride offers two very different experiences. The question you have to ask yourself is "to swing or not to swing?" If you want your gondola to swing back and forth, along with the moving wheel, be prepared for a thrill ride. If you like a gentle ride, then opt for the non-swinging gondola.

I prefer the stationery gondola. However, our five-year-old loves the thrill of the swinging gondola. She will laugh and scream as the gondola swings back and forth.

When I go along for the ride, I typically squeeze my eyes shut, and I clutch the sides with both hands. If you're feeling a little queasy, motion sickness bags are tucked inside a side pocket of each car.

Mickey's Fun Wheel and Screamin' roller coaster on Paradise Pier.

This is a great ride if you have multiple people with you. The cars are spacious, and can accommodate up to six people at a time. Whether you pick the swinging or stationary gondola, riding Mickey's Fun Wheel will get you a great view of Paradise Pier, the rest of the park, and even some of nearby Anaheim. The view from the top of the Wheel is not to be missed.

Peter Pan's Flight

One of the busiest and most-loved rides at Disneyland is Peter Pan's Flight. This is one of the first rides you'll see after walking through the middle of Sleeping Beauty's Castle into Fantasyland. This ride is popular with everyone; it's one of our favorite rides. Due to the location and popularity of this attraction, the line gets long quickly.

Suspended by a overhead track, you take flight in a three person galleon. You'll be swooped right into the Darling's nursery, then down into a sleepy London. A spin around London will give you a nighttime view of Big Ben and the Tower Bridge. You'll eventually make your way through almost every scene from the original animated feature. Ultimately, Peter Pan rescues his friends and leaves Captain Hook to the crocodiles.

If you want to take flight over London and Neverland, get there early. This ride only holds two-three people at a time, so it takes longer to wind your way through the line and load onto the ride. My advice is to make this your first ride of the day. This way, you won't miss out on a favorite, and you can enjoy the shorter lines elsewhere in Fantasyland.

Avoiding sore feet

There's a lot of walking involved when you're at Disneyland. Obviously, one of the best ways to avoid those aching feet is to wear comfortable shoes. However, even with great shoes, the best of us still get tired of walking, but we want to push on. If your feet start to ache, get off them and rest. There are tons of benches scattered throughout each park if you'd just like to sit and people-watch. There are also several things you can do to get off your feet and still have fun.

Catch the Disneyland Railroad at one of their four stops every fifteen minutes. You can hop on at Main Street U.S.A., New Orleans Square, Mickey's Toontown, or Tomorrowland. If you're near Main Street, you can also grab one of the Main Street Vehicles. The fire engine, horse-drawn carriage, horseless carriage, and the Omnibus offer one-way trips down Main Street to and from the castle. Our daughter loves riding the fire engine so she can ring the bell while traveling down the street.

A horse-drawn trolley car heads down Main Street, U.S.A.

You can also give your feet a brief rest by sitting down at one of the many of the shows around either park. At Disneyland, there are shows like the Jedi Training Academy in Tomorrowland, Billy Hill and the Hillbillies at the Golden Horseshoe, and the classic Enchanted Tiki Room at the entrance to Adventureland. In California Adventure, there's Disney Junior, Aladdin, and any of the featurettes inside the Animation Building.

Staying cool on hot days

Anaheim can get hot. There are several ways to keep cool while you are in the park. First, hit the park early. Note the attractions you'll need to ride that are in direct sunlight. Visit those attractions first, so you don't have to wait in long lines in the middle of the day when it's hottest. Enjoy the cool air on indoor rides like Star Tours, Pirates of the Caribbean, and The Haunted Mansion.

Don't forget about the Enchanted Tiki Room. Grab some fresh pineapple or a Pineapple Dole Whip out front at the Tiki Juice Bar and enjoy the show. When it's hot outside, this is the perfect time to see *Aladdin*, *It's Tough to Be a Bug*, *Disney Junior*, *Captain EO* or the new, *Mickey and the Magical Map.* The Disney Animation Building in DCA also features several fun air-conditioned ways to spend a hot afternoon. Plus, you might learn something new about animation, or how to draw your favorite Disney Character. Make sure you catch a wave with Turtle Talk too!

If you don't mind getting wet, the middle of a hot day is the perfect time to hit Splash Mountain, Grizzly River Run, Princess Dot Puddle Park, or get a quick cool down in the mist at Condor Flats. Just remember to have a small towel with you. I've seen people soaked head to toe, especially on Grizzly River Run.

Plan at least one sit down meal indoors when the park is crowded and when temperatures are at their peak. This will get you recharged before you head back out. Also, hop in the stores and get your souvenirs during these times too. Even a few minutes out of the heat will help cool down your body temperature. Take a break mid-day and spend some time at your hotel pool. And most importantly, stay hydrated and plan ahead when you know the temperatures are on the rise.

Parade seating

Disney parades are fantastic. They're full of action, lots of Characters, and energetic music. I've seen the same parade more times than I can count, but it never gets old. Most importantly, my children love the parades. The key to enjoying any parade is to find a moderately comfortable spot with a good view. The parade route typically runs from It's a Small World to the Town Square promenade. Sometimes it runs in reverse, but the route is typically the same.

There are several locations along the parade route that offer good views. Spots around Town Square, all the way along Main Street, near Plaza Inn, and in front of It's a Small World will offer the best views. The parade draws big crowds, so expect to find and claim a spot at least an hour before the parade begins. Want to sit on a bench? You'll need to grab it even earlier.

Belles of the Disneyland parade on Main Street, U.S.A.

If you're visiting with several people, take turns reserving your spot. As the parade start time draws closer, expect more assertive behavior from other folks trying to find a last-minute spot of their own. Make sure your entire party is back at your spot at least fifteen minutes before the parade starts. Dense crowds make moving along the parade routes a very slow and difficult process, especially if you have a stroller.

I'll offer one last piece of parade-seating advice. Don't lay a blanket down along the parade route, and expect that you can leave it unattended in attempt to reserve your spot. Disney Cast Members routinely monitor the parade route, and will immediately remove unclaimed blankets and belongings.

5
DINING

Best Character Dining experience

Get ready to sing, dance, and give out lots of hugs. Character dining can be a once-in-a-lifetime experience. With several options available at the Disneyland Resort, you may be left wondering which Character Dining option is the best for you. Each Character Dining experience has a theme. Disneyland and California Adventure offer five different dining options. Ariel's Grotto, Disney's PCH Grill, Goofy's Kitchen, Plaza Inn, and Storyteller's Cafe all have different experiences available.

Encounter a wide range of Characters at Goofy's Kitchen.

Find out which Characters your family would most like to see. If princesses are a top priority, Ariel's Grotto will allow you to see all of them at once. For a wide variety of animal, hero, and villain Characters, Goofy's

Kitchen tops the list, and will also give you the largest selection of food on their buffet. Want a quick bite to eat while you're in the park, but still have a full Character experience, then the Plaza Inn at the end of Main Street is the best option. If you're staying at one of the Disney hotels, consider a Character Dining experience for an early breakfast before you enter the park.

If this sounds like something your family or group would enjoy, I recommend doing research in advance of your trip, and choose a Character Dining experience that makes the most sense given its theme and location. Make your reservations in advance, and you'll cut down your wait time dramatically, possibly down to nothing.

Dining packages

For those of you who purchase packages through Disney or other travel planning services, you may be able to purchase a Disney Dining Plan. These plans don't offer a discount, but are intended to help budget in your meals. These plans are purchased ahead of time, along with your resort package. Vouchers can be used inside the park and at Disney hotels. You'll be able to select your dining plan, but most offer enough for three meals a day, plus a snack.

We've purchased dining plans before. Although we were able to pre-pay for our meals, we were also limited to dining at the Disneyland parks and hotels. Vouchers can't be used at most Downtown Disney locations.

If you plan on staying on-site at a Disney hotel and you'll be spending most of your time in the parks, consider a dining plan. However, if you're staying off-site, and you like flexibility with your time and money, a Disney dining plan might not be a good fit for you. Instead, set aside the money you would have paid for the dining plan and use those funds for your dining budget.

Breakfast at Disneyland

One of the best things about getting to the park is the smaller crowd. You may be able to ride more rides in your first hour than you will all day long. It's important that you either eat breakfast before you get to the park, or eat a later breakfast once you've taken advantage of the first hour of rides and attractions. You (and especially younger children) will need the energy throughout the day.

Mickey-shaped waffles, available for breakfast at many of the restaurants at Disneyland.

If you're staying in the area, I recommend getting out of your room a little early and grabbing a bite at Downtown Disney. Whether you prefer a sit-down meal, or a quick bite from the counter, La Brea Cafe has something for everyone. It's also steps away from the park entrance. A Starbucks will also open here sometime during Winder 2014.

If you want to hit the park and eat later, I love the newly renovated Market House Starbucks or Carnation Cafe on Main Street. Jolly Holiday Bakery is another great spot just at the end of Main Street. All three of these offer a variety of breakfast foods, baked goods, and basic coffee and tea. Main Street is usually open a half hour prior to the official park opening, or "rope drop." Guests are allowed into the park, up to the end of Main Street. Cast Members will drop the rope barrier at the scheduled opening time. Carnation Cafe and Minnie's Storyteller Cafe are both open before the drop, and you can make reservations for either in advance. Plan your morning accordingly, and you'll always be able to start the day off right.

Grown-up dinner with kids

We like to have at least one nice dinner out when we're on vacation, even if we have the kids with us. That's what makes dining at Disneyland easy. At Disneyland, you can have a nice dinner in a great atmosphere without the worry that you might ruin someone else's experience. Even if your children can't sit still long enough for the food to hit the table, dining at Disneyland isn't pretentious, and kids are welcome everywhere.

If you want a nice meal out, consider making reservations at The Blue Bayou, Carthay Circle, or our personal favorite, Wine Country Trattoria. The food is fantastic, reasonably priced, and it beats eating more fried food. How often would you think of eating well-prepared Italian food inside a Disney park, maybe paired with a glass of wine? We sit outside with our children, and about two dozen others. They have high chairs and booster seats for smaller children and offer a complete kid's menu. One that goes beyond the basic mac and cheese.

The Caprese salad from Wine Country Trattoria.

If you'd like an experience at one of the nicer restaurants, you absolutely should make a reservation in advance. A few restaurants may have availability same-day, or as a walk-up. But most of them will be booked days in advance, if not weeks or months. For the restaurants that take walk-ups, you may discover the wait time may push up to two hours at the busiest times of the year. When you have tired, hungry kids with you, who can stomach that kind of wait?

Dinner and a show

Disneyland isn't just for kids. Over the years, Disney has found ways to bring more and more adults into the park. Disney's California Adventure has several eateries perfect for an adult-only night out. As mentioned earlier, one of our favorite places, with or without kids, is Wine Country Trattoria. Wine Country Trattoria offers a Tuscan-style menu aimed at pleasing the adult palette. They have over twenty-five different wines to pair with your dinner. They also offer Sangria and have an extensive beer selection. Don't worry, they also have an extensive children's menu if dining alone isn't an option.

If you are bringing the kids, make reservations and ask to sit by the main thoroughfare. This way you might get a great view of the Pixar parade. We've been able to see the parade several times while enjoying our dinner. You can also make reservations for a World of Color package. These packages are available for lunch and dinner. With your three-course meal and special seating in the Center Stage Viewing Area, you'll also receive a Fastpass. Tickets for the dinner show run $42 per adult and $22 per child.

Boardwalk Pizza and Pasta

We always try to maintain a consistent routine when traveling, especially when it comes to meals. This can be challenging at an amusement park when you're trying to get from one place to the next. We believe that having at least one sit-down meal each day is important. I also like the opportunity for a little downtime. We found a place in California Adventure that fills both those needs. Boardwalk Pizza and Pasta, located at one end of Paradise Pier, offers the perfect combination of a quick and relaxing meal.

This location can be hard to find, which is one of the reasons why we enjoy it so much. Located between Goofy's Sky School and The Silly Symphony Swings, it's easy to miss. This area looks more like a garden than a dining location. It's not too busy and offers a nice covered outdoor venue to enjoy your meal. I also like this location because the green Toy Story Army Men perform just steps away. If you plan your meal times accordingly, you'll have a great view of the performance.

Following a hefty meal of pizza and spaghetti, my children always need to be cleaned up. Getting the extra sauce off their hands and faces is easy to do with the secret restroom located just steps away. This rest room is in the back corner of the restaurant area and is seldom used.

The Monte Cristo

One of the must-eats at Disneyland is a Monte Cristo sandwich. It's on the menu at Blue Bayou and at Cafe Orleans. If you've never had a Monte Cristo before, it's a richer variation of the already rich French croque monsieur. Disney's Monte Cristo is turkey, ham, and swiss, deep-fried in batter, and dusted with powdered sugar.

The Monte Cristo sandwich from Cafe Orleans.

If you're looking for a more formal experience, and you're prepared to pay a little more, try the Blue Bayou. Ask for a table out on the Bayou so you can watch the riders on Pirates of the Caribbean get ready for their big plunge. Be prepared for a table with low lighting.

Here's a little secret. If you just want to try the sandwich, hit Cafe Orleans instead of Blue Bayou. The sandwich is the same at both places. There's no difference, other than the presentation and small sides it comes with. Sit outside along the pathway and people watch with the boats heading out to Tom Sawyer's Island in the background.

I recommend ordering only one Monte Cristo for the table—they're very rich. Share the sandwich and order a bowl of gumbo to go with it! You can't go wrong.

Cozy Cone cuisine

Cars Land is the newest and most loved area of DCA. And for good reason. Each time you walk into Cars Land, it feels like you just stepped onto the set of Cars, the movie. The reproduction of Flo's V8 Cafe and Luigi's Tires looks just like you remember it from the movie.

Signage of the Cozy Cone Motel and Flo's V8 Cafe in Cars Land.

If you're looking for a little snack to hold you over between meals, or an after-dinner treat, check out another of the small reproductions of Radiator Springs: the Cozy Cone Motel. Inspired directly from the movie, this charming motel sits on the main stretch of the small town. Here you'll find oversized cone-shaped motel rooms, each serving up different snacks, and all in small cone-shaped cups. Each cone has a different menu, so make sure you're in the right line.

In addition to several beverages to choose from (including a "route beer float"), you can also choose from popcorn, chili cone queso, chicken verde, ice cream, churros, and pretzel bites. The Cozy Cone is open for breakfast. But I recommend stopping by for a mid-day or a late-night snack. This is the perfect road stop with something for everyone.

And as an added bonus, you'll often see full-size Cars Characters like Mater or Lightning McQueen parked out front of the Cozy Cone, waiting to pose for a picture, and talk with you and your kids.

The corn dog secret is out

This is one of the only places on earth I'd be willing to stand in a long line for a corn dog. Disney perfected the corn dog and the secret is out. There was a time when you could walk right up to the Little Red Wagon at the end of Main Street, and grab a corn dog to go. Not anymore. The lines are sometimes long, but the wait is worth it.

The corn dog is perfectly breaded in a cornbread batter, crispy on the outside, and moist on the inside. These dogs are huge. For $5.99 you'll get the corn dog, plus a choice of chips or apple slices. There are three locations to get these secret recipe corn dogs. You can find them at the Little Red Wagon or the Stage Door

Café in Disneyland, or at Corn Dog Castle in California Adventure.

Smoked turkey legs

For meat-loving Disney guests, the smoked turkey leg is a must-try, at least once. Disney sells over 1.5 million turkey legs each year. You'll inevitably see guests walking around enjoying these moist, savory treats that taste like a cross between bacon and smoked ham. Turkey legs are huge, and I'm sure people question whether they're really turkey. I've been assured that they are 100% turkey. I just don't often think about turkey legs being this large.

Enormous smoked turkey legs serve as an oversized snack.

If you're intimidated by the size, they can easily be shared with others in your party. I'm not a huge fan of dark meat, so I'll typically share a leg with my mother. This way, I can still enjoy smoked turkey without committing to the entire leg.

Turkey legs are available at two locations in Disneyland. You can find them at a cart between Fantasyland and the Matterhorn, or inside Frontierland across from Big Thunder Mountain Railroad. They're also available at two locations in California Adventure: one just outside the Hollywood Backlot, and one across from Toy Story Mania.

These legs are good, and seem to have a true cult following. For die-hard turkey leg fans, t-shirts, watches, even air fresheners (?!?) are available from DisneyStore. com.

Mickey beignets

A trip through New Orleans Square wouldn't be complete without a stop at the small Mint Julep Bar, just behind the French Market Restaurant, to enjoy a few Mickey-shaped beignets. These fried, puffy, Mickey-shaped, donut-like treats are dusted in powdered sugar, were brought to Disneyland from New Orleans. The powdered sugar coats each beignet with sweetly dusted goodness.

When you order beignets from the Mint Julep Bar, they'll come in a plain paper bag with lots of extra powdered sugar sitting in the bottom. They're made fresh for each order, so be warned that they'll be hot when they hand you your order. You could eat them there on the patio, which is usually quiet in the morning. Or we suggest taking your bag o' beignets down to the water's edge, and hopefully enjoy some Jazz music playing in the background.

Perfectly dusted Mickey beignets from Café Orleans.

You can also order Mickey beignets from Café Orleans. Here, you'll receive four to five beignets neatly stacked on a plate with sides of vanilla and raspberry dipping sauces.

If you're celebrating a special occasion at Disneyland, make sure to get a button from City Hall, and wear it! The Mint Julep Bar is one of the locations that may sneak a few extras into your order if they notice a birthday girl or boy, or an anniversary couple. On our last trip, we were pleasantly surprised to discover a few extra beignets had snuck their way into our bag because of a birthday button in our family.

Best cup of coffee

Anyone who has visited Disneyland in recent years knows that Disney hasn't historically done coffee very well. I can't count the number of times that I've had a mediocre to undrinkable cup of coffee at Disneyland. However, I'm happy to report the coffee situation at Disneyland has improved dramatically. The newly renovated Carnation Cafe and Jolly Holiday Bakery offer a refined set of coffees. I can now enjoy a nice cup of coffee with a fresh pastry, or perhaps some Mickey Mouse waffles.

The new Market House Starbucks location on Main Street.

I might be alone on this one, but I was thrilled when Starbucks first came into Disney's California Adventure Park. This gives us another option when searching for a good cup of java. Recently, another Starbucks opened on

Main Street at the Market House location. Outside the parks, you can find coffee in several Downtown Disney locations, including La Brea Cafe and Bakery. Starbucks will also be opening two new locations in Downtown Disney during winter 2014.

Visiting caffeine addicts can finally rest at ease, knowing a decent, predictable cup of coffee can more easily be found in multiple places throughout the resort.

6
LESSER-KNOWN EXPERIENCES

Ride the Monorail in style

The Monorail is a great way to get around Disneyland. It's close to the Disneyland Hotel and Paradise Pier, so if you're staying at either of those hotels, this is a must ride for you. If you have a little extra time, ask the Pilot if you can ride in the front. Riding in the front will let you give you a panoramic view as you speed along into the park. And at night, these views are incredible.

Before you board, make sure you ask a Cast Member if the space up front is available. The front compartment can only hold four people, so plan ahead. You might have to wait for the next train for a turn, but it's worth the wait. A side note, if it's hot outside, you won't be able to ride in the front of the monorail. The front compartment has no air, nor any open-able windows, and the nearly all-glass compartment gets too hot in the hot sun.

Snow White's Grotto

Sleeping Beauty's Castle is a wonderful spot for a photo opportunity. Due to its popularity, it creates a lot of congestion on the way into Fantasyland.

One of my favorite shortcuts, and a great way to avoid the crowd, is just to the right of the castle. Take the little path around the moat to the right, and you'll walk right into Snow White's Grotto. This hidden-in-plain-sight treasure is somehow overlooked. That is, until Snow White and the Evil Queen make an infrequent stop at the Grotto.

The Grotto itself is a quiet little nook where a magical waterfall hosts Snow White, the seven dwarfs, and a few of her animal friends. The Wishing Well sits in front of the Grotto. At any time during the day and you'll be serenaded by sounds of Snow White singing sweetly from the waterfall, and echoing from the well. There are also several tunes by her animal friends and bells playing in the background.

The Wishing Well, tucked away in Snow White's Grotto.

Not only is this a great area for a photo, but the well also has a special meaning for many young children. The coins tossed into the Wishing Well are donated to local children's charities. Look for the inscription, "Your wishes will help children everywhere," printed on the well. Next time, toss in a few extra wishes. You'll get to help other children's wishes come true.

Get a Jungle Cruise map

We've ridden the Jungle Cruise more times than I can count. Because of the colorful personalities of the Cast Members and their deadpan delivery of jungle cruise puns, each experience is different. Although we've been on the cruise so many times, I don't think I could tell you about any route specifics. That is, until recently.

Did you know there's an official Jungle Cruise map that Disney created? My daughter loves maps. Even though she's only five, she can give the best directions. The Jungle Cruise map is definitely one for the collection.

Cast Members keep a stash of secret Jungle Cruise maps.

As you're getting off the cruise, don't forget to ask a Cast Member for your free map of the Jungle Cruise. This is such a great keepsake for any Disney fan. Not many people know about this special treasure!

Pilot the Mark Twain Riverboat

Ever wonder who pilots the Mark Twain Riverboat? If you plan ahead next time, it could be your little one. What a great story that would be!

If your child wants to see where the Captain sits, or maybe steer the boat on their own, just ask a Cast Member at the boarding dock. One lucky passenger is allowed each trip to help pilot the boat. You and your child will be led up a narrow passageway to the wheelhouse, where you will be introduced to the Captain and your little one will get a chance to steer the ship. Don't forget to have them ring the bell as you make your way around the river!

At the end of your journey, your child will receive a certificate to let everyone know she or he is a trained pilot of the Mark Twain Riverboat.

Free lockers at Grizzly River Run

As you walk beyond Condor Flats inside California Adventure, you may notice other patrons walking past you and their clothes that are dripping wet. Even their shoes squeak as water sloshes out with each step. I've told you how to stay cool at Disneyland. But do you know how to keep your items from getting wet on those fun water rides? When it gets really hot during summer months, I'm sure you'll be thinking of riding the Grizzly River Run. Consider using the complimentary lockers here.

These lockers are free for you to use while you enjoy this ride. This way, you know your personal items are secure. And they won't be lost or waterlogged when you get off the ride.

These lockers can be used for free, for up to two hours. Find these lockers beside the Grizzly River Run exit.

Redwood Creek Challenge Trail

We just finished watching Disney-Pixar's movie, *Up*. If you haven't seen it yet, grab a box of tissues, and watch it now. It's such a cute movie, and perfect for the whole family.

It took three trips to Disney's California Adventure before we finally discovered the Redwood Creek Challenge Trail. This is an amazing two-acre course where you'll hike, climb, slide, and swing your way through nature, earning your Wilderness Badge along the way. Russell, the boy, and Dug, the dog from *Up*, will give you clues along the way to help you earn your badge.

It's easy to miss this mammoth trail. If you're speed walking to the next big attraction, you may not notice the guides encouraging you to take the challenge. It's located along the outer path of the Golden State, between Grizzly River Run and Ariel's Undersea Adventure. There is rarely a line, and once inside, you can stay as long as you want. I love this area—it's a great place for kids and adults to get out extra energy while spending time in a nature camp environment.

Beast's Library and Ursula's Grotto

Have you ever wondered what Disney Character or villain you're most like? Inside the Disney Animation

Building in Hollywood Land, take a few steps beyond the Sorcerer's Workshop and you'll stumble into Beast's Library from *Beauty and the Beast*. When you walk in, you'll see several stations around the room. Each station has an interactive exhibit where you can answer a few questions, watch videos, and even eventually be told which Character best matches your personality. Ironically, our daughter ended up being most like Ursula. Not everyone is a princess, right?

Beast's spacious library underneath the Animation Building.

This hidden space is often missed. It took us several visits before we realized we were missing out on this treasure below the Animation Building. The room itself is magical, and filled with a facade of books that goes all the way to the ornate ceiling. Every few minutes, the room changes lighting, from the dark halls of the Castle, to the bright open space shared with Belle. Make sure you stay the entire time to experience the effects, and don't miss the fireplace and magical rose at the far end of the library.

As you walk through the exhibit, you'll leave Beast's Library and end up in Ursula's Grotto. This cave-like space is dark and cool. Flotsam and Jetsam, Ursula's pets, weave their way around the room and can be a bit frightening for the itty-bitty children. This space has several interactive exhibits. Once you make your way through the Grotto, you'll end up back in the main courtyard of the Animation Building.

Look for the Sorcerer's Workshop signs directly ahead as you enter the Animation Building, and follow the ramp down into the castle below. You don't want to miss this special exhibit.

7
CHARACTERS

Introducing kids to Characters

Like everything new, it's hard to tell how kids are going to react when they meet their favorite Characters in real life. I remember the first time my daughter saw Brother Bear and Goofy, she feared for her life. Seeing animated Characters jump around on screen is entirely different once they're four times your height, and they look like they could eat you or carry you away. However, when kids see a less threatening princess like Cinderella or Belle, they're often beaming from ear-to-ear.

First-time introductions to larger-than-life Characters.

There's a simple way to gage how your child will react to certain Characters before you go into the park. Schedule a Character Dining experience, where your entire family will get a good dose of Characters as they visit each table.

In my opinion, one of the best Character Dining experiences is at Goofy's Kitchen. You get a great feel for a wide variety of live and animated Characters, all in one place, in a short amount of time. The buffet offers a wide selection of family-friendly food options. This way, you'll get to see how your child reacts to certain types of Characters. By the time you enter the park, you'll have a good idea of what to expect.

Note that Character Dining can be expensive. If you booked a trip through a travel agent, like Costco or AAA, ask for a dining package that includes Character Dining. If you don't get to visit Disneyland very often, this is an experience that's worth the cost.

Finding the Characters

Years ago, you could walk around Disneyland and ran-domly encounter Disney Characters throughout the park. As the parks get more popular, those times seem long gone. Now, you need to seek out Characters at des-ignated meet-and-greet locations and times. It may seem like you keep missing your favorite Character by a few seconds as they get whisked away to their next location. If you're looking for a specific photo opportunity with a favorite Character, you'll need to do a little planning ahead of time.

Disney makes it easy to find your favorite Characters throughout the day. Visit the Central Plaza board on Main Street in Disneyland, or the Information Station on Buena Vista Street in California Adventure. These boards provide up-to-the-minute details about your friends. Cast Members are always available here to answer any questions. Scheduled times and locations are also listed on the daily itinerary sheet obtained from the Main Gate.

Finding Goofy in Mickey's Toontown.

Another great way to see a set of Characters is to splurge for one of the five Character Dining experiences. I heavily recommend making reservations in advance or your visit. Reservations are accepted for Ariel's Grotto, Disney's PCH Grill, Goofy's Kitchen, Storyteller's Cafe, and the Plaza Inn. Character Dining is a great way to see how your little one feels about meeting their friends in real life. To make dining reservations, contact Disney Dining at 714-781-DINE.

The new Fantasy Faire

There's a lot of love about the Disney Princesses. Last year, Disneyland created a new venue for park visitors to meet them in person. The new Fantasy Faire location is just to the left of Sleeping Beauty's Castle. The new Fantasy Faire opened in March 2013, and has been a huge hit ever since. There's so much to this experience; everyone in your family will enjoy it.

The new location is now home to a theater, snack shop, shopping, and a whole new meet-and-greet area. When you stop by the Bavarian storybook village square, you never really know whom you might run into. Meet friends here from The Little Mermaid, Sleeping Beauty, and Tangled.

Meeting Princess Belle for the first time.

Get to the Fantasy Faire early. Unless you're doing a Character dining experience, this is the only place to easily and predictably meet multiple Princesses. Wait times can run up to 45 minutes. If you're a Disneyland hotel guest, take advantage of Extra Magic Hour in the park to get in early. Note that not all of the Princesses will be here at one time. There are usually three Princesses at the Faire at any given time, and they rotate out frequently. If you happen to miss your favorite Princess, stop back later. She'll likely return soon enough.

Visit Mickey and Minnie in Toontown

Toontown is a great place to meet the original crew. Mickey, Minnie, Donald, Daisy, Goofy, Pluto, and Chip and Dale all spend a lot of time around Toontown. Mickey, Minnie, Donald, and Goofy can frequently be seen greeting guests in front of their own homes here. A trip through each of their homes is a must for your little ones. When you walk into Minnie's house, you can actually feel Minnie's personality displayed throughout. Everything has her personal touch, and you'll find her signature bows everywhere.

Over at Mickey's, you'll be surprised at how big his house really is. You'll walk through his living room, laundry room, backyard, and see how Mickey lives his everyday life. Make sure you take note of the little things. Mickey's TV is playing classic cartoons, and there is a cabinet with a photo of Mickey and his good friend Walt. His house holds special memories that Walt created just for Mickey. These are treasures not to be missed.

Greeted by a special hostess inside Minnie's house in Toontown.

You can visit the houses at Toontown anytime, but they tend to be busy when Mickey and Minnie are actually home. Wait times can reach up to an hour to get a peek inside.

Where is Mary Poppins?

The Sherman brothers really pulled one over on those of us trying to learn and say "supercalifragilisticexpialidocious!" I'll never forget the first time our oldest daughter saw Mary Poppins. Having seen the movie several times, she couldn't believe there was a real-life Mary Poppins standing in front of us. Maybe it's because Mary Poppins is in Character the entire time you talk with her that makes it magical. Whatever it is, you need to see her.

Bert and Mary Poppins are hard to locate since they don't have a set meet-and-greet location like other Characters. They typically hang out around the Jolly Holiday Bakery and Carnation Cafe on Main Street, U.S.A. There's also an unpublished show with the Pearly Band in front of Sleeping Beauty's Castle. Bert and Mary Poppins are usually hanging around the band. After the performance, you can usually see and talk with them at Snow White's Grotto before they head off to London.

If you can't find them during your park stay, you are sure to get a glimpse of them during one of the two parades. Mary Poppins is also known to show up during certain Character Dining experiences. With the new movie, *Saving Mr. Banks*, I'm sure we'll be seeing even more of Bert and Mary throughout the park.

8
ENTERTAINMENT

Entertainment around the park

One of my favorite things about Disneyland is the live entertainment. If you're hustling from one spot to another, the different performances are easily missed. Most of these live events will not be published anywhere. Each section of the park has its own tailored performers; stand still long enough and you're sure to hear the beat of a drum or the sound of a trumpet playing not too far away.

The Dapper Dans entertain guests on Main Street, U.S.A.

A few of my favorites are the Hook and Ladder Company, The Dapper Dans, The Pearly Band, and The Refreshment Corner Pianist. The Trash Can Trio, in Tomorrowland, is also a huge hit with little ones. It's these performances that really make Disneyland set aside from other amusement parks. The live music and entertainment really add to the atmosphere.

If you know the name of the entertainers you'd like to watch, ask a Cast Member in the area. They're likely to know times and locations of what will happen next. One of our favorite things to do is to grab lunch at the French Market or Cafe Orleans. These two eateries in the New Orleans Square area are a hot spot for live entertainment. Try to sit as close to the outer railing as possible. Not only will you have a great meal, you'll also have a front row seat to the next spontaneous show.

Theatrical shows

One of Disneyland's most overlooked treasures is their live stage entertainment. Two shows in particular need to be on top of your must-see list. *Aladdin* and *Mickey and the Magical Map* offer two phenomenal performances.

In Fantasyland, you can find the old Fantasyland Theater. This theater has been used for various performances over the years. With five performances each day of *Mickey and the Magical Map*, I think they finally created a show that is going to keep this location busy for years to come. This incredible variety show includes as many stories as possible in a 25-minute performance. There are appearances and songs from King Louis from The Jungle Book, Pocahontas, Mulan, Rapunzel and Flynn Rider from Tangled, Princess Tiana from The Princess and the Frog, and Sebastian from The Little Mermaid. And, of course, this show wouldn't be complete without Mickey Mouse bringing the stage to life.

Aladdin offers the same excitement on the stage. This performance is located in The Hyperion Theater at California Adventure's Hollywood Land, and is easily missed because of the facade of the building. During the 40-minute show, you'll experience the entire story of Aladdin. This show is perfect for the whole family, even our toddler sat through the majority of the show. There are typically only four shows each day, so plan accordingly.

The Golden Horseshoe

The Golden Horseshoe is one of the last original buildings in Disneyland. It sits near the entrance of Frontierland, but is easy to miss if you're hurriedly rushing past it toward Pirates or the Haunted Mansion. The Horseshoe is a classic Western-style, small-stage theater with tables on the bottom floor, and a U-shaped balcony above. The theater was one of Walt's favorite spots in the park. He kept a private box reserved just so he could stop in to see the revue anytime he wanted. Today, that box is open and anyone can sit there.

The Revue that once ran at the Horseshoe is no longer there. However, it's been replaced by a bluegrass music show named Billy Hill and the Hillbillies. It's music and comedy combined into one, and the four guys usually have kids and adults alike bursting out loud in laughter throughout the show.

The Golden Horseshoe sits near the entrance to Frontierland.

The best way to get your money's worth is to show up a little early before the show. Sit in the alcove on the left side of the stage to enjoy your meal. Have your kids sit right up against the railing during the show (which they'll do without you having to tell them). The main Character always has a little fun surprising the kids there during the show. The crowd goes crazy, and your kids will leave with a special memory of this historical place.

Best seats in the Tiki Room

With its Polynesian theme and over 225 singing animatronic Cast Members, Disney's Enchanted Tiki Room is one of my favorite places. On a hot day, the Tiki Bar out front offers Dole pineapple whips to help you cool off. And the show is inside a large air-conditioned room. The

Tiki tune, written by the Sherman Brothers, is a classic and not to be missed. And the Enchanted Tiki Room just celebrated its 50th anniversary!

The tropical entrance of the Enchanted Tiki Room.

A lot happens inside the Enchanted Tiki Room. The main stars of the show are four macaws. They bring to life a world like no other inside Disneyland. If you want to take in all the happenings, sit towards the back of the room. If you sit in the front row, it's harder to see all the elements of the show, and you'll be craning your neck upwards to see everything above. Many of the focal points are in the center of the room and get lowered down from the ceiling. Sit towards the back and you'll get the best view of the show.

Although the Tiki Room show is great for families, there are a few tense moments that might be frightful for smaller children. The Tiki Room lights go dim for the show, and you'll weather a mock thunderstorm toward the end. Hopefully this won't scare your young children away. There's plenty of singing along to make this a fun break for everyone. Our daughters love it. We've been taking them since before they could talk.

A secret of the Tiki Room is the seldom-used, somewhat hidden restroom inside. The Tiki Room was originally intended to be a restaurant, so it was built with its own restroom and air conditioning.

Be prepared to be singing "In the Tiki, Tiki, Tiki, Tiki, Tiki Room..." in your head for several hours after you see the show!

Tinker Bell's night flight

One of the best moments at Disneyland is when Tinker Bell takes her nighttime flight from the top of the Matterhorn and over Sleeping Beauty's Castle. This longtime Disneyland tradition started in 1961 and is still a huge crowd pleaser.

At dusk, find a good seat for the fireworks show, making sure you have a clear view of the Matterhorn and Castle. Pay close attention during the show. Tinker Bell's journey is a quick thirty seconds. It can be easily missed because it's so short, and Tinker Bell is tiny. If you know what you're looking for and where to look, it's a fun sight to see. Amid all the explosions of light, a tiny little fairy flying high over the castle is a great reminder of the magic you'll find at Disneyland.

Turtle Talk with Crush

Turtle Talk with Crush is an interactive show in which the animated Crush (from Finding Nemo) talks directly with kids and adults in the small theater. He's able to ask questions, comment on answers, make kids laugh, and teach them how to properly say "Duuude!" No two shows are ever alike.

The show takes place in front of a big window looking into the ocean. During each visit with Crush, he's able to see children through the glass and call them out by what they are wearing, where they're sitting, or other unique identifying characteristics.

Crush interacts directly with the crowd in Turtle Talk.

My daughter was sitting in the front row off to the side. When Crush asked "the dudette with the purple glasses" her name, he began to have an in-depth conversation with my daughter about lunch. She was thrilled Crush had picked her. It was like this animated Character had truly come to life. Crush seems to favor children who sit closer to the front of the theater, as it's probably where he can best see or hear the kids.

Turtle Talk is a huge hit with young ones, and adults will be left wondering how Disney pulled off the magic of this experience. Since no two shows are alike, you can come back to see it again and again. Each talk with Crush lasts about fifteen minutes; check show times in advance.

Disney Junior show

Disney California Adventure occasionally updates the *Disney Junior–Live on Stage!* show to stay current with modern programming. This show has always been a favorite for us. Our daughter was thrilled to hear that Sofia the First and Doc McStuffins joined Mickey Mouse Clubhouse and Jake and the Neverland Pirates. This is the perfect show for preschoolers. Even our thirteen-month-old daughter loved the lights, sounds, and Characters. It's a great place to sit and take a break while interacting with some of the favorite Characters from Disney Junior. Although we loved the original show, the new version is refreshing. Each segment offers a life lesson, while keeping the kids on their toes.

Find the Disney Junior show in Hollywood Land at California Adventure. The show runs 22 minutes. Get there early. You'll be sitting on the floor, but the best seating toward the front goes quickly. If you're sitting too far on the sides, your child won't be able to interact with the bubbles, streamers, or "gold doubloons."

Check the weekly schedule for current show times.

Animation Academy

As you're cruising down the street through Hollywood Land in DCA, you can't miss a large deco sign for the Disney Animation building. Whether you're a kid, or a kid at heart, do not skip what looks to be another facade of a building.

Among several opportunities within the Animation building, don't miss the Animation Academy, which is off to the left as you enter the inner courtyard. Once inside the mini theater and pseudo art studio, you'll get your own lapboard, a piece of paper, and a pencil. A live Disney Animator greets you from the stage, and proceeds to teach you how to draw one of the popular Disney Characters. A schedule of which Characters you'll be drawing is mounted at the entrance to the Animation Building.

Fear not if you're no artist dripping with magical eye-popping talent. There's no harm in trying your hand at applying pencil to paper. An overhead screen projects exactly what the animator draws, as he or she slowly walks you through each step using simple shapes, guides, and curves. You may impress yourself and others in your group that you ended up with something that actually resembles the Character you tried to draw.

Not only do you get to take your artwork with you. When you can quickly sketch out Goofy or Mickey on a napkin at a restaurant, you'll be the hit of the table among your kids or friends, and probably the server too. Not content being a one-trick pony? Simply go back for another visit to the Animation Academy, and learn to draw another Character!

World of Color

Disney took everything it learned from Fantasmic at Disneyland and upped the game when they created the infrastructure for World of Color inside California Adventure. Imagine taking the fountains in front of Bellagio and combining the water-projected graphics of Fantasmic.

There are two preferred vantage points for enjoying World of Color. I think everybody should see the show from both views, but it will require seeing the show twice.

The options for the show are to sit close to the lake and get drenched (bring a rain poncho), but really feel like you're part of the show, or stand in the upper level and have a broader, dryer view of the entire event.

There's something very special about both. Without giving too much away, the up-close crowd will marvel at the feeling of being in the show as it's happening. Those watching from the back will remain dry. They will also be more of spectators, which isn't all bad. It's amazing to be able to see the entire show from a distance. Whether you're close up, or near the back, this is a beautiful show that you should see at least once.

I suggest seeing it twice: once from each vantage point. You'll want to get your Fastpass early in the day for World of Color. Fastpasses can run out quickly, especially during peak tourist seasons.

9
MEMORABILIA

Mickey ears

We have quite a few Mickey ears around our house. Mickey Mouse ears are a timeless keepsake and the perfect must-have souvenir. I'm not talking about the headbands with ears, although those are cute too. I'm talking about the traditional Mickey Mouse ear hats with plastic ears attached to a small dome-shaped hat. The traditional Mickey hat is around $14, and you can get it personalized with a name or short phrase on the back.

Classic Minnie ears, available to order online before your trip.

When I was a kid, Disney didn't have the selection it does now. Today you can get Mickey, Minnie, Princess, Goofy, Buzz, Perry, Bridal, Baby, and even Oswald ears. Regardless of which ears you choose, this is my number one, must-have souvenir for a first trip.

After your first set of ears, the question becomes: do you take them with you on each trip, or do you buy a new pair? Even though we have several hats to choose from, we come home with a new set of ears after each visit.

If you know you want a pair of Mickey ears, you can order them online (before your trip) from the Disney Store. Personalize them for an additional $5.95. This could save you a few minutes seeking them out inside the park, and you'll get to show off your new ears as you enter the Main Gate.

The Mad Hatter

It's always hard not to walk into the first shop at Disneyland and buy those Mickey ears you've been wanting. But you might want to wait until you've been to the Mad Hatter. While there's an entrance near the beginning of Main Street, I recommend the location in Fantasyland. It's right next to the Mad Tea Party (aka, the Tea Cups) and Alice in Wonderland. Here, you'll find the best hat shop in Disneyland.

The Mad Hatter has hundreds of hats to choose from. Not only do they have every set of mouse ears available, they have baseball hats, hats for kids, and everything in between with glitter and feathers. Don't forget that you can personalize your hat with your name or a special date.

The Mad Hatter wouldn't be complete without a visit from the Cheshire Cat. Watch the mirror behind the registers, and you might see him make a quick appearance. You'll need to look fast... he doesn't stick around for long.

Capture the moment with PhotoPass

The quality of cameras on today's smart phones means you're likely capturing a lot of memories without needing to lug around a large camera with you wherever you go. Disneyland is no exception to this benefit. Lots of great, spontaneous photos can be captured by snapping a quick pic with your phone.

However, there are key spots throughout the parks where you may want to take advantage of Disney's PhotoPass photographers. Want a photo of your entire group beside the statue of Walt and Mickey with Sleeping Beauty's castle in the background? Just approach any uniformed PhotoPass photographer and ask to have your picture taken. They'll capture a few photos with their high-powered cameras, then hand you a free (and reusable) PhotoPass card for later retrieval of your photos. The photographers don't have anything to sell, and there's no pressure to purchase anything.

At the end of your trip, either view your photos at the Photo Center on Main Street, or at home using the code on the back of the PhotoPass card. Low-resolution photos are free to view for thirty days. Higher resolution prints or digital files are available for purchase. And Disney provides several ready-made options to turn your images into souvenir gifts that can get shipped to any location.

Bonus tip: PhotoPass photographers will also gladly take the same photo for you with your own camera or smart phone. Not only does this make for a good backup of what you can access from PhotoPass later. It gives you a photo you can immediately share online, or send off to relatives and friends.

Family photos in the same spot

Our last few visits, we've taken a family photo in the same spot. We didn't do it intentionally, it just kind of happened. It's fun to see how much everyone has changed in just a short time. Or in our case, how our family grew. I enjoy looking back at each photo to see the changes.

When you pick your spot, try to think ahead. Pick a spot that is most likely going to be there in the years ahead. Sadly, I'm sure people have come back to their favorite spot only to have it missing or converted into something else.

Pin trading

Pin trading is a huge Disney phenomenon that has exploded in popularity. It started in 1999 when Disneyland introduced the Millennium pin sets. Today, you can buy and trade pins at almost every Disney park location. My mother has been actively trading pins with Cast Members for years. She's been able to pick up different pins from various Disney Stores, the Walt Disney Family Museum, D23, and Aulani, making her collection swap-worthy. Cast Members are always excited to see new pins from different locations.

Our oldest daughter caught the pin-trading bug. She gets really excited when she sees a cast member with a lanyard full of pins. Cast Members are usually just as excited to get a chance to see a new pin. There are a few pin trading guidelines you'll need to follow:

- Pins need to be authentic. If you are unsure of a pin's authenticity, ask a Cast Member to verify whether it's genuine. Cast Members will generally avoid trading a pin they recognize as a cheap knockoff.
- Look, but don't touch. Always ask the person with whom you're trading to remove their own pins, and they'll expect you to do the same with your pins.
- Always put the back on your pin before handing it over.
- Pins should be in good condition to trade.
- Most importantly, have fun.

The best way to start trading pins is to buy a starter set at one of the many Pin Trader locations. The starter sets, which come with a lanyard, start at about $15. If you think pin trading is in your future, start saving up before you go. Like any collectible, pin trading can get costly. But the souvenirs you'll go home with will remind you of the fun memories you created at Disneyland.

Silhouette Studio

We've walked down Main Street, U.S.A. countless times. Each time we passed the Silhouette Studio, I thought to myself that we should have our daughter's portrait done. But we passed it by each time, in a hurry to get to something further into the park. I can't believe it took several years of going to Disneyland before we finally stopped in this cute little shop. Little did I know, in less than a minute of hand-cutting black paper, I'd see a beautiful silhouette of my daughter, perfectly frozen in time.

The Silhouette Studio is a timeless classic on Main Street. They've been around for almost fifty-five years. Each silhouette is hand-cut with a pair of scissors. Yes, hand cut in less than a minute. It's amazing to see. I can't even draw a picture of my daughter. How someone can cut out a realistic-looking silhouette of her so quickly with basic scissors and paper is beyond me.

Bonnie and Sylvia, who have been cutting out these portraits for over thirty years, keep this classic tradition alive. It's unbelievable. For only $9, you get two silhouettes mounted to nice little cards. They have frames available for an additional cost as well.

The Silhouette Studio storefront on Main Street.

Bonnie informed us the Silhouette Studio might not be around much longer. Sales of the silhouettes are not as popular as they once were. So perhaps Disney is thinking of replacing the studio with something more modern. It would be a true shame to lose such a beautiful part of the original Main Street attractions. If you're going to Disneyland in the near future, and have ever considered getting a silhouette of your kids, don't hesitate. Nine dollars, and you'll have a little piece of history as a perfect souvenir of your trip, and a reminder of how small and innocent your little ones once were.

Pressed pennies

Who says no one uses pennies anymore? Whoever did should talk to our oldest daughter; she has the perfect use for those pennies lingering in your pocket.

My daughter loves pressed pennies from Disneyland. These machines can be found along Main Street, and around the exit of popular attractions throughout Disneyland and California Adventure. You can also find them in Downtown Disney, the Disney hotels, and even at a few Good Neighbor hotels. A pressed penny only costs fifty cents, plus the penny you'll be getting pressed. There are also a few popular or seasonal machines that take silver coins. If you visit the parks during the holidays, you can get a pressed quarter for Tim Burton's *The Nightmare Before Christmas* in New Orleans Square, and a seasonal nickel set is available on Main Street, U.S.A. These pressed coins are rare and fun to show off if you can get them.

We already have a collection of Pooh and friends, Tinker Bell, Mickey Mouse, and several princesses. Most recently, Fozzie from the Muppets was added to our collection. A complete list of locations and coin press collectibles is available at Guest Relations at City Hall in Disneyland.

Marceline's Confectionery

I often kick myself for not grabbing a gift for our house sitter or a special treat to enjoy on the way home. Especially our favorite treat, chocolate and caramel-dipped marshmallow wands!

Sorcerer Mickey apples from Marceline's.

If you've left the park and forgot to pick up one of your favorite sweet treats, fret not. You have another chance if you leave by way of Downtown Disney. Stop by Marceline's Confectionery, located about halfway through Downtown Disney. Marceline's has a lot of the favorite treats from the park. Here, you'll find Mickey rice crispy treats, Minnie cookies, chocolate pretzels, and many more nostalgic candied goodies.

Marceline's opens at 10:00am, and stays open late each night. They have a big glass storefront window for you to watch confectioners working on the latest sugar concoctions. It's fascinating to see them working on Mickey or Minnie apples and how perfect each one turns out. If you're visiting during the holiday season, make sure to at least stop by the window. You're sure to see something spectacular in the making.

10

CHILDREN

Follow your child's lead

One of the hardest parts of going to Disneyland for the first time is knowing how your children are going to react. Whether they are fearless or apprehensive, always follow their leads. Don't push them to do more than they can handle. This is a hard tip to follow, especially when your time is limited and you want to do as much as you can. If your children get overly tired, or become afraid, your visit can go downhill fast. Take your time, go with the flow, and have fun. Getting through the entire park in one day is hard to do, especially if you have children in tow.

Take a nap, stop for a show, skip the parade, or ride one more ride. Whatever is going to make your trip most enjoyable is the best way to experience the park. Your children will be happier, and so will you. I don't think there's anything worse that seeing a miserable family at The Happiest Place on Earth.

Disneyland with newborns

Just because you have little ones doesn't mean you have to skip Disneyland until they can walk on their own. We've taken both of our girls at very early ages, and have enjoyed our time despite their age. There will be some rides that you'll skip, but taking your little ones to the park will bring on an entirely different experience for you.

One of the key things to remember about Disneyland is that it's not just about the rides. There's so much more to do that everyone can enjoy. You can visit Characters, watch a parade, see a show, take the train or monorail; the options are many, even when you have a newborn with you. For those who are a little more adventurous, a few rides are perfect for families with babies. Toontown is great for anyone under 40 inches tall. Our younger daughter loves playing in Goofy's Playhouse garden while the older one rides Gadget's Go Coaster.

A few attractions are appropriate for all ages, even if you're wearing a newborn in a carrier. Alice in Wonderland, Casey Jr. Circus Train, Disneyland Railroad, Finding Nemo Submarines, Jungle Cruise, Peter Pan, Small World, Storybook Canal Boats, Tiki Room, Winnie the Pooh, and of course, Dumbo are all good options for parents wearing a baby in a carrier.

Strollers

You'll likely encounter the highest ratio of strollers to walking adults at one of the Disney parks. Strollers are everywhere, because everyone ends up walking a lot. So much that your feet will ache by the end of the day. So even if your child is at a good walking age, they'll tire out easily. You may save yourself a midday breakdown (or breaking your own back from carrying your child) by having a stroller to plop them into once they're tired. In less crowded areas, you also tend to move a little faster if your child is in a stroller.

Even if you don't normally use a stroller for your slightly older toddler, another benefit of having one is the small storage baskets they typically have under the seat. These come in useful for storing extra jackets, sweatshirts, sunscreen, or small souvenirs you might accumulate during your visit.

If you're not into the idea of traveling with your own stroller, Disney offers strollers for rent at both Disneyland and California Adventure. $15 per day rents one stroller, or you can rent two for $25. Note that double strollers are NOT available for rent. Stroller rental is located just outside the Main Gate, to the right of the entrance to Disneyland. While rental strollers are allowed in both parks, you cannot take them into Downtown Disney or to the Disney Hotels.

Strollers are available for rent outside the Main Gate.

If you're visiting the parks over multiple days, I recommend bringing your own stroller, especially if it's one of the small, lighter-weight varieties. This will save you a few dollars, and your own stroller will be easier to identify in the sea of light blue rentals that stack up in stroller parking areas.

Lost children

The first few times we went to Disneyland, I was scared we would lose our daughter. Not that she would get lost, but we would somehow lose her in a sea of strollers and people. Since that first trip, we've learned several things that help keep our family safe and together.

Our first daughter was only fifteen months old the first time we went to Disneyland. She's not one to stray away from us, but it was a constant chore to make sure she was in the stroller and strapped in. As she got older, her curiosity would get the best of her and she would venture a few feet away from us. I was the parent that had her child on a backpack leash. I was perfectly ok with it because I knew that I wasn't going to lose her this way. But as she became more mobile and sturdy on her feet, we just relied on the stroller and our instincts.

Kids are most likely to get separated in crowded areas. Keep extra watch around Characters, parades, and play areas. On average, ten kids get separated or lost at Disneyland each day. Disneyland holds a perfect record of reuniting families. They are ready and prepared for lost children or parents. Disney has a Baby Care Center set up just for lost children.

Disneyland is prepared to help lost children (and parents).

Have a plan in place before you go. We use temporary tattoos that have our name and number just in case. You can also purchase hard-to-remove identifying wristbands from Amazon for the same purpose. We also taught our daughter how to identify a Cast Member just in case she gets lost or separated from us. However, if you and your little one get separated, don't hesitate. Notify the nearest Cast Member immediately. They're trained and can call ahead to Security and the Baby Care Center to help locate your child as soon as possible.

Playgrounds

Until I had children, I didn't know Disneyland had designated play areas. I had walked by them probably a thousand times, but never stopped. Once we had our first child, we were more in tune to finding appropriate areas for her to stretch out and walk on her wobbly legs. Goofy's Playhouse garden is perfect for children under three. This play area has padded play turf, and plenty to climb and slide on. There are benches that surround the area; parents can watch as their toddlers explore.

Tom Sawyer's Island also has a play area. This play area is a little more rustic and offers an adventurous feel. Kids can climb and run around on the isolated island. Plan on staying for a bit; it usually takes 45 minutes or so to tour the island. The island is very kid-friendly, perfect for those active, restless five-year-olds.

Over in DCA, you have Flik's Fun Fair and the Redwood Creek Trail. Both of these areas are great for children of all ages to explore. If you don't mind your kids getting a little wet, let them explore the Princess Dot Puddle Park in Bug's Land. Keep a towel handy in the event your child gets a little too wet.

If you plan on hitting up any of these play areas, make sure your kids have on the proper shoes. Tom Sawyer's Island and the Redwood Creek Trails offer a lot of climbing options. You'll want to make sure your little ones can handle the trails. Glass slippers and flip flops won't work very well in these locations.

Balloon replacement

As soon as we hit Disneyland, our kids see those $12 Mickey balloons and want one immediately. I really don't mind getting one, as long as it's the first day of the trip. These balloons are great and usually last the week.

10 · CHILDREN

However, the last time we did this, our balloon deflated rather quickly. A Disney Cast Member was close by, noticed our balloon, and gave us a voucher for a new one.

Mickey balloons, typically available on Main Street.

If your balloon suffers an injury or breaks away, a Disney Cast Member will give you a new one. Also, if your balloon deflates, you can also get it refilled for free. Just ask any Disney cast member and they'll direct you to the nearest balloon repair.

Face painting

Ever since my daughter entered preschool, she has come home with her face painted several times a month. Our older daughter loves to have her face painted! She would rather use her spending money on face painting than on chocolate.

I should be proud. But there are always a few tears when the paint starts to wear off after a really long day.

The great thing about the Disney face painters is that they'll paint whatever you want. Starting around $10, you can get anything from a small butterfly to your entire face painted. I'm happy our daughter still chooses smaller objects, so we can still recognize her smiling face.

One day soon she's going to want her face painted like Jake from the Neverland Pirates! Until then, I'm going to enjoy the flowers and butterflies.

Jedi Training Academy

Fighting off Darth Vader takes a lot of training. Over at Tomorrowland Terrace Theater, you'll find the Jedi Training Academy, where your child can learn how to fight off Darth Vader and Darth Maul. The Academy takes about thirty children at a time, and instructors teach them how to use light sabers, preparing them for battle. Robes are issued, sabers are swinging around, and kids are thrilled when they get to fight Darth Vader, face to face. Upon completion of their challenge, children are rewarded with Jedi Training Academy diplomas.

If you think your child will participate in the Jedi Training, make sure you get there early. There will be a lot of children eagerly awaiting a turn. Trainers typically pick children sitting in the first couple of rows. The ones picked are energetic and are vocal about their desire to participate. If your child doesn't get picked the first time around, don't worry. The Jedi Training Academy has multiple show times per day.

Top five Disneyland rides for kids under 42"

Disneyland has so many great rides for children. Fantasyland is full of wonder, but there are so many other attractions outside of Fantasyland that are perfect for children aren't tall enough for the major attractions. Here are the top five attractions our daughter loves at Disneyland:

1. **Gadget's Go Coaster** This roller coaster takes a quick whirl around the track, but offers a thrill for the whole family. The lines are seldom long, allowing us to ride this little gem over and over.

2. **Buzz Lightyear Astro Blasters** This is a fun ride where our daughter loves to try to get the highest score. You'll cruise along in a spaceship shooting a laser gun at stationary and moving targets.

3. **Jungle Cruise** If you have a funny Cast Member leading the way, the Jungle Cruise can feel like hitting a stand-up comedy club. Our daughter loves to sit as close to the front as possible.

4. **Haunted Mansion** This one is not for the easily frightened. The Haunted Mansion involves a mysterious dwelling and looks to give you a scare. Although our daughter might jump a time or two, she still loves this ride.

5. **Astro Orbiter** This is a Disney classic and has been a favorite since we stepped foot into Tomorrowland. On the Orbiter, you get a birds eye view of the park. It's a fun ride, similar to Dumbo, with a little more speed and height.

There are so many more great attractions for kids under forty-two inches. Make sure you check your child's height before you go, so you'll have an idea ahead of time what rides they can enjoy.

Top five DCA rides for kids under 42"

Disney California Adventure Park is full of some of the best attractions for kids. However, the height requirements can keep some of the smaller children from experiencing those great rides. Most five-year-olds tend to be right around forty-two inches tall. Here are the top five attractions our daughter loves at California Adventure:

1. **Radiator Springs Racers** These race cars are a favorite for everyone. They offer the thrill and excitement of a fast-paced ride while traveling through Radiator Springs.

2. **Ariel's Undersea Adventure** One of our daughter's favorite movies is Little Mermaid, so it's no surprise she picked this as a favorite. Travel under the sea with Ariel as she begins her journey to the mainland to find love.

3. **Jumpin' Jellyfish** This was our daughter's first ride when she hit 40 inches. For months she watched this ride go up and down with anticipation that, one day, she too, would get to ride the Jellies.

4. **Mickey's Fun Wheel** This one is not for the weak-kneed. In fact, I usually sit this one out. There are two different gondola types on the Fun Wheel. Make sure you watch it go around a couple of times before you pick your car type. Our daughter loves the thrill of the swinging gondola!

5. **Mater's Junkyard Jamboree** This is Cars Land version of the Teacups. Not only is the ride a hit, but our daughter loves the music and listening to Mater chat away. This is another ride that's fun for the whole family.

California Adventure has more rides for kids under forty-two inches. Again, just check your child's height before you go, and have an idea of what rides will be appropriate given their height.

Bring a towel for Bug's Land

I think A Bug's Land is one of the best areas in the Disneyland and California Adventure parks for children under 35 inches. One of my favorite areas of A Bug's Land is the Princess Dot Puddle Park. On a hot day, this is a great place to cool off and let the kids play in the water. There's a giant sprinkler in the middle of the play area and kids try to avoid getting wet, but that's not likely. The giant splash pad is fun for all ages. Our older daughter has loved this area since she was just a toddler, and still wants to go there today. Regardless of age, make sure you have a towel and maybe even a change of clothes. If your little one gets too wet, the nearby restrooms offer two family restrooms to make changing easier.

Don't let getting a little wet keep you from this area; it's so much fun to watch the kids anticipate where the next jet of water will come from.

11
ADULTS

Drinks at Carthay Circle

After a long day in the park, a little downtime to enjoy a cocktail is well-deserved. The renovation of Disney's California Adventure brought us Carthay Circle Theatre, located on Buena Vista Street. The restaurant upstairs offers fine dining and spirits. However, the lounge on the first floor is the perfect spot to enjoy on its own, or to make the time go faster while you're waiting for table upstairs.

Carthay Circle was inspired by the Golden Age of Hollywood.

The lounge is beautifully designed and appointed. Step into the lounge, find a spot to call home for a short bit, and you'll feel like you just stepped back in time into one of the finest drinking establishments of the early 20th century. Everything you order here is painstakingly crafted and poured into its own special glassware that pays homage to each libation. Consider ordering one of Walt's favorite drinks, the Scotch Mist. Elegant versions of traditional appetizers and bar foods are available to complement your drink selection.

The lounge ambiance is perfect for a nice quiet evening, as children aren't allowed in the lounge. We enjoyed several different appetizers and fancied a few drinks; such a great ending to an already perfect day. Reservations are not required when visiting the Carthay Circle Lounge. But note that seating is available on a first come, first-served basis.

Beer and wine tasting

Wine Country Trattoria in California Adventure has been a family favorite since it opened. The Tuscan style setting allows you to escape the park (without leaving it) when you're in need of a little reprieve. The Trattoria has both indoor and outdoor patio seating that feel entirely and welcomely different to normal amusement park dining. The menu includes traditional Italian and Californian wine country favorites, as well as a variety of options for wine by the glass.

There are also several overlooked spaces immediately adjacent to the Trattoria. There's an actual winery right on site. Adults can stop by the Mendocino Terrace and enjoy wine tasting from Golden Vine Winery. There are twenty-five different selections available to delight your palate. A typical tasting will consist of three to four selections and run you about $15 per person. If wine isn't your thing, the Sonoma Terrace next door offers a selection of more than fifteen California craft beers. From IPAs, to lagers and pilsners, there's sure to be something that appeals to your tastes. Order up a Bavarian pretzel, or a meat and cheese plate, and enjoy an adult break, all right inside the park.

If you have a little extra time, stop by Blue Sky Cellar while you're in the area. Here you can watch a short ten-minute film on the making of Disney's California Adventure. True Disney fans love this mini-tour. You'll get an in-depth look into beginning concepts, see models on display, and there's even an interactive Cars Land game for the true enthusiast. Allow about 30 minutes to experience this tour. This little enclave of California Adventure is a perfect way to end an adult evening in the park.

The Cove Bar

Some might say that California Adventure is more for adults than kids. While there's plenty for kids inside DCA, many rides and shows cater to adults or older kids. Plus it's the only park where you can purchase and consume alcoholic beverages.

If you're looking for a relaxing afternoon by the water, head over to The Cove Bar on Paradise Pier. Just a few steps away from the entrance to Ariel's Grotto, you'll find a bar perched on the end of the pier. They offer signature drinks, wine, and beer, as well as decent bar food and appetizers. The Cove is open daily during regular park hours.

Tasty appetizers and drinks from the Cove Bar.

Not only will you find decent food and drink here. You'll also take in an exceptional view overlooking Paradise Bay. You can watch the California Screamin' roller coaster speed off, gaze at Mickey's Fun Wheel as it spins around, and overdose on people-watching over the Boardwalk. At night, the pier attractions are all lit up and makes for a beautiful sight to behold.

12
CAUTIONS

Don't come up short

Before you jump in the car, walk on the airplane, or board the train to Disneyland... If you're visiting with small children, make sure you know their height, and ideally, some of the height requirements for any key attractions you might be interested in. One of the things I love about Disney is their commitment to safety. Cast Members will check your child's height, even if he or she seems taller the height indicator.

Checking the 40-inch height requirement at Space Mountain.

We had to wait a year for our first child to hit the forty-inch mark. Forty inches is a minimum height for many of the basic rides at Disneyland and at DCA. Each trip, we would check and double check in hopes our daughter had grown enough. Don't worry if your little rider doesn't meet the height requirement; the Cast Member will give your child a special pass to get him or her to the front of the line on the next visit (once they meet the height requirement).

Don't get disappointed, and don't let your kids get disappointed either. There are so many things to take advantage of at Disneyland. If height is an issue, find areas of the park that better suit your child's size. Fantasyland and Bugs Land cater to smaller children. Very few of the rides there have height requirements. Also, take in a show like *Disney Junior, Live on Stage*, or *Mickey and the Magical Map* as a good alternative. No height requirements here either.

Most importantly, your child will have fun if you make the most of what's available for their age groups. Just avoid any unnecessary let-downs by checking their height before you go.

It's Tough To Be a Bug warning

Bugs Land is one of the best areas for children under forty inches. However, here's a small caution for *It's Tough To Be a Bug*, a 3D film in a theater near the entrance to Bugs Land. It can be intense for little ones. As we sat and watched, I was nervous for my daughter. She loves the thrill of a ride, but this was entirely different. This movie is dark, loud, and can be scary for young children. You get a pair of 3D glasses as you enter the theater, so the action of bugs (some small, some very large) flying directly at you can be a little much.

Hopper greets visitors at the entrance to It's Tough To Be a Bug.

If you're set on seeing this show, I recommend waiting until your children are a bit older. Well beyond the preschool recommended age. Also, if you're questioning whether or not your child could handle the intensity, perhaps waiting is best. You can ask parents exiting the theater what they thought of the film, and make a judgment from their response. We haven't been back to try it yet. I'm waiting a couple more years when our youngest daughter will be a little older.

Motion sickness on Star Tours

In 2011, Disney renovated Star Tours and gave it a significant update. You're still taking flight in a simulator, but the chances of taking the same flight twice are slim. The space flight now has over fifty story variations. Just when you think you're on the same path, the story changes and you get a slightly adjusted experience. Get ready to take flight and immerse yourself in the Star Wars saga. Even if you aren't a Star Wars fan, this ride might just change your mind.

With the complete overhaul came a new state-of-the-art 3D screen, which is amazing. Unless you're the type to experience motion sickness. For those who tend to have motion sickness, the new screen, the simulated diving, the twisting, and all of the bumps might just make a sensitive stomach upset. If you can handle it, this ride is worth it. But if you experience motion sickness, you might want to sit this one out.

If you want to ride Star Tours, and it's not going to be your first ride of the day, get a Fastpass. Without one, you can expect over an hour wait for this extremely popular attraction. Fastpasses are usually out of distribution by mid-day, so make sure you get yours early on or use the single rider line.

Scare factor

Some children, like mine, will try anything. Even before our older daughter could form sentences, we knew she'd be a daredevil. She loves the thrill of the rides. As soon as she's off, she wants right back on to ride it again. Her little sister seems to be following in her older sister's footsteps.

However, some children may not be as thrilled. I've seen parents trying to force their kids onto a ride. This is a recipe for disaster. Some rides are scary. Beware of the caution signs located on the ride information board at the entrance to each ride. When our daughter hit the forty-inch mark, I was still hesitant to let her ride Space Mountain. It's dark, fast, and loud. This might be a little much for younger children. Even I get a little nervous riding the ride.

If you're traveling with smaller children, beware of the scare factors. If you have doubts, ask a Cast Member. Even though all children are different, I will always ask parents with smaller children exiting the ride how their child reacted. When in doubt, don't ride. Once a child has been scared on a ride, you might have difficulty getting them to try it again.

13

SPECIAL NEEDS

Baby Care Centers

When we were getting ready for our first trip to Disneyland with a baby. I didn't know what amenities would be available. Fortunately, Disney makes it easy for families with babies in tow. If you'd like to feed in private or change a diaper, head to the Baby Care Center.

Disneyland's Baby Care Center, at the end of Main Street, U.S.A.

Whether breastfeeding or bottle-feeding, there is a quiet, private area to sit and feed your baby. If you need to heat up or mix a bottle, there's a small kitchen for your use. Each center has large changing tables with disposable liners. Diapers, wipes, and formula are available for purchase as well. Using cloth diapers? Not a problem. The Baby Care Center in Disneyland has a place for you to wash those dirty diapers. These centers are also equipped with rockers, swings, high chairs, TVs, and even toys.

Not only is the Baby Care Center great for babies, but you can also bring in toddlers under forty-two inches tall. Small, pint-sized commodes are available for those in the midst of potty training. My daughter loved being able to use a potty more her size without worrying about falling into those big, grown-up potties.

Baby Care Centers are tucked away in low-traffic areas of each park. At Disneyland, the center is tucked in an alley behind the old photo supply store at the castle end of Main Street. And at California Adventure, it's nestled in a corner beside the Ghirardelli Chocolate Shop.

Food allergies

Disney takes pride in how it treats their guest. Because we are guests, they want to make sure our needs are met. Over the years, Disney Parks have managed to accommodate more and more special need situations, including food allergies. Our daughter has a citrus allergy, so we need to take a little extra care to ensure her meals are safe for her.

We don't have this issue at Disneyland. Any time we have questions about food safety, a Chef is available to answer our questions. They are also able, and more than willing, to create a meal that will be safe for you or your child. Sometimes this even means the chef will go to another location in the park to have something created.

If you're concerned about food allergies, contact the Disneyland Resort Food & Beverage team. They are committed to accommodate guests with food allergies. When you make your dining reservations, let the Cast Member know of the specific allergy, and that your party may need special assistance. They will be happy to assist you. Outside food and beverages are generally not permitted. However, if you're still worried about food safety, and would like to bring your own food items, anyone with dietary restrictions can bring food into the park. If this is the case, you can contact Guest Services or Disney Dining at 714-781-DINE.

Eating gluten-free

So many people are now eating gluten free, and Disneyland has made dining stress-free for most special needs diets. Most hotel and park locations will accommodate your dietary restrictions; you just have to ask! Most of the time, the Chef will come out to talk with you to make sure your needs are being met. Disney also offers a full list of park locations that offer gluten-free dining. Pluto's Dog House, Hungry Bear Restaurant, and Flo's V-8 Cafe are just a few examples of dining locations that are designed to be, or are naturally, gluten-free. Most of the gluten-free foods available are processed in their own facilities, preventing cross contamination.

As a parent with a child who has allergies, I am always specific when ordering my food. Let the cashier or wait staff know in advance about your dietary restrictions. Your food order might take a few extra minutes, but this will put your mind at ease. With so many choices, don't be afraid to ask about special circumstances to ensure you enjoy your in-park dining experience.

Traveling with sick children

Having sick children is hard. Being on vacation with sick kids is even harder. If you're staying at one of the Disneyland hotels, they have a doctor on-site if needed. I knew there was a First Aid station inside both parks, but I knew nothing about an on-site doctor. It was reassuring to know that if I needed a doctor, one could be to our room within an hour.

For minor situations, you can get over-the-counter medications at a nearby Target, which is just a bus ride away if you don't have a car. The hotel gift shops and park gift stores also have several options as well. If you need additional care, there is a nearby Urgent Care center. The U.C. Irvine Medical Center is a full-service hospital, and is even closer.

So don't worry too much about you or your kids getting sick or injured during a family trip to The Happiest Place on Earth. It's great to know that if someone in your party gets sick, there are options nearby. Disney hotels have several options available, or the First Aid stations inside the park can help with minor issues. Use them—that's why they exist!

ABOUT THE AUTHOR

After spending many years trying to convince the guy (now her now husband) that she was "the one," Cam Bowman and her man jetted off to Paris for a weekend. Sharing a warm croissant early one morning in the middle of France, he finally realized that she was also "the one." So one and one became two. Fast forward a few years, these two multiplied and made two more. Cam now lives in San Francisco with her husband, two daughters, and an obnoxiously misbehaving chocolate lab, named Jackson. For the trouble he causes, Jackson should have gone to the pound by now. But the heart-strings tugged by Marley and Me somehow preserve his endangered role as the family dog.

When she's not baking, leading a Girl Scout meeting, or driving to the next swim lesson, Cam spends her days navigating between laughter and tears as she raises two high-energy girls. Most days, she doesn't know if she's coming or going. So she records some of the unique family moments, along with practical tips and ideas she picks up along the way on her site, *GrowingUpGoofy.com*. Find her on Twitter or Instagram by looking up @cambowman. Stop by and say hi anytime.

THANKS

To you, my readers. Thank you for purchasing and reading this book! If you enjoyed it (and I hope you did), I would be so grateful if you took a minute or two to leave a quick review of this book at your favorite bookseller.

To my husband. Thank you for listening to me at all hours of the day. For being patient with me, when I have no patience. This book would never have happened if it weren't for you. Ultimately, you were the driving force behind it. Had this book been about anything else, it simply wouldn't exist. Thank you for being a kid with me and loving Disney as much as I do. For showing me my Disney side, and living our dream together.

To my family and friends. Thank you for putting up with random questions about your trips and experiences. For letting me pick your brains, and listening to me ramble on and on about everything Disney. Yes, this appears to be one of our only vacation destinations. Thank you for going on this journey with us.

To my readers. Thank you for coming back day after day. It's because of you that I keep going. I love reading your comments, talking with you online, and building such a great community over the years.

To my tribe. You know who you are. We've spent countless hours over the last few years chatting on Twitter, private messaging, and passing through many Facebook groups. Regardless, you have helped me through this process and I'm forever indebted to you.

To Dennis, Dawn, and Roxanne. A very special thanks to you. I knew I could count on you in the eleventh hour to help get it done. Saying thank you will never be enough. Thank you for filling in the blanks when I couldn't.

To my mother. I know there were many times you wanted to pull your hair out when I asked you to watch the girls for "just one minute". I know it wasn't easy. Thank you for all your help. I wouldn't have finished this without it.

Last, but not least, to my two favorite girls, Emma and Addie. Thank you for showing us pure joy. We are beyond blessed to have two amazing, adventurous, children. It's because of you that we still see and feel the magic every time we step foot inside Disneyland.

DISCLAIMER AND TRADEMARKS

This is an unofficial book detailing personal experiences at Disneyland and recommendations for others who visit. This book is not endorsed nor published by The Walt Disney Company. The author is not officially connected to, or affiliated with Disney in any way.

Content of this book refers to Disney, Disneyland, DCA, and Characters trademarked by The Walt Disney Company. Use of this information is provided as editorial content covered by the Fair Use Doctrine. No permission needed. All content and photos were taken at the Disneyland Resort by the author. Any specific photo pertaining to Disney marketing is copyright by Disney. General use covered for editorial purposes.

The names listed below are used in accordance with the Fair Use Doctrine:

Adventureland, Big Thunder Mountain Railroad, Boudin Bakery, Buena Vista Street, Cars Land, Condor Flats, Critter Country, Disney California Adventure, Disneyland Resort, Disney's Paradise Pier, Downtown Disney, Dole, Fantasyland, FASTPASS, Frontierland, Golden State, Grizzly Peak, Hollywood Lands, "it's a small world," It's Tough To Be a Bug, Jungle Cruise, Main Street, U.S.A., Mickey Mouse and Characters, Mickey's Toontown, Monorail, New Orleans Square, Pacific Wharf, Paradise Pier, Peter Pan's Flight, Radiator Springs Racers, Redwood Creek, Roger Rabbit, Starbucks, Space Mountain, Splash Mountain, Star Wars, Starbucks, Tomorrowland, Toy Story and Characters, Up

Characters, Winnie the Pooh and Characters, World of Color, and World of Disney. This may not be an exhaustive list of every trademarked name or reference in this book. All trademarks belong to their respective owners.

INDEX

AAA, 75
Adventureland, 2, 45
Aladdin, 45, 83-84
Alice in Wonderland, 4, 95, 105
allergies, 129-130
Anaheim, 13, 42, 45
Animation Academy, 90-91
Animation Building, 45, 70-72, 90
appetizers, 117-119
arrival, 19, 23
Baby Care Center, 107-108, 128-129
balloons, 109
bathroom, See restroom
Beauty and the Beast, 71
beer, 55, 59, 117-118
beignets, 8, 61-62
Belle, 23-24, 47, 71, 74, 77
benches, 43, 108
Big Thunder Mountain Railroad, 19, 61
Billy Hill and the Hillbillies, 44, 84
Blue Bayou, 54, 56-57
Blue Sky Cellar, 118
Boardwalk Pizza and Pasta, 56
bottle-feeding, 128
breakfast, 13, 51-53, 59
breastfeeding, 128
Bugs Land, 123
Captain Hook, 43

Carnation Cafe, 53, 63, 80
Cars Land, 58, 113, 118
Carthay Circle, 35, 54, 116-117
Casey Jr. Circus Train, 105
Castle, 43-44, 60, 66, 71-72, 77, 80, 87-88, 96, 129
Character Dining, 50-51, 74-76, 78, 80
Characters, 3, 6, 24, 46, 50, 59, 73-80, 89-90, 104, 107
Chef, 129-130
Cheshire Cat, 95
Chip and Dale, 78
chocolate, 26-27, 101-102, 110, 129
Christmas, 19, 31, 100
churros, 59
Cinderella, 74
City Hall, 7-8, 18, 23, 62, 101
climbing, 109
closures, 19, 35
clothing, 18
Club 33, 18
coffee, 17, 38, 53, 63-64
collectible, 98, 101
complimentary, 13, 69
Condor Flats, 45, 69
cookies, 27, 102
Corn Dog, 59-60
Cove Bar, 118-119
Cozy Cone Motel, 58
Critter Country, 26

crowds, 7, 23, 30, 32, 36, 46-47
Crush, 88-89
Daisy, 78
Dapper Dans, 82
Darth Vader, 110-111
diapers, 128
dietary restrictions, 130
discount, 4-5, 10, 51
Disney Junior, 45, 89, 123
Disneyland hotel, 5, 12-13, 20, 27, 66, 78, 131
Disney Store, 6, 95, 97
DL Waits, 9-10
doctor, 131
Dole Whip, 3, 45
Donald, 78
Downtown Disney, 13, 27-28, 51, 53, 64, 100, 102, 106
drawing, 90
drinks, 116-119
Dumbo, 4, 105, 112
Enchanted Tiki Room, 3, 17, 45, 85-86
entertainment, 9, 13, 27-28, 81-83
Extra Magic Hour, 78
face painting, 110
fairy, 87
Fantasy Faire, 77-78
Fantasyland, 2, 4, 43, 61, 66, 83, 95, 111, 123
Fantasyland Theater, 83
Fastpass, 25, 31-32, 36-39, 55, 92, 125
Finding Nemo, 88, 105

fire engine, 44
Firehouse, 23
fireworks, 87
First Aid, 131
flying, 88, 123
Flynn Rider, 83
formula, 128
French Market, 61, 83
Frontierland, 19, 61, 84-85
Ghirardelli, 129
Glass slipper, 109
gluten-free, 130
Golden Horseshoe, 45, 84-85
Golden Vine Winery, 117
Good Neighbor hotel, 5, 12-13, 100
Goofy, 5, 39, 50, 56, 74-76, 78, 91, 94, 105, 108
Great Moments with Mr. Lincoln, 17
green Toy Story Army Men, 56
Grizzly River Run, 33, 39, 45, 69-70
Guest Relations, 8, 33, 101
gumbo, 58
Halloween, 19
Happiest Place on Earth, 3, 6, 30, 104, 131
Haunted Mansion, 45, 84, 112
height, 74, 112-113, 122-123
hidden Mickey, 18, 20
Hollywood, 61, 70, 84, 89-90, 116
Hook and Ladder Company, 82
horse-drawn carriage, 44

hotels, 4, 7, 12-13, 20, 27, 51, 66, 100, 106, 131

Hungry Bear, 130

hydrate, 46

ice cream, 3, 27, 59

Indiana Jones, 17, 34, 39

Jake and the Neverland Pirates, 89

Jazz, 62

Jedi Training, 44, 110-111

Jolly Holiday Bakery, 34, 53, 63, 80

Jungle Book, 83

Jungle Cruise, 17, 34, 68, 105, 111

La Brea Cafe, 53, 64

lanyard, 97-98

Library, 70-72

Lightning McQueen, 59

Lilly Belle, 23-24

lines, 9, 17-18, 30-32, 34, 36, 38-40, 43, 45, 59, 98, 111

Little Mermaid, 77, 83, 113

Little Red Wagon, 59

live entertainment, 28, 82-83

lockers, 32-34, 69-70

lost, 34, 69, 106-108

Lost and Found, 34

lost children, 106-107

lounge, 116-117

Mad Hatter, 8, 95

Mad Tea Party, 95

Magic Mornings, 16, 31

Main Gate, 16-18, 33, 76, 95, 106

Main Street, U.S.A., 20-22, 44, 47, 80, 82, 98, 100, 128

Main Street Vehicles, 44

maps, 9, 68

Market House, 53, 63-64

Mark Twain, 69

Mary Poppins, 79-80

Mater, 59, 113

Matterhorn, 39, 61, 87

Memorabilia, 93

merchandise, 4

Mickey, 2-3, 16-18, 20-22, 24-25, 41-42, 44-45, 52, 61-63, 76, 78-79, 83, 89, 91, 94-96, 101-102, 109, 113, 119, 123

Mickey and the Magical Map, 3, 17, 45, 83, 123

Mickey ears, 94-95

Minnie, 16, 53, 78-79, 94, 102

Mint Julep Bar, 8, 61-62

monorail, 12, 27, 66, 105

Monte Cristo, 56-58

motion sickness, 42, 124-125

MouseWait, 9-10

Mulan, 83

Muppets, 101

nervous, 123, 126

newborns, 104

New Orleans Square, 22, 44, 61, 83, 100

New Years, 17, 31

Omnibus, 44

parade, 3, 34, 46-47, 55, 80, 104-105, 107

Paradise Pier, 12, 42, 56, 66,
  118
Paradise Pier Hotel, 12
parking, 7, 13, 31, 106
passes, 4-5, 10, 27, 31-32, 37-
  40, 92, 125
Pasta, 56
PCH Grill, 50, 76
Pearly Band, 80, 82
personalized, 94
Peter Pan, 4, 43, 105
photo, 5, 17, 66-67, 75, 78, 96-
  97, 129
photographers, 96
PhotoPass, 17, 96
pineapple, 45, 85
pin trading, 97-98
Pirates of the Caribbean, 17,
  45, 57
pizza, 56
Playground, 108
Plaza Inn, 46, 50-51, 76
Pluto, 78, 130
Pocahontas, 83
Pooh, 26-27, 101, 105
pool, 13, 46
popcorn, 59
portraits, 99
potty training, 129
pressed pennies, 100
pretzels, 102
Princess and the Frog, 83
Princess Dot Puddle Park, 45,
  108, 113
Princesses, 6, 50, 77-78, 101

Radiator Springs, 38-39, 58,
  112
Radiator Springs Racers, 38-39,
  112
Railroad, 18-19, 22, 44, 61, 105
Rapunzel, 83
Redwood Creek, 70, 108-109
Redwood Creek Challenge
  Trail, 70
Refreshment Corner Pianist, 82
renovations, 19
rentals, 106
reservations, 5-6, 19, 28, 36, 51,
  53-55, 76, 117, 130
restroom, 9, 17, 56, 87, 114
Rider switch passes, 40
rope drop, 53
Roy O. Disney, 22
Saving Mr. Banks, 80
scare factor, 125-126
schedule, 18, 23, 26, 32, 36, 53,
  74, 76, 90
Scotch Mist, 117
Sebastian, 83
shopping, 3, 6-7, 27, 77
shuttle service, 13
sick, 42, 124-125, 131
silhouette, 20, 98-100
Silhouette Studio, 98-100
Silly Symphony Swings, 56
single-rider, 39
Sleeping Beauty, 4, 43, 66, 77,
  80, 87, 96
Small World, 2, 46, 105
smartphone, 9, 35

smoked turkey leg, 60

Snow White, 4, 66-67, 80

souvenir pin, 19

Space Mountain, 17, 122, 126

spaghetti, 56

special needs, 9, 127, 130

spectators, 91

spirits, 116

Splash Mountain, 39, 45

Starbucks, 53, 63-64

Star Tours, 45, 124-125

Star Wars, 7, 125

storage, 105

Storybook Canal, 105

strollers, 105-106

summer, 30, 36, 69

sunscreen, 17, 106

supercalifragilisticexpialidocious, 79

Tangled, 77, 83

Tea Cups, 95

temperatures, 46

Thanksgiving, 31

theater, 77, 83-84, 88-90, 110,
123-124

thrill, 8, 40-41, 63, 89, 111-113,
123, 125

Tiana, 83

ticket booths, 31

tickets, 27, 31, 38, 55

Tigger, 26-27

Tigger Tails, 26-27

Tiki Room, 3, 17, 45, 85-87,
105

Tinker Bell, 6, 87, 101

tired, 43, 55, 104-105

toddlers, 108, 129

Tomorrowland, 2, 12, 22, 27,
44, 82, 110, 112

Toontown, 2, 20, 22, 24-25, 44,
76, 78-79, 105

tours, 4, 18-19, 45, 124-125

Town Square, 18, 46

toys, 129

Toy Story, 56, 61

Toy Story Mania, 61

Trash Can Trio, 82

Turtle Talk, 45, 88-89

Up, 70

Urgent Care, 131

villain, 50, 70

Vouchers, 51

wait times, 3, 7, 9, 34-35, 78-79

walking, 13, 22, 26, 37, 43, 60,
69-70, 105

Walt Disney, 3, 21, 23, 40, 97

Walt Disney Family Museum,
97

water, 62, 66-67, 69, 91, 114,
118

wifi, 13

Wilderness Badge, 70

windows, 21, 66

Wine Country Trattoria, 54-55,
117

wine tasting, 117

winter, 64

wipes, 128

Wishing Well, 67

World of Color, 55, 91-92

the

dog owner's

manual

[front] [left side]

[right side] [back]

the

dog
owner's manual

OPERATING INSTRUCTIONS, TROUBLESHOOTING
TIPS, AND ADVICE ON LIFETIME MAINTENANCE

by Dr. David Brunner and Sam Stall

Illustrated by Paul Kepple and Jude Buffum

QUIRK BOOKS
PHILADELPHIA

Library of Congress Cataloging in Publication Number: 2003096236

ISBN: 1-931686-85-8

Printed in Singapore

Typeset in Swiss

Designed by Paul Kepple and Jude Buffum @ Headcase Design
www.headcasedesign.com

Distributed in North America by Chronicle Books
85 Second Street
San Francisco, CA 94105

10 9 8 7 6 5 4 3

Quirk Books
215 Church Street
Philadelphia, PA 19106
www.quirkbooks.com

Contents

WELCOME TO YOUR NEW DOG! 10

The Dog: Diagram and Parts List 13

    ■ The Head 13

    ■ The Body 14

    ■ Sensor Specifications 15

Memory Capacity 19

Product Life Span 19

CHAPTER 1:

OVERVIEW OF MAKES AND MODELS 20

A Brief Product History 22

Survey of Brands 24

Top-Selling Models 26

Nonstandard, Off-Brand Models 38

Selecting an Appropriate Model 40

New Versus Used Models 42

Selecting a Gender 43

Selecting a Vendor 43

Puppy Pre-acquisition Inspection Checklist 46

Adult Dog Pre-acquisition Inspection Checklist 48

CHAPTER 2:

HOME INSTALLATION 50

Preparing the Home 52

Recommended Accessories 53

Initial Introduction 56

    ■ Interfacing with Children 57

    ■ Interfacing with Other Dogs 60

    ■ Interfacing with Cats 63

First Night at Home 66

Selecting a Name 67

CHAPTER 3:
DAILY INTERACTION 68

Audio Cues and Body Language 70
Dogs and Human Speech 72
Sleep Mode 72
Dog Identification Methods 73
Exercise and Fitness 74
Yard Containment Protocol 77
Waste Disposal Protocols 81
  ▪ Crate Training 81
  ▪ House-Training 84
  ▪ Dealing with Unauthorized Downloads 84

CHAPTER 4:
BASIC PROGRAMMING 86

Overview of Factory-Installed Software 88
Establishing Dominance 89
Training Options (Software Add-Ons) 92
  ▪ Socialization 92
  ▪ Leash Training 92
  ▪ Sit 94
  ▪ Stay 94
  ▪ Heel 97
  ▪ Coming When Called 98
Selecting an Obedience Program 101

CHAPTER 5:
FUEL REQUIREMENTS 102

Types of Fuel 104
Selecting a Brand 106
How to Feed 107

Fuel Supplements (Snacks) 111
Managing the Dog's Weight 112
  ▪ Weight Reduction 114

CHAPTER 6:
EXTERIOR MAINTENANCE 116

Understanding the Coat 118
Overview of Dog Hair Varieties 119
General Coat Maintenance 122
Selecting a Professional Groomer 123
  ▪ Removing Mats 124
  ▪ Bathing 125
  ▪ Ears 128
  ▪ Eyes 129
  ▪ Teeth 129
  ▪ Anal Glands 129
  ▪ Nails 130
Emergency Cleanups 132

CHAPTER 7:
GROWTH AND DEVELOPMENT 134

Puppy Growth Stages 136
  ▪ Birth to 8 Weeks 136
  ▪ 8 to 15 Weeks 136
  ▪ 16 Weeks to 11 Months 137
  ▪ 12 Months 137
Calculating Age in "Dog Years" 140
Teeth Development 140
Diet Requirements 141
Sexual Maturity 141
  ▪ Spaying and Neutering 142

CHAPTER 8:
INTERIOR MAINTENANCE 144

Selecting a Service Provider 146
Conducting a Home Maintenance Inspection 147
Visiting Your Service Provider 149
  ▪ Age 6–8 Weeks 149
  ▪ Age 10–12 Weeks 149
  ▪ Age 14–16 Weeks 150
  ▪ Annually 150
Potentially Major Hardware Glitches 151
Minor Hardware Glitches 154
Medicinal Compounds 156
Administering Pills 157
Measuring the Dog's Heart Rate 158
Measuring the Dog's Core Temperature 159

CHAPTER 9:
EMERGENCY MAINTENANCE 160

Contagious Diseases 162
Chronic Diseases 164
Hereditary Diseases 166
Allergies 167
Poisons 168
Trauma 170
Bugs in the System 172
  ▪ Internal Parasites 172
  ▪ External Parasites 175
Behavioral/Psychological Disorders 178
Emergency Transport Techniques 180
The Heimlich Maneuver 183
Artificial Respiration and CPR 184
Pet Insurance 187

CHAPTER 10:
ADVANCED FUNCTIONS 188

Home and Personal Defense 190
Contests 191
Hardware Modifications 195
Reproduction 196
  ■ Selecting a Mate 196
  ■ Mating 197
  ■ Pregnancy 198
  ■ Prenatal Monitoring 198
  ■ Preparing for Birth 199
  ■ Birth 199
Canine Travel 200
  ■ Automobile Travel 200
  ■ Air Travel 202
Old Age 203
Obsolescence and Deactivation 204

APPENDIX 206
  ■ Troubleshooting 207
  ■ Technical Support 216
  ■ Glossary of Terms 217
INDEX 219
ABOUT THE AUTHORS 224

Welcome
to Your New Dog!

[UNPACK CAREFULLY]

dog

Model: ☑ Puppy ☐ Adult
Not intended for resale

FRAGILE

THIS
END UP

Contents: One (1) Jack Russell Terrier

ATTENTION!

Before beginning this manual, please inspect your model carefully. If any of the standard parts shown on pages 16–17 appear to be missing or inoperative, consult your dog's service provider immediately.

Whether you have just acquired a new dog or are contemplating getting one, congratulations. This product's legendary utility has inspired unprecedented customer loyalty among humans of every culture, age, and locale. With proper care and maintenance, it can accomplish almost any task its owner cares to assign.

The dog is surprisingly similar to other high-tech devices you may already own. Like cars, dogs are available in numerous makes and models. Like PCs, they can be configured to serve different functions. And like home security systems, they can keep you and your property safe and sound.

However, while most such highly developed consumer products come with instruction manuals, dogs do not. This is a major oversight, since the complexity of their programming far exceeds that of even the fastest computers, and their mechanical functions are more varied and subtle than those of the finest automobiles. With proper guidance, this near-autonomous system can master numerous desirable behaviors. It can even provide companionship and love. But used improperly, it can manifest traits inconvenient and/or harmful to you, your family, and your possessions.

Hence this book. *The Dog Owner's Manual* is a comprehensive user's guide that explains how to derive maximum enjoyment from your canine. It is not necessary to read it from cover to cover. For ease of use, this book has been divided into 11 sections. If you have a question or problem, turn to any of the following chapters:

OVERVIEW OF MAKES AND MODELS (pages 20–49) offers a primer on the literally hundreds of available dog types, a quick look at important hardware and software variations, and guidance on making the right choice for your lifestyle.

HOME INSTALLATION (pages 50–67) explains how to safely introduce a dog into your home and to its new human and/or animal companions.

DAILY INTERACTION (pages 68–85) covers elementary maintenance issues such as deciphering dog behavior, body language, and play preferences.

BASIC PROGRAMMING (pages 86–101) offers an overview of factory-installed software (instinctive behaviors) and owner-installed software add-ons (training).

FUEL REQUIREMENTS (pages 102–115) discusses your dog's nutritional requirements, including when to feed, what to feed, and how much to feed.

EXTERIOR MAINTENANCE (pages 116–133) explains how to handle body-work and detailing issues, including grooming, bathing, and nail clipping.

GROWTH AND DEVELOPMENT (pages 134–143) covers puppy growth milestones, neutering/spaying, and how to calculate your dog's physio-logical age.

INTERIOR MAINTENANCE (pages 144–159) explains how to monitor a dog's mechanical systems for signs of trouble and how to select an author-ized service provider for technical support. Covers everything from minor dings to major realignments.

EMERGENCY MAINTENANCE (pages 160–187) lists major medical con-ditions that may afflict canines and outlines possible treatment alternatives.

ADVANCED FUNCTIONS (pages 188–205) surveys additional program-ming options for dogs and offers a brief look at hardware modifications and reproduction.

TROUBLESHOOTING (pages 206–215) addresses frequently asked ques-tions about common software glitches, from undue aggression to exces-sive barking.

When used properly, a dog can provide its owner with endless hours of fun, companionship, and service. Remember, however, that mastering such a complex system requires energy and commitment. As you cope with training setbacks, unauthorized bodily discharges, and programming bugs, remember that the final result—a loyal, loving pet—is well worth the effort.

Congratulations and welcome to the world of dog ownership!

The Dog: Diagram and Parts List

Though canine physical attributes can vary substantially from one breed to the next, all have the same complement of preinstalled parts and capabilities. If your pet is missing one or more of the parts or systems herein described, contact an authorized service provider immediately.

The Head

Eyes: Most dog breeds come with brown or black eyes, though some varieties are fitted with blue, green, yellow, or even a combination of colors. Each eye has three eyelids—upper, lower, and a "third" lid in the inner corner. The third lid functions as a "windshield wiper," clearing dust and debris from the surface of the eye.

Ears: May come in several styles, including button, floppy, and rose ears. The "erect ear" (seen on such breeds as German shepherds and huskies) is the standard model once used by all ancient dogs.

Nose: As with the ears, the nose can take many forms and lengths. Colors can vary from black to liver; the color often lightens during winter. In general, the longer the nose the more well-developed the dog's sense of smell. Its wetness increases its effectiveness by dissolving incoming scent molecules for easy analysis. Contrary to legend, a dry nose does not necessarily indicate sickness.

Tongue: While frequently used to taste potential food, the canine tongue is also used to vent excess heat. The movement of air back and forth across its surface (via panting), combined with the evaporation of saliva, serves to regulate body temperature.

Teeth: Dogs have 42 teeth, including six pairs of incisors in front that are bracketed by two pairs of large canines. The rest are molars and premolars, allowing dogs (unlike some predators) to easily add vegetarian fare to their diets, if circumstances dictate.

The Body

Coat: All dogs, even the so-called "hairless" varieties, have a covering of fur. Its color and/or combination of colors can vary widely, even among members of the same breed. Muscles in the skin allow the hairs to stand up or "bristle." Excess shedding or a dull, brittle coat may indicate health problems. (See "Exterior Maintenance," pages 116–133.)

Output Port: The dog's waste discharge system also functions as a means for identification. The anus is bracketed by two internal anal glands that secrete a strong, pungent odor along with each bowel movement. This acts as an olfactory "calling card" to other dogs. When canines sniff each other's hindquarters, they are in fact investigating the anal glands.

Genitals: Male dogs reach sexual maturity at approximately 8 months of age. Females become sexually mature at 9 to 15 months.

Paws: Most of the dog's sense of touch is located here. Dogs can also sweat through their paw pads.

Tail: Used primarily to signal emotions. The number of bones in a dog's tail (and therefore its length) varies from animal to animal.

Nipples: These docking ports for peripherals come preinstalled on both female and male models. However, the circuitry of the male model renders these valves inoperative.

Weight: Dog weights vary markedly, from a maximum of more than 200 pounds (91 kg) to a minimum of 2 or 3 pounds (1–1.5 kg). In general, male dogs weigh about 10 percent more than females of the same breed.

Height: As with weight, canine dimensions vary wildly from breed to breed. While the Irish wolfhound stands roughly 32 inches (81 cm) tall at the shoulders, the Chihuahua can be as short as 5 inches (13 cm).

Sensor Specifications

All dogs possess a highly developed suite of environmental sensors. The data they furnish provide canines with a situational awareness far superior to that of humans.

Visual Sensors: The dog's vision is a legacy system from the wolf. It is excellent for spotting moving targets at great distances and in poor lighting.

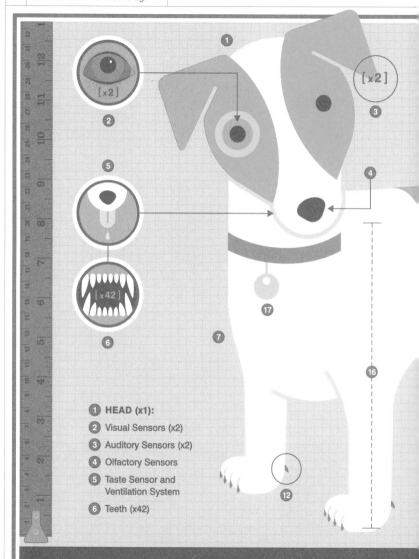

1 **HEAD (x1):**

2 Visual Sensors (x2)

3 Auditory Sensors (x2)

4 Olfactory Sensors

5 Taste Sensor and Ventilation System

6 Teeth (x42)

STANDARD COMPONENTS LIST: Check your model carefully. If any of

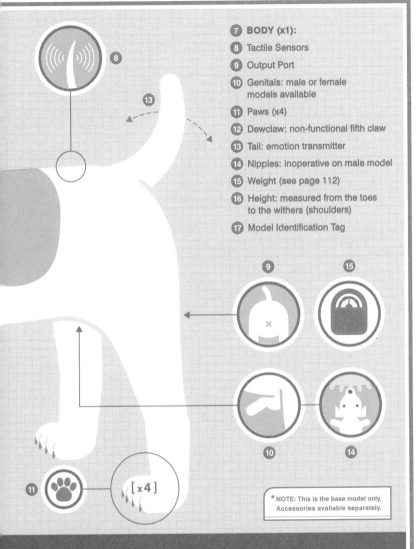

7 **BODY (x1):**

8 Tactile Sensors

9 Output Port

10 Genitals: male or female models available

11 Paws (x4)

12 Dewclaw: non-functional fifth claw

13 Tail: emotion transmitter

14 Nipples: inoperative on male model

15 Weight (see page 112)

16 Height: measured from the toes to the withers (shoulders)

17 Model Identification Tag

[x4]

*NOTE: This is the base model only. Accessories available separately.

the parts shown above are missing, notify your service provider immediately.

However, dogs see fewer colors than humans and cannot discern fine detail. At close range they rely heavily on their sense of smell, which is almost unequaled in the animal world.

Olfactory Sensors: While human noses contain between 5 million and 20 million scent-analyzing cells, dogs can carry 200 million or more. The bloodhound, famed for its tracking skills, possesses 300 million. To handle all this data, the olfactory processing center of a dog's brain is 40 times larger than that of humans. This faculty allows rescue dogs to detect humans buried under an avalanche and enables tracking hounds to follow scent trails that are 3 days old.

Auditory Sensors: Dog ears can move independently of each other, allowing them to pinpoint the origins of specific sounds in a fraction of a second. Dogs can also hear extremely high frequencies (as high as 40,000 cycles per second, compared to 20,000 per second for humans) and detect noises at roughly four times the range of humans. In other words, what you hear at 50 feet (15 m), a dog can hear at 200 feet (60 m).

Tactile Sensors: Each hair in a dog's coat acts as an antenna, feeding environmental data to a *mechanoreceptor* nerve at its base. This data allows the canine to be acutely aware of its immediate surroundings.

Taste Sensors: Dogs possess only about 1,700 taste buds compared to roughly 9,000 in humans. This relative lack of taste explains their undiscriminating palates, allowing them to eat almost any food without complaint (and to lick themselves without gagging).

Memory Capacity

Experts debate the exact intelligence quotient of dogs and even whether it is possible to gauge the IQ of a nonhuman species. What can be said with certainty is that the average dog's memory capacity and problem-solving skills far exceed those of the most powerful computers. Consider the fact that while supercomputers can play master-level chess, they can't begin to tackle such complex tasks as foxhunting or guiding a blind person down a city street.

Similarly, comparing the acuity of different breeds can be a very subjective exercise. Some models excel at mental traits—trainability, energy, inquisitiveness—desired by humans. This may make them appear "smarter" than other canines. However, these traits aren't always a plus. Many dogs with high "intelligence," such as Border collies and terriers, require plenty of exercise, mental stimulation, and "face time" with their owners. Conversely, allegedly less intelligent breeds can be much more laid-back and easier to live with.

Product Life Span

The operational life span of dogs averages 12 years, but your model's mileage may vary. As a rule of thumb, larger varieties depreciate much more rapidly than compact ones. For instance, a 7-year-old mastiff or Great Dane is very close to obsolescence. However, a poodle, beagle, or similar small dog could easily function twice that long or longer. The oldest documented canine life span was 29 years.

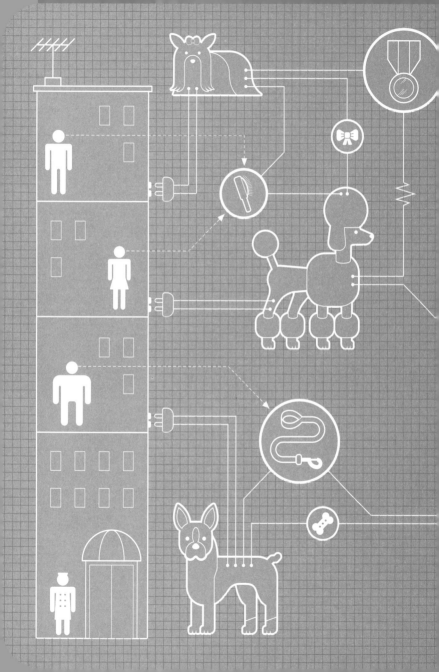

Chapter 1

Overview of Makes and Models

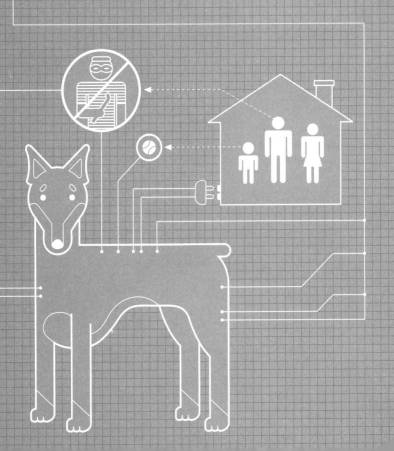

A Brief Product History

Since before the dawn of civilization, dogs have been a valued and welcome component of human society. But because the animal's association with man is so ancient, we know very little about the long-gone days when it was created.

Experts theorize that the dog, or *Canis familiaris*, was developed from its wild cousin, the wolf (*Canis lupus*). Though the wolf is a far less user-friendly system (Fig. A), it carries much of the basic programming (loyalty, courage, and highly developed social skills) that humans covet in dogs. Over many generations, wolf behavior was altered by selective breeding to enhance those desirable characteristics and to suppress undesirable ones, such as extreme aggression. The result has become one of marketing's greatest success stories. Today there are approximately 60 million dogs in the United States alone (Fig. B), compared to only about 100,000 wolves worldwide.

The physical differences between *Canis familiaris* and *Canis lupus* can be quite radical. While wolves adhere to one standard physical template, dogs come in a variety of shapes and sizes. Every trait from coat length to hair color will vary from breed to breed—and from individual to individual.

The same, however, can't be said of a dog's programming. Except for a few key modifications, dogs and wolves still share the same basic operating system. For instance, a dog's willingness to cohabit with human families springs directly from its wild progenitor's preference for living and hunting in packs. The dog's legendary courage in territorial and personal defense, its ability to understand and obey instructions, even its devotion to children, are all attributes of pack behavior.

Of course, not all of the dog's undesirable programming has been deleted. Like wolves, they constantly seek to upgrade their status in the pack—usually by dominating lesser members. In the wild this means that the strongest animal leads. In a domestic situation, a dog who tries to dominate its master may become aggressive, uncontrollable, or, at the very least, annoying.

Fortunately, in most cases, these programming glitches can be fixed with careful socialization and firm discipline—both of which will be explained in upcoming pages.

CANIS LUPUS VS. CANIS FAMILIARIS

(Fig. A)
Canis lupus, 10,000 B.C.

(Fig. B)
Canis familiaris, Today

Survey of Brands

The majority of the world's dogs are undifferentiated varieties produced by random interbreeding. These are called "mixed breeds" or "mutts." However, there are also numerous selectively bred models that reliably produce a particular body type and/or emphasize specific behaviors. Dogs created in this way are called "purebreds." America's leading purebred association, the American Kennel Club, divides them into seven major groups:

Sporting Dogs: This division is composed mostly of pointers, retrievers, setters, and spaniels, including the golden retriever, Labrador retriever, Weimaraner, cocker spaniel, and Irish setter. *Best Features:* All have active, energetic personalities. *Caveat:* Members of the sporting group usually require regular, vigorous exercise.

Working Dogs: Developed for such things as guard duty and rescue work, working dogs are among the strongest and hardiest of all breeds. The list includes the Great Dane, Doberman pinscher, Alaskan malamute, Newfoundland, Saint Bernard, and Rottweiler. *Best Features:* Their courage and large size make many models in this group ideal for home defense. *Caveat:* These powerful dogs require careful training and socialization.

Toys: Members of the toy group are, for the most part, tiny. Not surprisingly, many are classic lapdogs. Toy models include the Maltese, Chihuahua, Shih Tzu, Pekingese, and Pomeranian. *Best Features:* Perfect for apartment dwellers with little space to spare. **Caveat:** Not all lapdogs are placid. Chihuahuas and Pomeranians, in particular, can present numerous behavioral challenges.

Terriers: Developed to pursue, corner, and kill everything from rats to badgers, members of the terrier group are famous for their distinctive (some would say *challenging*) personalities. These energetic dogs are best-suited to an energetic owner. Models include the cairn terrier, Jack Russell terrier, bull terrier, Border terrier, and the American Staffordshire terrier. **Best Features:** Terriers are known for their vitality and colorful attitudes. **Caveat:** They can be very combative with other dogs and may try to dominate an overly passive owner.

Hounds: A loose grouping encompassing several models originally designed for hunting animals in open country, most are now utilized primarily as house pets. The hound group includes the beagle, basset hound, Rhodesian ridgeback, greyhound, and borzoi. **Best Features:** When not actually hunting, many hound models display placid, laid-back personalities. **Caveat:** Some hounds, such as beagles, regularly emit a loud, drawn-out bark/howl called a "bay." Learn if the particular model you desire does this, and experience it for yourself, before acquiring one.

Nonsporting Dogs: A catchall category that includes breeds of diverse size, shape, and temperament, these dogs are best defined by what they *aren't* (not a hound, not a terrier, not a working dog) rather than what they are. Well-

known nonsporting models include the bichon frise, bulldog, poodle, and Dalmatian. ***Best Features:*** From guard dogs to lapdogs, this group offers models for every lifestyle. ***Caveat:*** The diversity of this category makes generalizations about behavior and/or physical requirements impossible.

Herding Dogs: As the name implies, all members of this group excel at controlling the movements of other animals. The group includes the collie, Border collie, Old English sheepdog, and the Welsh corgi (a tiny, slow-moving model that nevertheless can herd cattle by nipping at their heels). ***Best Features:*** Many herding breeds, such as the Border collie, are renowned for their intelligence and energy. ***Caveat:*** When it comes to herding dogs, the line between "intelligent and energetic" and "nervous and high-strung" can be very thin. If a herder does not receive regular, stimulating exercise, it may "exercise itself" by destroying your personal property.

Top-Selling Models

Though there are hundreds of dog breeds, a relative handful enjoy near-universal popularity and acceptance. The following models are either extremely common or so well-known that they merit special mention. If any interest you, consult a veterinarian or local breed club for more information. Always buy a purebred from a reputable breeder.

Akita Inu: Originally bred for fighting and guarding, the Akita is the national dog of Japan. ***Height:*** 25–28 inches (64–71 cm). ***Weight:*** 66–100 pounds (34–45 kg). ***Exterior:*** Thick coated; strong resemblance to Western working breeds such as German shepherds and huskies; powerfully built with a curling, bristly tail. ***Best Features:*** High intelligence and loyalty to master. ***Caveat:*** Can dominate a weak owner. Aggressive toward other dogs. ***Special Programming:*** Excellent memory. ***Ideal Owner:*** Strong, energetic person willing to satisfy the Akita's need for exercise and firm handling.

American Staffordshire Terrier: Originally bred for pit fighting and bull baiting, it is, pound for pound, arguably the strongest dog in the world. ***Height:*** 16–18 inches (41–46 cm). ***Weight:*** 37–44 pounds (17–20 kg). ***Exterior:*** Short, smooth coat in a variety of colors. Extremely powerfully built, with a barrel chest, obvious muscle development, and extra-wide jaws. ***Best Features:*** Properly bred models make steady, loyal companions. ***Caveat:*** A poorly bred model in the hands of an abusive or otherwise incompetent owner can be extremely dangerous. ***Special Programming:*** Indifferent to pain, completely fearless. ***Ideal Owner:*** Strong, energetic person capable of developing this model's tender side.

Basset Hound: A descendant of the bloodhound, the basset's short legs were developed so human hunters could stand a better chance of keeping up with it in the field. ***Height:*** 15 inches (38 cm). ***Weight:*** 40–51 pounds (18–23 kg). ***Exterior:*** Short, smooth coat, short legs, long ears that can drag on the ground. ***Best Features:*** Patient to a fault, devoted to its family, good with children, all but incapable of aggression. ***Caveat:*** Can be difficult to house-train—or to train at all. ***Special Programming:*** The basset's sense of smell is one of the dog world's keenest. ***Ideal Owner:*** A person who will give it proper exercise (bassets gain weight easily) and plenty of personal attention.

Beagle: One of the oldest European hunting models, it dates at least to the 14th century. ***Height:*** 13–16 inches (33–41 cm). ***Weight:*** 26–33 pounds

(12–15 kg). ***Exterior:*** Smooth coat, floppy ears. ***Best Features:*** Good with children and families; shows almost no aggression. ***Caveat:*** Easily distracted. If it catches an interesting scent, an unleashed beagle will simply vanish. Also, they tend to overeat. ***Special Programming:*** Beagles announce the arrival of strangers with a hair-raising, drawn-out bark/howl called a "bay." ***Ideal Owner:*** A family with children.

Boxer: So-named because of its alleged proclivity for rearing onto its hind legs and "boxing" with its forearms. ***Height:*** 21–25 inches (53–63 cm). ***Weight:*** 53–70 pounds (24–32 kg). ***Exterior:*** Short, smooth coat, well-muscled body, flat nose, and an intimidating facial expression. ***Best Features:*** An excellent watchdog, but also good with children. ***Caveat:*** Has a relatively short life span (usually less than 10 years). ***Special Programming:*** The boxer, though exuberant, tends to display much less aggression than other popular guarding breeds, such as the German shepherd and Rottweiler. ***Ideal Owner:*** A family with children.

Chihuahua: Arguably developed in pre-Colombian Mexico, it is the world's smallest dog breed. ***Height:*** 5–9 inches (15–23 cm). ***Weight:*** 1–6 pounds (.5–3 kg). ***Exterior:*** Coat can be short or long. Head shapes include "deer" (longish face with well-developed muzzle) and "apple" (large eyes, large skull, shortened muzzle) varieties. ***Best Features:*** This sprightly dog has a fiery, entertaining personality. It is also an excellent watchdog. ***Caveat:*** Its small stature makes it somewhat fragile. Mature dogs have a small opening in the tops of their skulls, making them vulnerable to head injury. ***Special Programming:*** Chihuahuas don't seem to realize how little they are. They will, without hesitation, attack dogs 20 times their size. *Do not allow them to do this.* ***Ideal Owner:*** Apartment dwellers and senior citizens.

Collie: Originally developed in the Scottish Highlands as a herding dog. **Height:** 22–24 inches (56–61 cm). **Weight:** 48–70 pounds (22–32 kg). **Exterior:** One of the most aesthetically pleasing of all dogs, collies' luxurious coats come in sable, tricolor, and blue merle patterns. A shorthaired "smooth" model is also available. **Best Features:** A steady, highly intelligent dog. **Caveat:** Can be somewhat tricky to train—headstrong, yet also sensitive and timid. **Special Programming:** Collies, originally developed to herd, often seize any opportunity to implement this portion of their programming. They have been known to "herd" children, other pets, even groups of adults. **Ideal Owner:** Anyone willing to shoulder the prodigious costs of grooming (and who doesn't mind having large amounts of sable, tricolor, or blue merle hairs on their home furnishings).

Dachshund: Developed to hunt prey in its lair, the dachshund's name means "badger dog." **Height:** 8–10 inches (20–25 cm). **Weight:** 12–15 pounds (5–7 kg). **Exterior:** This short-legged, long-bodied model comes in longhaired, shorthaired, and wirehaired varieties. **Best Features:** A well-tempered dog with few programming glitches. **Caveat:** Can be problematic around children. Resistant to training. **Special Programming:** Dachshunds were designed to be fearless hunters. Though they resemble lapdogs, they act like terriers. Owners expecting a placid couch companion will be disappointed. **Ideal Owner:** A person willing to invest the time to train a dachshund properly.

Doberman Pinscher: Developed in the 1860s by a German dogcatcher named Louis Dobermann. **Height:** 27–28 inches (69–71 cm). **Weight:** 66–88 pounds (30–40 kg). **Exterior:** Short, smooth, mostly black coat (though color variations such as blue and red are available). Powerfully muscled, graceful body. Floppy ears that are sometimes "cropped" to a point. **Best Features:** A peerless, highly disciplined guard dog. **Caveat:**

TOP-SELLING MODELS: There are many breeds to choose from. The

models shown above (and on pages 36–37) represent some of the most popular canines.

Can be very aggressive if not handled properly. **Special Programming:** Dobermans are extremely intelligent and can accept a great deal of complicated training. Males can be markedly more aggressive than females. **Ideal Owner:** An experienced handler who can offer thorough training and consistent discipline. These dogs are not intended for novices.

German Shepherd: Originally developed as a herding dog. **Height:** 22–26 inches (56–66 cm). **Weight:** 62–77 pounds (28–35 kg). **Exterior:** Most commonly a short, tan coat with a black "saddle" across the back. However, solid black models are available (along with other color combinations), plus medium-haired and longhaired varieties. **Best Features:** Highly intelligent and trainable. **Caveat:** Coat sheds perpetually. **Special Programming:** Shepherds love to work and excel at everything from guarding to rescue. **Ideal Owner:** Someone who can give the dog plenty to do—and can control its natural aggressive tendencies.

Golden Retriever: The entire breed reportedly stems from the 19th-century pairing of a yellow wavy-coated retriever to a Tweed water spaniel. **Height:** 20–24 inches (51–61 cm). **Weight:** 59–81 pounds (27–37 kg). **Exterior:** Straight or slightly wavy golden coat. Friendly, perpetually pleasant expression. **Best Features:** Amiable, playful, and gentle, the golden is a family dog without peer. **Caveat:** It is completely useless for personal protection or home defense. **Special Programming:** Originally bred as a hunting dog, it is still sometimes used for that purpose. **Ideal Owner:** Anyone willing to give it the attention and daily exercise it requires.

Greyhound: The fastest of all dogs, it can run at speeds exceeding 40 mph (64 kmph). **Height:** 27–31 inches (69–79 cm). **Weight:** 55–66 pounds (25–30 kg). **Exterior:** Short coat in a variety of shades. Lithe, powerfully built body.

Best Features: Though famous for its explosive speed, the greyhound also makes a docile, well-mannered pet. **Caveat:** Greyhounds need a great deal of exercise. **Special Programming:** The urge to pursue game is so deeply ingrained that no amount of remedial work can overcome it. Greyhounds must always be leashed in public. They are easily distracted by moving objects and/or small animals (including cats), which they may chase over great distances and—if not stopped—kill. **Ideal Owner:** An athletic person willing to give the dog the exercise it needs.

Jack Russell Terrier: Developed in the 19th century by English clergyman and dog breeder Parson Jack Russell. **Height:** 13–14 inches (33–36 cm). **Weight:** 9–18 pounds (4–8 kg). **Exterior:** Available in wirehaired and smooth-coated versions. Body shape, leg length, and facial structure vary far more widely from individual to individual than is generally seen in a recognized breed. **Best Features:** A highly intelligent, breathtakingly athletic companion dog with one of the canine world's most vivacious personalities. **Caveat:** Possibly the most belligerent and high-tempered of all terriers. **Special Programming:** Jacks were originally bred to chase game into (or out of) underground lairs. As such, they are adept at pursuit, fighting, and digging up back yards. **Ideal Owner:** An experienced dog owner who can supply the extensive training and firm hand this model requires.

Labrador Retriever: The most popular dog model in the United States. **Height:** 21–24 inches (53–61 cm). **Weight:** 55–79 pounds (25–36 kg). **Exterior:** Available in black, chocolate, and yellow. To facilitate swimming, its coat is waterproof and its toes are webbed. **Best Features:** Excellent family dog. Loves children. Accepting of guests. **Caveat:** No guarding skills whatsoever. Tends to overeat. **Special Programming:** Because Labradors were designed to retrieve game from the water, they love to swim and get wet. ***Ideal Owner:*** A family with lakefront property and a very high tolerance for the game of fetch.

Newfoundland: A working dog once used by fishermen to carry burdens and to help haul in nets. ***Height:*** 26–28 inches (66–71 cm). ***Weight:*** 99–150 pounds (45–68 kg). ***Exterior:*** Long, waterproof black or brown coat. Massive, stocky body and webbed toes to facilitate swimming. ***Best Features:*** Though its size and phenomenal strength make it intimidating, the Newfoundland is, in fact, quite mellow, making it a good family dog. ***Caveat:*** "Newfies" drool excessively and their coats require regular, careful grooming. ***Special Programming:*** Because of their strength and affinity for the water, Newfoundlands are sometimes employed as water rescue dogs. ***Ideal Owner:*** A family with a large house and yard. Newfoundlands are not apartment dwellers.

Pekingese: Formerly a fixture at the imperial Chinese court, it was brought to the West in the 19th century. ***Height:*** 6–9 inches (15–23 cm). ***Weight:*** 10–13 pounds (5–6 kg). ***Exterior:*** Long, silky coat with a black face surrounded by a lionlike mane. Available in numerous colors. ***Best Features:*** The dog displays a placid demeanor and devotes itself to its master. ***Caveat:*** Has little patience with children. Obedience training is very difficult, if not impossible. ***Special Programming:*** Although "Pekes" are difficult to train, their basic temperament is easygoing and cooperative. They generally avoid trouble. ***Ideal Owner:*** Anyone who wants a small dog to dote on.

Poodle: Originally a hunting dog with a strong affinity for water, its name derives from the German word *pudeln*, which means "splash." These dogs come in four different sizes: standard, medium, miniature, and toy. ***Height:*** Standard, 18–23 inches (46–58 cm); Medium, 14–18 inches (36–46 kg); Miniature, 11–14 inches (28–36 cm); Toy, up to 10 inches (25 cm). ***Weight:***

Standard, 48 pounds (22 kg); Medium, 26 pounds (12 kg); Miniature, 15 pounds (7 kg); Toy, up to 11 pounds (5 kg). **Exterior:** All possess thick, woolly coats that come in a variety of shades. **Best Features:** Poodles are highly intelligent with amiable, steady personalities. **Caveat:** Though most poodles are famously even-tempered, toys and miniatures display a tendency to bite. **Special Programming:** Besides being intelligent, poodles are eager to learn and easy to train. **Ideal Owner:** Virtually anyone.

Pug: Legend says that the pug was brought to Europe by Genghis Khan. **Height:** 10–12 inches (25–30 cm). **Weight:** 14–18 pounds (6–8 kg). **Exterior:** Short, smooth coat in silver, black, or beige, but always with a black face. Pushed-in nose and large, expressive eyes. Very stocky body. **Best Features:** An entertaining little dog that makes few physical or psychological demands on its owner. Good with children. **Caveat:** Given to loud, relentless snoring. **Special Programming:** Adaptable to almost any living arrangement, from a small apartment with one resident to a large house full of children. **Ideal Owner:** Anyone who can tolerate snoring.

Shih Tzu: A Chinese dog, possibly a cross between a Pekingese and a Lhasa apso. **Height:** 8–11 inches (20–28 cm). **Weight:** 9–16 pounds (4–7 kg). **Exterior:** Long, silky hair in a variety of shades. **Best Features:** The perfect lapdog—just as it was in China, where it was a favorite of the imperial court. **Caveat:** Other than for cuddling, it has no particular talents. **Special Programming:** Very placid personality; devoted to its owner. **Ideal Owner:** Anyone seeking a low-maintenance dog. Everything about the Shih Tzu (except its coat) is low maintenance.

Yorkshire Terrier: Originally developed in Yorkshire, England, to rid coal mines of rats. **Height:** 7–9 inches (18–23 cm). **Weight:** 7 pounds (3 kg). **Exterior:**

TOP-SELLING MODELS: There are many breeds to choose from. The

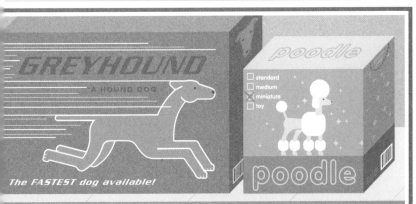

GREYHOUND

A HOUND DOG

The FASTEST dog available!

poodle

- [ ] standard
- [ ] medium
- [x] miniature
- [ ] toy

poodle

Yorkshire Terrier

Yorkshire Terrier

Yorkshire Terrier

GOLDEN RETRIEVER

GOLDEN RETRIEVER

SPORTING DOG

FUN FOR THE ENTIRE FAMILY!

Silky and Elegant

Shih Tzu

*Bow not included

PUG

IMPORT

BEIGE EXTERIOR!

PUG

IMP

BEIGE EXTERIOR!

models shown above (and on pages 30–31) represent some of the most popular canines.

Long, shiny, finely textured coat that is golden on the head, chest, and legs, but is steel blue everywhere else. *Best Features:* A happy, lively dog with all the spirit of bigger terriers. *Caveat:* Will try to attack much larger dogs. Can be difficult to train. Hair (if kept long) requires regular grooming. *Special Programming:* "Yorkies" only look like lapdogs. Inside they carry the same aggressive, energetic programming as other terriers. *Ideal Owner:* Anyone willing to undertake the management of a very energetic dog.

Nonstandard, Off-Brand Models

There are more than 500 dog breeds, but their numbers are dwarfed by the worldwide population of mixed breeds, or mutts. Available primarily through informal distribution channels (private owners, animal shelters), their highly individualized software packages and mechanical layouts carry both advantages and disadvantages. While the programming of a purebred is designed to accentuate one or more behaviors (herding in a Border collie, territoriality in a German shepherd), a mutt's programming is not. Temperaments and skill sets vary; the only way to discover what a particular model offers is to study it closely.

Conversely, mutts enjoy some important mechanical advantages. The controlled breeding that accentuates certain physical and mental traits in purebreds also magnifies genetic defects, predisposing them to everything from hip problems to various skin conditions. Mutts, because of their cosmopolitan genetic makeup, display few such weaknesses.

If you're interested in a specific, very expensive breed, one option is to select a mutt that obviously incorporates traits from that model (based on a visual inspection or data supplied by its current owner) into its lineage. With luck, you can get all the positive characteristics of the desired model in a healthier, more affordable animal.

EXAMPLES OF MIXED BREEDS

(Fig. A)
"DARBY"

Doberman	Pekingese	Pug
42%	11%	47%

(Fig. B)
"HUXLEY"

Akita	Boston Terrier	Schnauzer
23%	31%	46%

(Fig. C)
"POMPOM"

Basset Hound	Dachshund	Poodle
9%	49%	42%

(Fig. D)
"GIZMO"

Collie	Shih Tzu	Yorkie
26%	58%	16%

Selecting an Appropriate Model

Picking the right model from such an extensive product line takes careful deliberation. To determine what breed, size, and temperament is right for you, consider the following factors:

Size: As a rule of thumb, bigger breeds are inappropriate if you live in a small apartment or a home with a small or unfenced yard. However, this is not always the case. Some more-relaxed large models, such as the golden retriever, are better suited for small spaces than, say, an energetic schnauzer. When selecting a breed, temperament and activity level are equally as important as size.

Coat Type: Longhaired breeds usually shed prodigiously and require regular, costly, professional grooming. Shorthaired varieties require less maintenance, though they can shed just as much. Dog dander (tiny skin flakes) can also aggravate human allergies. Some models, such as poodles, are less troublesome in this regard.

Temperament: Since purebreds display well-understood mental characteristics, it is important to pick a model that complements your lifestyle. Consult breed guides and also, if possible, spend time with someone who already owns the type you're considering. It is especially important to spend preacquisition time with a mutt, so you can gauge its mental properties. If its parents appear to be two related breeds, then determining its personality may be straightforward. A model of more diverse parentage (say, a German shepherd and a terrier) may be tougher to evaluate.

Physical Requirements: If you like outdoor activities and want your dog to tag along, consider a large, sporting breed or energetic terrier. If you enjoy watching sports on TV rather than playing them, consider a model that makes fewer physical demands.

Schedule Demands: During workdays, will you return home at regular hours to provide your dog with exercise and bathroom breaks? Remember that while some models (Shetland sheepdog, bloodhound, and golden retriever) don't mind being left alone, many (including Border collies and wheaten terriers) can suffer separation anxiety. (See "Behavioral/Psychological Disorders," page 178.)

Familial Considerations: Before acquiring a dog, make sure every member of the family wants to own one. Remember that models predisposed to biting or aggressive behavior are, in most cases, inappropriate for families with younger children. Also, consider the reactions of pets you already own.

Financial Obligations: Dog ownership is an ongoing expense. Food, veterinary bills, grooming, and other costs will require hundreds of dollars annually. If that price seems too steep, consider more affordable pets such as parakeets or gerbils.

⚠ CAUTION: *Adding a dog to one's home is a life-changing decision requiring careful forethought. For that reason, canines must never, ever be given as unexpected gifts to third parties. Animal shelters euthanize such "surprises" by the hundreds of thousands each year.*

Advantages of Dog Ownership

The psychological benefits of owning a canine are well known. A carefully trained animal companion can offer fellowship, unconditional love, and often a friendship as intimate as any human bond. Dogs can also become an integral part of the family. Indeed, most adults, when asked to recall their earliest memories, will usually mention an encounter with their dog.

Canines also assist us during crises by helping to bear our emotional and psychological baggage. This function has important physiological benefits as well. Studies show that owning a dog—or even being near one—lowers human blood pressure and decreases stress levels. Over the long term this can prevent heart disease and lower health care costs, because dog owners make fewer doctor visits. A good-natured dog can also help fight depression and loneliness—one of the reasons they are used extensively to visit nursing homes and hospitals. Considering the benefits, the relatively nominal cost of keeping a dog seems like a wise investment.

New Versus Used Models

Puppies

Advantages: A puppy's programming can (to a certain degree) be modified to suit your needs. Puppies also have an easier time adjusting to new surroundings and accepting family members. *Disadvantages:* Training a puppy can be a difficult, time-consuming, and expensive task. Destruction can be considerable, ranging from carpet stains during house-training to chew-damaged furniture and mangled personal belongings.

Adult Dogs

Advantages: Quality adult dogs are usually "plug-and-play systems" equipped with all the software (housebreaking, socialization, rudimentary obedience training) necessary for family life. *Disadvantages:* Adult dogs may have trouble adjusting to new surroundings. Also, some models may carry deeply encoded software "glitches" (excessive aggression, destructive behavior) either hardwired or mistakenly installed by a previous owner.

The dog should be carefully screened for such problems before acquisition. An obedience expert or veterinarian can assess how much work would be necessary to bring the canine up to spec.

Selecting a Gender

In general (though there can be exceptions), female dogs tend to be less territorial and aggressive than males. However, having a male dog neutered (which should be done under almost all circumstances) in many cases mitigates these behaviors. Female dogs are also somewhat easier to train. This does not, however, mean that all females of all breeds are passive and pliant. For instance, though a female Rottweiler may be less aggressive and assertive than her male counterpart, she will still be far more aggressive and assertive than most other dogs of any breed.

Selecting a Vendor

Numerous individuals and agencies offer dogs for sale or adoption. Often, depending on your needs, it is possible to acquire a well-trained model at little or no initial expense.

Animal Shelters

Advantages: Shelters offer a wide choice of pre-owned models, many already user-friendly and configured for immediate home use. These facilities usually screen their stock (which ranges from mutts to the most exclusive purebreds) for undesirable traits; they will also conduct a careful physical inspection. Fees for these animals (especially when compared to those charged by pet stores and breeders) are generally nominal. Some facilities may require a waiting period, background check, and/or proof that you will have the animal spayed or neutered, if necessary. **Disadvantages:** None. The only important thing to remember is that the personality of a shelter dog should be carefully evaluated. Be aware that most are surrendered not for any fault of their own, but because of their owners' ignorance of canine care as well as changing lifestyles and/or pet preferences.

Pet Stores

Advantages: These businesses can be found in almost every large shopping mall. **Disadvantages:** Purebreds sold by pet stores can be of questionable lineage and in poor health. In spite of this, they are usually sold for premium prices. Since they are raised in a confined space, they are often poorly socialized and extremely difficult to house-train. For this reason, most dog experts advise against patronizing these establishments. At the very least, puppies purchased in such places should be carefully inspected by a veterinarian for physical and mental defects.

Breeders

Advantages: A qualified breeder (consult a veterinarian or a local or national breed club to find one in your area) is often the best source for carefully raised purebred puppies. They can often answer even the most detailed questions about your model's ancestry, genetic foibles, and personality. **Disadvantages:** Make sure you find a *qualified* breeder. Such a person will allow you to inspect his facility; supply the names of previous customers; offer detailed information about your puppy and its lineage; ensure that the puppy has received all vaccinations and medical care appropriate for its age; and include a written guarantee of its good health. If any of these items are lacking, find someone else.

Breed Rescue Groups

Advantages: These organizations devote themselves to "rescuing" owner-less dogs of specific breeds and then finding them new homes. The Internet provides information on numerous such groups specializing in everything from Jack Russell terriers to Newfoundlands. They are an excellent resource for those in search of a specific model. *Disadvantages:* The particular animal you want may not be in your area, so adopting it might necessitate travel.

Private Individuals

Advantages: Newspapers are full of advertisements for puppies. These are usually mixed breeds, offered "free to a good home" or for a nominal fee. In many cases such pets make fine animal companions—provided you carefully examine the puppies, their surroundings, and, if possible, their parents. (See "Puppy Preacquisition Inspection Checklist," page 46.) *Disadvantages:* In some cases, such litters may not have received veterinary care or proper socialization. Also, they increase the already-serious problem of pet overpopulation. If you do nothing else, encourage the owner to have the mother (and father, if possible) spayed and/or neutered.

⚠ **EXPERT TIP:** *If your own dog has not been spayed or neutered, have this done immediately or as soon as feasible. (See "Sexual Maturity," page 141.)*

Puppy Preacquisition Inspection

When examining a puppy, ask yourself the following questions. Ideally, all of your

○ Yes
○ No
If possible, inspect the puppy's mother. Is she free of major physical and/or mental shortcomings that might be passed to her offspring? (Remember that a puppy will look and behave like its parents.)

○ Yes
○ No
Is the puppy at least 8 weeks old? (Puppies younger than 8 weeks should not be separated from their mother and siblings.)

○ Yes
○ No
Does the puppy seem alert, happy, and eager to socialize with you? (A shy, withdrawn puppy may grow up to be a shy, withdrawn dog.)

○ Yes
○ No
Does the puppy seem gentle and amiable? (Be extremely wary of a dog that shows undue aggressive tendencies—growling, determined biting—at such an early age. This can indicate a significant software glitch.)

○ Yes
○ No
Has the puppy received all vaccinations and/or medical care appropriate for its age? (See "Visiting Your Service Provider," page 149.)

○ Yes
○ No
Is the puppy's stool firm? (A stool exam for intestinal parasites should be done by 8 weeks of age. A thin puppy may be malnourished or have worms.)

○ Yes
○ No
Are its eyes clear and free of discharge?

Checklist

answers should be "yes." Even a single "no" should be cause for careful consideration.

○ Yes ○ No	**Are its ears and nose free of discharge?**
○ Yes ○ No	**Is its coat clean and shiny?**
○ Yes ○ No	**Is its breathing regular, with no coughing and/or wheezing?**
○ Yes ○ No	**Is its body physically sound, with no lameness or tenderness anywhere?**

It is also important to make sure the puppy is screened for the specific genetic disorders (hip dysplasia, heart disease, blindness, etc.) common to its breed. Finally, no matter what sort of dog you plan to acquire, you should make any sale contingent on an examination and approval by your veterinarian. Detecting a heart murmur, orthopedic problem, or some other major malfunction at this early stage allows you to return the puppy before becoming emotionally attached.

⚠ *CAUTION: If you have young children, wait until they are at least 6 years old before acquiring a very large dog. Also, remember that the workload associated with caring for a new puppy can be similar to that required for supporting a human infant. The premature addition of a puppy to a family with very young children may trigger overload and breakdown of the home's primary caregiver.*

Adult Dog Preacquisition Inspection

When examining an adult dog, ask yourself the following questions. Ideally, all of you

○ Yes ○ No	**Can you contact the dog's previous owner?**
○ Yes ○ No	**Is there any record of the dog's previous history and why it is being offered for sale/adoption?**
○ Yes ○ No	**Are you sure the dog isn't being given up by its previous owner because of aggression and/or destructiveness? (This is not necessarily a deal breaker. In many cases, loving attention and proper obedience training can clear up bad habits.)**
○ Yes ○ No	**Is the dog housebroken?**
○ Yes ○ No	**Does the dog seem friendly, amiable, and interested in you?**
○ Yes ○ No	**If the dog will live among children, was it raised with any?**
○ Yes ○ No	**Has the dog received appropriate medical care? Are there records to prove it?**
○ Yes ○ No	**Is the dog's stool firm?**

Checklist

answers should be "yes." Even a single "no" should be cause for careful consideration.

◯ Yes ◯ No	**Are its eyes clear and free of discharge?**
◯ Yes ◯ No	**Are its ears and nose free of discharge?**
◯ Yes ◯ No	**Is its coat clean and shiny?**
◯ Yes ◯ No	**Is its breathing regular, with no coughing and/or wheezing?**
◯ Yes ◯ No	**Is its body physically sound, with no lameness or tenderness anywhere?**

Plan to spend considerable time with an adult dog before adoption, to make sure you understand its personality. Additionally, take the dog to a veterinarian for a pre-adoption checkup. Finally, remember that many of the canines surrendered to animal shelters are there not for insoluble problems, but due to their owners' ignorance and/or unwillingness to provide adequate training. A firm, loving hand could upgrade them to superior pets.

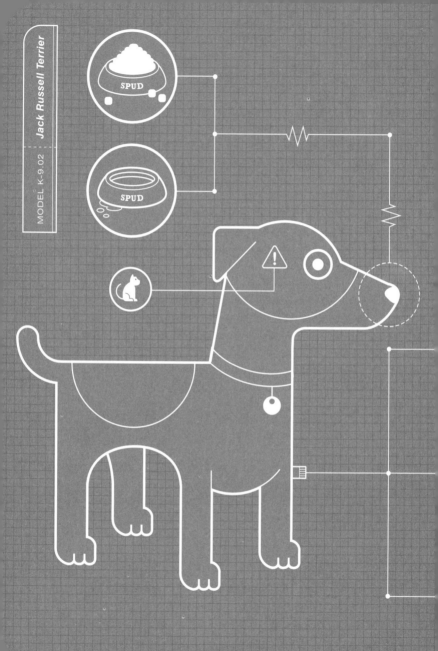

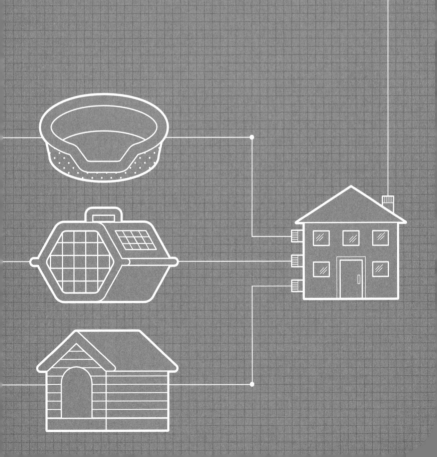

[Chapter 2]

Home Installation

Bringing a new dog into your home can be an exhilarating, albeit disruptive, experience. If your model is a puppy, you may face weeks of complex software downloads (otherwise known as "training"), plus maintenance of its complicated and ever-changing physical plant. While in most cases adult dogs don't require this level of commitment, they still need firm guidance as they find their place in a new setting. For this reason it is advisable, if possible, to stay home with your new canine during its first two or three days.

Preparing the Home

Before bringing the dog into your home, it is recommended that you take the following precautions:

◼ Make sure all household cleaning products are put away.

◼ Secure all medications (drugs such as Motrin and Tylenol can cause fatal liver damage in dogs).

◼ Secure all unauthorized foods (chocolate, for instance, can be deadly to canines).

◼ Secure all toxic chemicals stowed in your laundry room, basement, and garage—particularly antifreeze, which dogs find attractive because of its sweetness. Even a small amount, if ingested, can be lethal.

■ Secure tight spaces (such as the area behind your refrigerator) where a puppy or small dog might get stuck.

■ Position electrical cords out of reach so puppies cannot chew them.

■ If you own a swimming pool, make sure the dog cannot fall in.

■ Secure (at least for a while) any clothing, heirloom furniture, or family artifacts that should not be chewed and/or urinated upon.

■ Secure houseplants, some of which (such as philodendron) are toxic.

Recommended Accessories

Commercial retailers offer thousands of products designed to complement the life cycle of standard puppies and adult dogs. While a great number of these add-ons are not mandatory, most owners choose to invest in the following:

Bed: A purpose-made cushion (perhaps stuffed with flea-repelling cedar shavings) is a good choice. Be sure the outer covering can be removed for laundering. Avoid wicker baskets; some dogs like to chew on them. Also avoid investing in an expensive dog bed until you learn whether your dog likes to destroy bedding. In the interim, old blankets and/or a pillow will suffice.

Toys: Fleece toys are excellent for puppies. Adult canines appreciate hard rubber balls (choose one that is too large to swallow or become lodged in the dog's mouth). Avoid real bones (which may splinter) or household items such as old shoes, which may convey the idea that *all* shoes are for chewing.

Comb and/or Brush: Different types are available for various coat styles. (See "General Coat Maintenance," page 122.)

CANINE ACCESSORIES (sold separately) These products can assist

Food Bowl

Water Bowl

Dog Food

Biscuits

Treats

Leash

Collar

Waste Bags

Pooper-scooper

Scissors   Hair Clippers   Shampoo   Flea & Tick Bath   Currycomb   Shedding Tool

Dog Bed

Doghouse

with the installation, handling, and maintenance of your canine.

| Rope Tug | Tennis Balls | Squeaky Toy | Fleece Toy | Flying Disc |

  Name Tags Bows Bandanas Rain Poncho Winter Sweater

Undercoat Rake Brush Comb Grooming Glove Nail Clippers Styptic Powder

KWIK KLOT

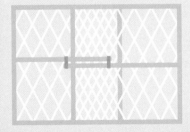 

Baby Gate Dog Crate

Collar/Tag: Put a leather or nylon collar on your dog, along with a tag containing its name and (at least) your telephone number, as soon as you acquire the animal. (See "Dog Identification Methods," page 73.)

Leash: This essential item is available at any pet store. Nylon models, which are lighter and less expensive than leather leashes, are a good choice.

Water/Food Bowls: Rubber-rimmed, stainless steel, nonskid models are best. For larger breeds or dogs with long ears, consider bowls that are elevated off the ground. Puppies may need a set of smaller, "starter" bowls.

Dog Crate: Select a model with a metal grate and a high-impact plastic body. It should be large enough for the dog, when fully grown, to turn around in. (See "Crate Training," page 81.)

Initial Introduction

Upon arriving home, offer the dog (who will undoubtedly be nervous) an immediate bathroom break. Then show it the location of its water and food bowls and encourage it to drink. However, do not offer food at this time.

Next, allow the dog several hours to explore the house under your supervision. Interface with children, other pets, and strangers should be avoided or minimized during this process. In adult dogs, expect some stress-triggered behavior regression—waste elimination "accidents," hiding, excessive shyness. Do not scold or correct a dog who acts in this way. The behaviors should vanish in a few days as the animal gains confidence in its new surroundings.

EXPERT TIP: A newly adopted adult dog may act extremely reserved for several days or even weeks while adjusting to its new environment. As it becomes more comfortable, its natural personality will reassert itself.

Interfacing with Children

Once the dog has gained a certain amount of familiarity with its new surroundings, you may begin the process of introducing it to younger human members of your family. This process should be handled in one of two ways, depending on whether the dog is a puppy or an adult. Refer to the illustrations on pages 58–59 for additional guidance.

Puppies

▪ Puppies tend to squirm and can easily be dropped by children (Fig. A). Have the child sit, then hand him or her the canine (Fig. B).

▪ Have the child present the puppy with a toy while holding it (Fig. C). Puppies tend to chew, and a toy may prevent them from nibbling on tiny fingers and arms.

▪ Encourage the child to feed and water the puppy (Fig. C). This will increase bonding. However, remember that adults are always ultimately responsible for the canine's health and maintenance.

▪ Stay in the room. Very young children (1–6 years old) should always be closely supervised when handling a puppy.

▪ If the children are approximately 10 years or older, they should participate in the puppy's obedience training.

Adult Dogs

▪ Leash the dog during initial introduction. At first glance, a larger dog may perceive small children as potential prey (Fig. D).

CHILD ---> PUPPY INTERFACE

(Fig. A)
PUPPY MAY SQUIRM AWAY

(Fig. B)
HAVE CHILD SIT BEFORE HANDING A PUPPY

(Fig. C)
CHILD SHOULD:

1. Give puppy a toy
2. Feed puppy
3. Water puppy
4. Always be under adult supervision

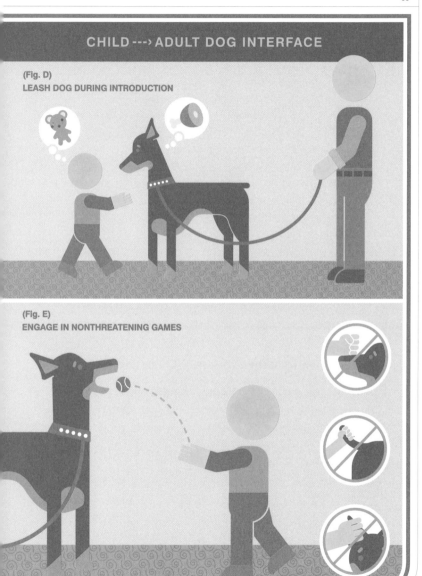

■ Prompt children to interface with the dog in safe, nonthreatening games. Toy accessories are especially useful here (Fig. E).

■ Do not let children interface with the dog while it is eating or sleeping.

■ Children should postpone aggressive hugging until the dog knows them well. Many canines find this behavior threatening.

■ Children should postpone rough play until the dog knows them well and its personality (and propensity for aggressive action) is well understood.

■ Do not allow children to tug on the dog's ears and/or tail. These are highly sensitive areas for the canine.

■ Any dog who will spend time with children should receive thorough obedience and socialization training.

⚠ *CAUTION: Very young children should never, under any circumstances, be left alone with a dog—even a dog that knows them and has shown no aggressive tendencies.*

Interfacing with Other Dogs

Introducing a new dog into a home that already contains one can be challenging. Canines must establish a "pecking order," with the most dominant animal becoming pack leader. If you bring a second or third dog into your home, this is the first issue the dogs will resolve. The key is to make sure it happens with minimal discord. Under close human supervision, this difficult but necessary aspect of canine behavior can be accommodated with minimal fuss.

[1] When you bring the new dog into your home, make sure your current pet is confined to a specific section of the house, out of sight.

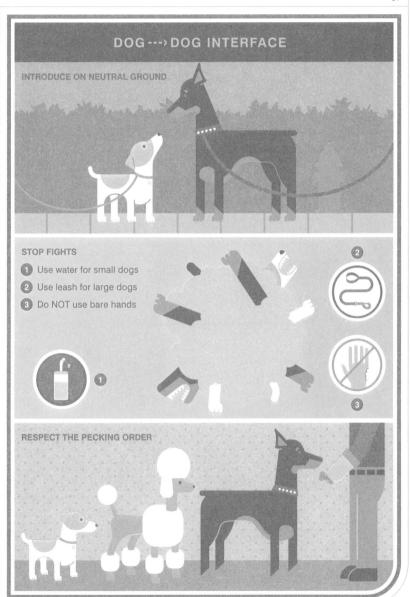

DOG ---> DOG INTERFACE

INTRODUCE ON NEUTRAL GROUND

STOP FIGHTS

1. Use water for small dogs
2. Use leash for large dogs
3. Do NOT use bare hands

RESPECT THE PECKING ORDER

[2] Allow the new model to roam the house for several hours. The new model will scent the current dog and become aware that it is not alone.

[3] Introduce the two dogs—not in your home but on neutral ground. Try the sidewalk in front of your house. This will eliminate issues of territorial defense. Both animals should be leashed. If the dogs are large, enlist another person to help.

[4] If the dogs appear to tolerate each other, take them both back to the house. However, do not leave them alone together. It can take weeks or even months for the dogs to develop a healthy relationship; until that happens, they should interact only under your direct supervision.

[5] If the dogs do not tolerate each other, try briefly crating the new dog and giving your current model the run of the house. Then briefly crate the current model and let the new dog out. After they become more familiar with each other, release both dogs and allow them to interact under your supervision.

[6] If the dogs fight, do not try to separate them with your hands. For smaller dogs, use a squeeze bottle of water to temporarily distract both canines. Larger dogs should be equipped with leashes, so they can be pulled apart.

[7] Give each dog separate food and water bowls, separate beds, and separate crates. Sharing such personal effects may lead to strife.

[8] Once your dogs establish a pecking order, respect it. Greet the pack leader first when you come home (it will be obvious who the pack leader is). This dog should also be fed first and should receive preferred access

to treats and attention. Ignoring the pecking order may cause the dogs to become confused or agitated.

⚠ **EXPERT TIP:** *A puppy will almost invariably submit to an older dog, even if the puppy is a Great Dane and the older dog is a Chihuahua. However, if the older dog is appreciably larger, do not let it attack or excessively bully the newcomer.*

Interfacing with Cats

The idea that dogs are hardwired to vex cats is not true. However, many dogs are programmed to chase small prey, which cats, unfortunately, resemble. Before interfacing your canine with a feline, be sure you understand the extent of your dog's "prey drive." For instance, a Shih Tzu will exhibit little or none, while hunters such as greyhounds (bred for the chase) and terriers (bred to fight and kill small game) may display quite a bit. To gauge the dog's prey drive, simply toss a favorite toy across the room. The dog may ignore it (low), pick it up and return it to you (medium), or aggressively chase it down, then shake and chew it (high). This does not necessarily mean the dog will try to kill your cat, but it may very much want to harass it.

Problems can be prevented by following these rules of introduction.

[1] When the new dog is first introduced to the home, confine your cat(s) to another section of the house. Allow the dog to orient itself and become less agitated.

[2] Once the dog has become acclimated, direct its attention to the (closed) door, behind which the cat resides. Allow the animals to sniff and perhaps touch each other under the door (Fig. A).

(Fig. A)
UNDER-THE-DOOR INTRODUCTION

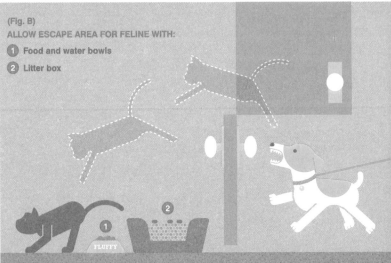

(Fig. B)
ALLOW ESCAPE AREA FOR FELINE WITH:

1 Food and water bowls

2 Litter box

DOG ---> CAT INTERFACE: Some dogs are hardwired to chase small prey,

(Fig. C)
GAUGE YOUR MODEL'S "PREY DRIVE"

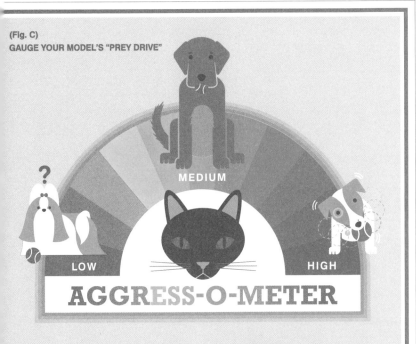

MEDIUM

LOW   HIGH

AGGRESS-O-METER

(Fig. D)
SHOW DOG THAT YOU VALUE THE CAT

which cats, unfortunately, resemble. Exercise caution when introducing them to each other.

[3] Introduce the two under close supervision. The dog should be leashed. Alternatively, you could crate the dog and release the cat.

[4] During these early encounters, offer the dog special treats or extra attention whenever the cat appears. This programs the canine to associate the cat with positive things.

[5] Give the cat a high shelf or gated room where it can retreat from the dog if it wishes (Fig. B).

[6] Stroke and hold the cat in the dog's presence. The dog will sense that you value the other animal (Fig. D).

[7] Place the cat's litter box someplace inaccessible to the dog. Canines like to eat cat feces, an action that could result in malfunction.

[8] Provide two sets of food bowls, water bowls, and beds in separate locations. The cat and the dog should each have its own sanctuary for eating and resting.

⚠️ **EXPERT TIP:** *It is not uncommon for cats to try to harass dogs. However, in most cases the dog can (and will) end the problem with a few loud barks.*

First Night at Home

Whatever sleeping arrangement you select for your dog, make sure its components are already in place when the animal arrives. In most cases a puppy should (for the first few nights at least) be allowed to sleep near your bed. This is for your convenience as well the canine's. The puppy will

probably whimper during the night, so comforting it will be as simple as reaching over the side of the mattress. However, do not allow the puppy to sleep with you; this creates a precedent that can be hard to change.

The puppy may be comforted by the presence of a hot-water bottle, a ticking alarm clock, or a softly playing radio. The puppy should not have unlimited access to the house at night. Move its crate into the bedroom, or close your bedroom door, or install a child gate to deter unauthorized elimination or chewing incidents. Make sure the puppy has toilet arrangements, such as a spread of newspapers, nearby. Be prepared for accidents—and to be awakened during the first few nights by whimpering. (See "Crate Training," page 81.)

Selecting a Name

Picking a name for your dog is a highly personal decision. However, a few rules may guide you in your quest.

■ Dogs have an easier time identifying a multisyllabic rather than a monosyllabic name. Consequently, Rover is better than Spot.

■ Use the dog's name often. Repeat it while petting, holding, or playing with it.

■ Do not use the dog's name with an angry tone or when disciplining it.

■ Make sure the dog's name doesn't sound like a commonly used command word. For instance, "Ray" and "stay."

■ If an adult dog has already been assigned a name, keep it. While "Bon Jovi" might not have been *your* first choice, trying to alter it will only add to your pet's adjustment issues.

⚠ **EXPERT TIP:** *Owners who bestow human names on their canines (Jenny, Ben, etc.) tend to hold their dogs in higher regard.*

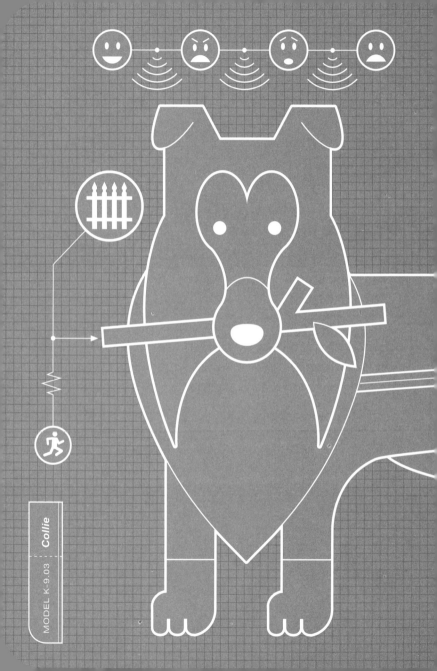

MODEL K-9.03 · *Collie*

Chapter 3

Daily Interaction

Audio Cues and Body Language

Audible dog communication typically assumes one of the following forms:

Howls: Wolves howl to locate other pack members over long distances. Many domestic dogs have kept this behavior. It can sometimes be initiated by such things as police sirens.

Growls: This sound is often associated with aggression, threats, and displays of dominance. However, dogs may growl during play as well. Study the dog's body language to distinguish one from the other.

Grunts: These are often heard when dogs greet humans or other dogs. They are the equivalent of a human sigh.

Whines: A form of communication over intermediate ranges that can signal anything from pain to submission to happiness at meeting someone.

Barks: As with howling, these can be used to get attention, to raise the alarm, or to identify an individual. A dog who is anxious tends to bark in a high pitch; a dog who is warning off an intruder barks at a lower pitch. Warning barks may become more rapid as a stranger gets closer.

BODY LANGUAGE

Canines will often display their emotions via these nonauditory cues.

(Fig. A)
PLAYFULNESS

(Fig. B)
SUBMISSION

(Fig. C)
AGGRESSION

(Fig. D)
FEAR

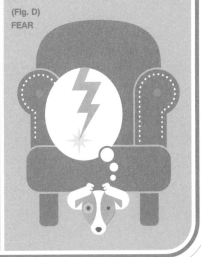

Dogs and Human Speech

Dogs do not "understand" human speech at all. However, they can associate audio cues (words) with the execution of various behaviors. For instance, though a collie does not comprehend that "stay" is a word, it does understand that this particular sound calls for a specific behavior. Some dogs can store dozens of words or other audio cues this way. In fact, the word itself may not be as important as how you say it. Dogs can gauge your mood by the tone of your voice, so saying something—anything—with an angry tone will usually elicit a fearful or submissive response. Likewise, saying "bad dog" in a cheerful voice will not achieve the desired effect.

Sleep Mode

Dogs sleep roughly 14 hours a day. Older or larger dogs (such as Saint Bernards or Newfoundlands) will sleep even more. Instead of sleeping in one continuous stretch—as most humans do—dogs will take naps of varying lengths throughout the day.

Canine sleep patterns mirror those of humans. When a canine first goes to sleep it enters a "quiet" phase, followed shortly thereafter by "active" or REM (rapid eye movement) sleep. The dog's eyes move under its eyelids, its legs jerk, and it may whine or softly bark. There is no way to know with certainty (because they have no way to tell their owners), but the dog gives every impression of dreaming.

EXPERT TIP: *If your dog has trouble sleeping through the night, consider increasing its play/exercise time.*

Dog Identification Methods

Your dog should wear its collar, with identification tags attached, at all times. The tag should include your name, address, and home and work telephone numbers. The dog's rabies vaccination and license tags (stamped with your veterinarian's name and telephone number) should also be attached. In many towns and cities, this is mandatory. Dogs can also be tattooed or fitted with an identification microchip (the veterinarian-preferred method for permanent identification). About the size of a grain of rice, the microchip is injected just under the skin between the shoulder blades. When scanned, it produces information that can assist the dog's finder in locating its owner. Chip scanners are used at all lost-dog intake locations, including humane societies, city pounds, and veterinary hospitals. However, a "chipped" dog still needs to wear a collar with identification.

EXPERT TIP: If you travel with your dog on vacation, update its tags by including your temporary phone number.

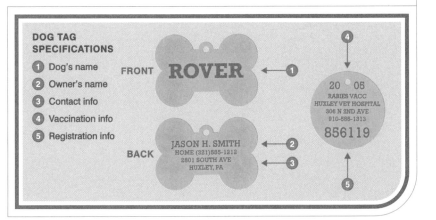

DOG TAG SPECIFICATIONS

1. Dog's name
2. Owner's name
3. Contact info
4. Vaccination info
5. Registration info

FRONT **ROVER** ← 1

4 →

20 • 05
RABIES VACC
HUXLEY VET HOSPITAL
306 N 2ND AVE
910-555-1313

856119

BACK
JASON H. SMITH ← 2
HOME (321)555-1212
2801 SOUTH AVE ← 3
HUXLEY, PA

↑ 5

Exercise and Fitness

Even the most sedentary models require a certain amount of physical exertion to stay healthy. Consider the following factors before determining the level of exercise appropriate for your pet.

Size: For small breeds such as pugs and Boston terriers, a walk around the block is the equivalent of a marathon. Larger animals are, in general, capable of longer jaunts and more strenuous activity.

Physical Stamina: How long and how hard a dog can play depends on its genetic makeup. Some models, including huskies and most terriers, were bred for stamina. They can run and play for a very, very long time. Others were designed for specific types of exertion. For instance, the greyhound is capable of great speed, but only over short distances. As a result, it makes a poor jogging companion. Models such as the German shorthaired pointer and the vizsla, however, were engineered to go the distance.

Physical Makeup: Various breeds, because of their design, have certain physiological disadvantages. For instance, "flat-faced" models such as boxers, pugs, and bulldogs have below-normal breathing capacity and therefore less stamina. Physical activity for these dogs should come in short bursts. Also, some models are prone to orthopedic problems (such as hip dysplasia) that can be aggravated by excessive exercise. Your veterinarian can help you create a suitable exercise plan for your dog.

Weather Conditions: Coat length also can determine how much exercise a particular model can handle. In winter, thin-coated dogs can tolerate less cold exposure than thick-coated dogs such as the Samoyed and Great Pyrenees. During the summer months, however, thin-coated dogs can tolerate

more heat than heavily coated breeds. In general, heat is a bigger problem for most dogs.

⚠️ **CAUTION:** *Be extremely careful with "flat-faced" breeds (bulldogs, pugs) during times of high heat and humidity. Their inability to dissipate heat during otherwise normal exertion can be potentially life-threatening.*

Physical Conditioning: Dogs, like humans, can become out of shape. Taking a normally sedentary dog on a 2-mile run can lead to orthopedic injuries (among other problems). Instead, build up the dog's capacity slowly over weeks and exercise it daily, if possible. A sedentary dog can be conditioned with a 20- to 60-minute walk 5 days a week. Swimming is also a good activity, because it eases strain on joints. Consult your veterinarian before beginning any sort of exercise program for an overweight, aged, and/or infirm canine.

⚠️ **CAUTION:** *A dog, in attempting to please its owner, may persist in a physical activity beyond the point of exhaustion, putting it in danger of mechanical damage. Monitor your dog's physical regimen and discontinue it at the first sign of serious fatigue.*

How to Teach "Fetch"

Fetch is a great all-purpose exercise. However, it is important to remember that not all dogs are programmed to play this game. Some breeds are not very "reactive"—that is, attuned to the sorts of quick movements a ball, stick, or Frisbee makes. But terriers, herding dogs, and retrievers often love the game. In such cases teaching can be simple. First toss the object (Fig. A). After the dog chases it down and collects

it, offer a treat (Fig. B) to entice the canine back to you (Fig. C). Give up the treat after the dog releases the object into your hand (Fig. D). Repeat until the dog understands what is expected. Soon you can offer praise (and another toss) as a reward, rather than food.

Yard Containment Protocol

If possible, dogs should have a secure outdoor area in which to exercise and/or download wastes. Containment options include the following.

Fencing: The standard method. Be sure the dog cannot crawl or tunnel under the enclosure. Also, be sure exterior access gates can be locked, to prevent unauthorized entry.

Invisible Fences: These "fences" are in fact electric lines buried around the perimeter of the dog owner's property. When the dog approaches the line, its collar sounds a warning signal, then delivers an uncomfortable electric shock if the canine continues forward. Dogs cannot dig their way under the system as they can with conventional fencing. However, a large or excited dog can escape simply by ignoring the shock. Also, nothing prevents unauthorized people and/or pets from entering your yard.

Chain: Should only be used when your dog is being let out to relieve himself—and only if your yard is not adequately fenced. Leaving a dog on a chain for any length of time is inhumane.

Dog Run: A small portion of the yard that is fenced and may contain a doghouse. Again, your model should not be confined for any length of time to a dog run. Because the area is small, it must be cleaned frequently.

1 FENCING

2 CHAIN

TINY

YARD CONTAINMENT PROTOCOL: The type of outdoor containment you

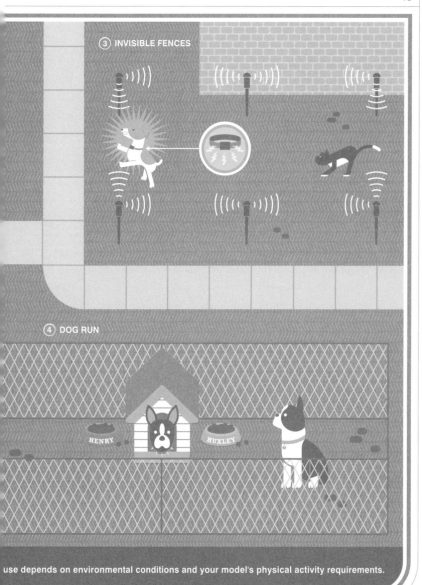

③ INVISIBLE FENCES

④ DOG RUN

HENRY   HUXLEY

use depends on environmental conditions and your model's physical activity requirements.

⚠ **CAUTION:** *If your dog is accustomed to being indoors, do not leave it outdoors and unattended for long periods of time. Such animals may develop severe emotional problems, become excessively dirty, and/or injure themselves.*

Outdoor Storage

Many dog models are suitable for outdoor storage, as long as they receive the necessary support equipment: a storage facility or "house" that is raised off the ground and large enough for the animal to turn around in easily. It should be located in a shaded area inside a contained space (fenced yard or dog run) and be equipped with hay or other bedding during winter. Water should always be available and frequently changed.

Be advised, however, that many experts believe prolonged outdoor storage can degrade a dog's performance. Canines want to be with their pack (in this case, you and your family), so confining them outdoors can be viewed by dogs as punishment. Also, outdoor dogs, because they receive less time with humans, tend to be less socialized. With proper training and attention to hygiene, even the largest breeds can be kept indoors.

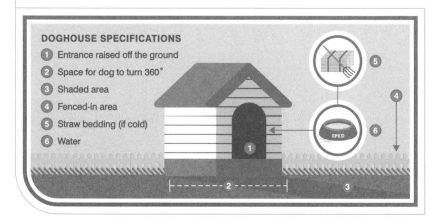

DOGHOUSE SPECIFICATIONS
1. Entrance raised off the ground
2. Space for dog to turn 360°
3. Shaded area
4. Fenced-in area
5. Straw bedding (if cold)
6. Water

Waste Disposal Protocols

Though dogs are usually considered to be "earth friendly" products, owners should remember that they can emit prodigious quantities of toxic waste. The following section outlines how to safely manage this problem.

Crate Training

This is a popular puppy house-training method that, when used properly, teaches a young canine where and when to relieve itself. It also provides the animal with a safe and secure retreat—a retreat that can be moved anywhere the owner desires. The method works because dogs are hardwired to not soil the place where they sleep. When executed correctly, this technique programs the puppy to "hold it" until it is allowed to go outside.

⚠️ **CAUTION:** *Crate training is not a long-term storage method. Puppies should not be left alone for extended periods in their crates. If the dog ever soils the crate, this can set back house-training by weeks.*

[1] Purchase a dog crate equipped with metal bars or a high-impact plastic body and metal grate. Be sure the crate is large enough for the dog to turn around in—but not too large. It should be used as a sleeping area, not a playpen.

[2] Line the crate with a blanket or soft towel. Add a couple of toys.

[3] Encourage the puppy to expel its waste before entering the crate.

[4] Place the puppy in the crate for a short period of time. Provide a

CRATE TRAINING

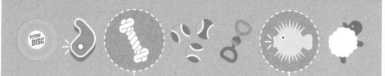

CRATE PREPARATIONS

1. Should only be large enough for dog to turn around in
2. Line with blanket or soft towel
3. Add a couple of toys
4. Allow waste disposal
5. Remove collar
6. Reward compliance

BEFORE CRATING . . .

small treat, so the puppy associates its confinement with good things. Stay nearby until the puppy settles down. Removing the puppy's collar will prevent it from getting snagged on any part of the crate.

[5] Never release the puppy when it barks. Wait until it stops barking before releasing.

[6] Begin placing the puppy in the crate for its naps and other downtimes. During the day, you should never leave the puppy in the crate for more than 4 hours at a time.

⚠️ **EXPERT TIP:** *A good rule of thumb is that the maximum number of hours a dog should remain in the crate is its age in months plus one. For instance, a 2-month-old puppy should never be crated more than 3 hours without (at least) a bathroom break.*

[7] The puppy should sleep in the crate during the night. Be aware that it will probably require at least one bathroom break midway through the night.

[8] After your puppy is released from the crate, immediately offer it the opportunity to expel its waste. If it does, praise the puppy and allow it to roam the house freely for a while. If not, return the puppy to the crate for 10 to 15 minutes. Then try again.

⚠️ **EXPERT TIP:** *Give the puppy plenty of opportunities to relieve itself. It should have a "bathroom break" first thing in the morning; after every meal; after every nap; after strenuous play sessions; last thing at night; and during the night if it appears restless. When escorting the puppy outside, always take it out the same door and to the same spot.*

[9] Puppies can be weaned from the crate at 5 or 6 months of age, after earning the owner's trust. However, the crate can always remain their "home." This will make transportation easy, because you can take their safe, secure environment anywhere you go.

House-Training

Even newly adopted adult dogs may require a "refresher course" on waste management. When you sense that the dog is ready to use the bathroom, quickly escort it outside to a spot you would like it to use (Fig. A). You might want to leash the dog to keep it from straying. If it uses the spot, praise it strongly and perhaps offer a treat. Afterward, keep a sharp eye on the dog and take it to the spot whenever it seems in need of relief. Regularly clear away feces. In no time the dog should start visiting the spot on its own—and requesting bathroom breaks when needed.

Dealing with Unauthorized Downloads

It is important to thoroughly clean up urine puddles in the house, because dogs tend to return to and reuse spots they have targeted earlier. Several commercial products remove stains and kill lingering odors. A homemade mix of 50 percent white vinegar and 50 percent water (Fig. B) will remove urine smells (but not the odor of feces).

EXPERT TIP: Do not admonish a dog (especially a puppy) if it urinates in the house (Fig. C). Negative reinforcement does not work with housebreaking. Unless you act while the dog is literally in the middle of soiling the carpet (Fig D), it will not associate the punishment with the unauthorized urination. Remember that accidents are often the result of inattentiveness by the owner.

HOUSE-TRAINING

(Fig. A)
ALWAYS USE SAME DOOR AND SPOT

(Fig. B)
CLEAN THOROUGHLY
Mix 50% White Vinegar
with 50% Water

50%
50%

(Fig. C)
WARNING: DO <u>NOT</u> PUNISH

(Fig. D)
ATTEMPT TO CANCEL UNAUTHORIZED DOWNLOADS

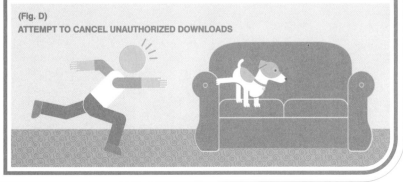

Chapter 4

Basic Programming

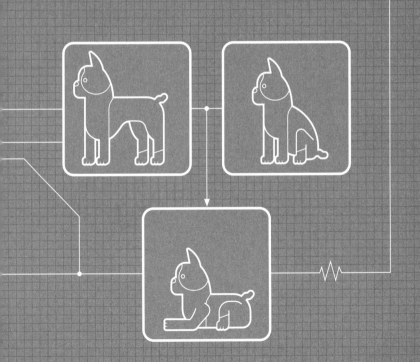

Overview of Factory-Installed Software

The dog comes with a great deal of pre-installed programming. Though its operating system is more or less the same one used by its wild cousin, the wolf, the software has been altered in important ways to make the dog more amenable to life with humans. Here are some of the key points.

Socialization: Because they were designed to live in groups, dogs are highly attuned to the moods of their pack mates—in this case, you and your family. That's why it is ideal for puppies to join their new families during the seventh or eighth week of life. This is the period in which they are most susceptible to imprinting.

Dominance: Dog packs are structured around a well-established pecking order, from the leader, or alpha, on down. To enjoy the maximum benefits of this software, you must establish yourself as the dog's alpha. (See "Establishing Dominance," next page.)

Hunting: This key aspect of wolf behavior has been altered in many important ways. In herding breeds, the urge to actually kill game has been suppressed, while the drive to stalk it has been accentuated. Many dog behaviors (nipping at heels, chasing tossed objects) are related to hunting.

Territoriality: Dogs are programmed to stake out and defend territory. In most cases this will be your house and (often) the yard. Canines who might be quite mild if they met a stranger on neutral territory can be highly aggressive if they encounter the same person or animal on their home terrain.

Territorial Marking: Dogs, like wolves, mark the limits of their domain with urine and feces. This behavior greatly eases the process of housebreaking. Since dogs will repeatedly mark the same spots, pick a location in the yard where you want your pet to expel its waste. After the dog has used the spot a few times, it will update its internal preferences and remember the spot forever.

Establishing Dominance

If you acquire a dog as a puppy, it will in most cases automatically—and forevermore—see you as its superior. As for adult dogs, the simple act of providing their food strongly reinforces your primacy. Also, dogs that are markedly smaller than you will usually accept your authority. However, some particularly high-spirited breeds (Jack Russells, Dobermans, Akitas) may choose, on occasion, to challenge. This can manifest itself in interesting ways: The dog may growl or snap if you try to move it off your bed; aggressively defend its food bowl; or even refuse to give you "right of way" when you pass. Such problems must be dealt with promptly, before they escalate into more serious challenges.

Troubleshooting Dominance Issues

■ If a dog is having trouble with one member of its human family, have that person start feeding the animal. When the canine sees where its food comes from, it will often submit to the provider.

■ A dog that stands on its hind legs, puts its forepaws on your chest or shoulders and looks you in the eye is trying to dominate you. Do not allow this behavior.

■ If a dog wants a treat or a toy, make it perform some trick or obey a command before providing it. This reinforces the chain of authority.

■ One of the perks of being the dominant pack member is "right of way"—

A:/SOCIALIZATION

B:/DOMINANCE

FACTORY-INSTALLED SOFTWARE: The dog includes numerous

C:/HUNTING

E:/TERRITORIAL MARKING

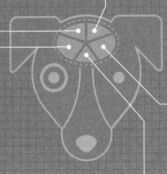

D:/TERRITORIALITY

pre-installed software applications.

animals with lower status must get out of your path. For this reason, if your dog is in your way, do not move. Make it move.

■ If your dog seems to develop dominance issues with a child, seek the help of a veterinarian and/or a professional trainer immediately.

Training Options (Software Add-ons)

While the home enthusiast can install the following software options himself, less-knowledgeable dog owners should consider attending an obedience class.

Socialization

Puppies should learn how to meet new people and pets without display-ing fear or aggression. One of the best ways to accomplish this is to introduce the puppy to many people. These sessions should be calm, brief experiences in which the puppy is handled and petted, but allowed to retreat if it tires of the encounter. Supervised sessions with other dogs are also a good idea—but only after the puppy has received its full set of vaccinations. The puppy can also participate in a socialization class, where it will meet other canines and people under controlled conditions.

Leash Training

A puppy can be introduced to a leash long before it is mature enough to attempt a proper "walk." Attach a small, lightweight version to the puppy's collar and allow it to walk around the yard (supervised) as the leash trails behind it. Later you can pick up the leash and nonchalantly "walk" the canine. Trying to guide the animal is unnecessary; you just want it to become familiar with the leash.

Once the dog has received its full set of vaccinations (see Chapter 8), it will be ready to undertake a proper walk. Bring the dog to an open space that is free from distractions (such as other dogs, children, and/or wild game). Place the dog on a leash and begin walking. Whenever the dog begins to pull, stop walking. Wait until the dog stops pulling, then offer praise and resume the walk.

Repeat the process for as many training sessions as necessary. It is acceptable to sternly say "no" if your puppy pulls constantly. However, patient, consistent handling is the real key to effective leash management.

EXPERT TIP: *Obedience sessions should take place twice a day, but each should last no more than 5 or 10 minutes. If they take too long, the dog may become bored.*

CAUTION: *"Choke" and "pinch" collars are unnecessary for leash training. They can even be harmful to smaller breeds. Should your dog pull excessively, consider a halter-type lead. This device places pressure on the dog's shoulders instead of its throat.*

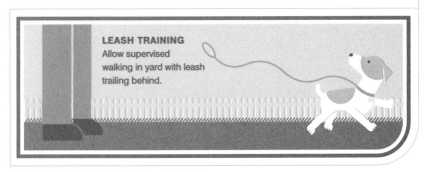

LEASH TRAINING
Allow supervised walking in yard with leash trailing behind.

Sit

[1] Begin training indoors. The room should be free of distractions.

[2] Summon the dog, then show it a treat. Hold the treat so that the dog points its nose upward (Fig. A). Move the treat backward over its head until the dog naturally lowers into a sitting position (Fig. B).

[3] As soon as it sits, give it the treat and offer ample praise.

[4] Repeat the exercise, this time saying "sit."

[5] Once the dog learns the command, try it in more distracting settings: the yard, on a sidewalk, and so on.

Stay

[1] Command the dog to sit.

[2] Once It assumes the position, say "stay" (Fig. C), then wait 2 seconds before praising and/or giving a reward. Be sure the dog holds the sit position during this time. Repeat as many times as necessary.

[3] Once it masters this step, tell it to stay, then take several steps back as the dog holds its position (Fig. D). Wait 2 seconds before rewarding dog.

[4] As the dog becomes more competent, add further distractions such as running in place or making odd noises (Fig. E). Also, increase the interval between the command and the reward. Do not move on to the next step until your dog complies with these new demands.

VOICE-ACTIVATED COMMANDS: "SIT" AND "STAY"

(Fig. A)
HOLD TREAT OVER DOG

(Fig. B)
MOVE TREAT SO DOG LOWERS
INTO THE SITTING POSITION

SIT

(Fig. C)
SPEAK "STAY" COMMAND

STAY

(Fig. D)
INCREASE DISTANCE

STAY STAY STAY

(Fig. E)
ADD FURTHER DISTRACTIONS

STAY

VOICE-ACTIVATED COMMAND: "HEEL"
(Fig. A)
ENGAGE SITTING POSITION
SIT
(Fig. B)
ACTIVATE "HEEL" COMMAND
ROVER
HEEL
(Fig. C)
TEST RUN
(Fig. D)
REPEAT "HEEL" COMMAND
ROVER
HEEL

[5] Gradually increase the length of time the dog stays and the distance you move from it.

[6] Pick a word or phrase, such as "free time," to let the dog know when it no longer has to stay. It should hold its position until it hears that phrase.

Heel

This important leash-walking protocol teaches the dog to walk by your knee, matching your pace and ignoring distractions.

[1] Hold the dog's leash in your right hand, taking up any slack with your left. The dog should stand at your left side.

[2] Command the dog to sit (Fig. A).

[3] While holding a treat in your left hand, bring it to the dog's nose and say its name, followed by "heel" (Fig. B).

[4] Walk for a short distance, keeping the food at your side (Fig. C).

[5] When you stop, say the dog's name, followed by the word "heel," and raise the treat so the dog sits (Fig. D).

[6] Give the dog its reward, then repeat the process until the dog walks faultlessly at your side, whether wearing a leash or not.

⚠ *CAUTION: Heel training is not a substitute for a leash, which should still be used in all public situations.*

Coming When Called

[1] Solicit help from a friend or family member. Each person should sit at opposite ends of a room. Take turns calling the canine from one person to the other, saying "come" in a pleasant, enthusiastic voice (Fig. A).

[2] Bribe the dog with treats and/or praise to win compliance. Make the idea of coming when called as attractive as possible.

[3] Later that day, call the dog at random times, whether the animal is a few feet away or in another room. Reward it amply when it responds.

[4] When the dog consistently comes the first time it is called, put it on a long leash and move the training outside (Fig. B). Take the dog for a walk, allowing it to put a fair distance between itself and you (but always on a leash). Ask it to come, and if it complies reward it with treats and praise. If it doesn't, tug firmly on the leash and pull, still calling to it in a friendly voice. When it finally returns to you, reward the dog lavishly. Repeat the process several times.

[5] Once the dog is competently trained, upgrade to a longer leash and repeat step 4.

[6] Next, practice off the leash in a fenced area (Fig. C). If your dog refuses to come when called, do not keep calling. Sit down on the ground or do something unusual (but nonthreatening) that it will want to investigate. When it returns, put the leash on. Go back to leash training for several days before attempting another leash-free session. Eventually the dog will catch on.

[7] Saying "come" should always be associated in the canine's mind with pleasant things. Never call a dog to punish it. Instead, go to the

VOICE-ACTIVATED COMMAND: "COME"
(Fig. A)
PHASE ONE: INDOORS WITH TWO PEOPLE
COME
COME
(Fig. B)
PHASE TWO: OUTDOORS WITH LONG LEASH
COME
(Fig. C)
PHASE THREE: OUTDOORS WITH NO LEASH
COME
COME =

canine. If the animal associates the word "come" with punishment, it may not respond.

Training Tips

■ If a dog exhibits an undesirable behavior, the best approach is to pointedly ignore the behavior and the animal. The dog will quickly realize that doing the wrong thing deprives it of what it desires most—attention. The only exception is when a dog becomes extremely aggressive; this type of undesirable behavior requires your immediate attention. (See "Establishing Dominance," page 89.)

■ Shouting at a dog when it does something wrong can have unintended consequences. Canines are programmed to crave attention—positive or negative. If one of their transgressions leads to an uproar, they may be tempted to repeat it.

■ Do not reprimand a dog for a transgression unless you catch the animal in the act of committing it. A dog will not understand that you are angry about something it did an hour ago. It will simply know that you are angry—perhaps about what it is doing at that moment.

■ Never strike or harshly reprimand a puppy or adult dog. This is always counterproductive because it teaches the canine, first and foremost, to fear you. In the case of guarding breeds with high levels of innate aggression, it can also be very dangerous.

■ Always end teaching sessions on a high note. If a dog is having trouble with a new lesson, have it finish by doing an already-mastered behavior that it can successfully execute. Praise it lavishly.

■ Hold instruction sessions at the same times and places each day.

■ Try to use command words such as "sit" with the same tone of voice each time. Dogs respond as much to *how* you say things as *what* you say.

■ Be sure you have the dog's attention before giving a command.

Selecting an Obedience Program

Most veterinarians can suggest qualified obedience programs in your area. These usually meet once a week over several weeks and cover such basics as socialization, walking on a leash, and simple commands. Understand, however, that attending a class does not free you from the responsibility of training your canine. The class will merely demonstrate techniques. You will still have to spend many hours applying them to your pet.

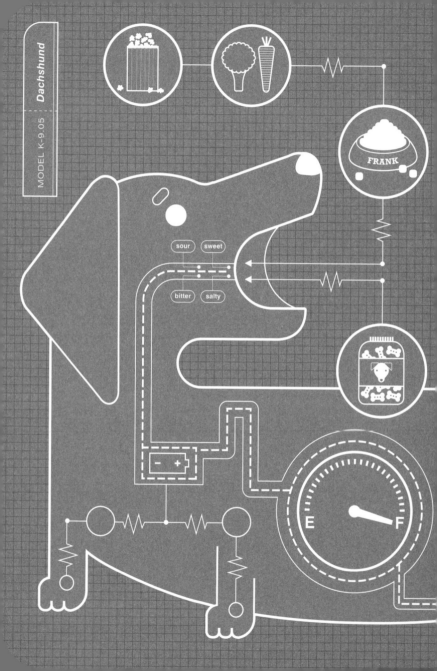

Chapter 5

Fuel Requirements

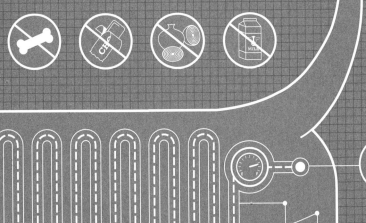

Types of Fuel

Dog foods are divided into broad categories—dry and canned. Dry is the most popular. It contains more nutrition by weight, is less expensive than canned, and its hardness may help reduce dental tartar. Canned food is favored by dogs themselves and includes fewer calories by volume (it is approximately 70 percent water).

Special foods are available to counter everything from diabetes to obesity to allergies. Lamb is often the centerpiece of such formulations because very few canines are allergic to it. Aging dogs may also have special dietary needs. Their kidneys handle protein less efficiently, sometimes necessitating a low-protein food. The onset of heart disease, liver and/or kidney difficulties, stomach problems, and other concerns can also call for special diets.

When feeding a commercially produced food, begin by offering your dog the recommended daily serving. Be prepared to alter this, however, because recommended portions tend to be slightly more than what dogs actually require to maintain their weight. Never give "high protein" or "puppy formula" foods to dogs more than a year old.

EXPERT TIP: *Unless you are prepared to work very hard at it, do not try to make your dog's food. Creating the proper balance of nutrients, minerals, and vitamins takes a great deal of effort.*

Fuel Facts

Nutritional needs vary from canine to canine and hinge on such things as size, activity level, and age.

■ Small dogs need more calories per pound of body mass than larger dogs.

■ A very sedentary dog may need 30 percent fewer calories than an average dog of the same size.

- Very active dogs may require 40 to 50 percent more calories than an average dog.
- Pregnant or lactating dogs may need 30 to 50 percent more calories than usual—sometimes even double their normal serving.
- During winter, dogs who spend time outside may need additional food, because maintaining a constant body temperature requires more calories.

Approximate Daily Fuel Requirements

	DAILY CALORIC INTAKE	
Weight	Puppies	Adult Dogs
■ 5 pounds/2 kg	■ 500	■ 250
■ 10 pounds/4.5 kg	■ 850	■ 450
■ 20 pounds/9 kg	■ 1400	■ 700
■ 30 pounds/13.5 kg	■ 1800	■ 900
■ 40 pounds/18 kg	■ 2300	■ 1200
■ 50 pounds/22.5 kg	■ 2700	■ 1400
■ 60 pounds/27 kg	■ 3200	■ 1600
■ 70 pounds/31.5 kg	■ 3600	■ 1500
■ 80 pounds/36 kg	———	■ 1800
■ 90 pounds/40.5 kg	———	■ 2100
■ 100 pounds/45 kg	———	■ 2300

Selecting a Brand

The makers of dog food, just like the makers of processed human foods, are required by law to post nutritional information on their labels. Such labels must list, among other things, the ingredients and a statement of nutritional purpose and adequacy (basically, an explanation as to what sort of dog the food is meant for).

Examine the statement of nutritional purpose and adequacy first. For instance, a product formulated for puppies and pregnant females might read, "Complete and balanced nutrition for growth and reproduction." Or a food for adult canines might say, "Complete and balanced nutrition for growth and maintenance of adult dogs." Top products will state that these claims are based on "Association of American Feed Control Officials (AAFCO) feeding protocols." Lesser products may base their assertions solely on a nutrient analysis that "meets AAFCO nutrient profile recommendations." In short, the higher-quality product was subjected to a feeding study; the lesser product only to a lab test.

After selecting a balanced, nutritionally complete product that is designed to meet your dog's needs, examine the ingredients. The heaviest ingredient by weight is listed first. Wet foods will almost always list a meat product first, while in dry preparations meat may appear farther down the roster. This is because in wet foods the meat is hydrated and therefore heavier. Dry products may contain just as much meat, but because it weighs less it sits slightly lower on the ingredient list.

In general, some form of meat should be near the top of any list. Meat by-products (these can range from bonemeal to poultry feathers) are generally of a lower quality. Cereals and soy are also important ingredients and should appear prominently. Plant hulls are low-quality foods, but may be added to increase fiber. Vitamins, minerals, and preservatives, used in minute amounts, will appear last on any ingredients list.

If you wish to compare brands, examine the guaranteed analysis printed on the container. This explains what percentage of the product is made up of protein, fat, fiber, and moisture. To make such comparisons meaningful, ask your veterinarian what percentages are right for your dog.

How to Feed

Do not "free feed"—that is, leave a bowl of food sitting out all day so that the canine can serve itself. This may lead to obesity. Pick a time to offer a meal, present the food, then, after perhaps half an hour, put away the bowl until the next feeding. Twice-daily feedings (once in the morning, once in the evening) will suffice for most models.

Puppies up to 12 weeks of age should receive three meals a day and twice-daily feedings thereafter. Small-breed puppies may need more frequent feedings to avoid hypoglycemia. At 9 to 12 months puppies should be switched to adult food and less-frequent feedings. Nutritional supplements not recommended by a veterinarian should be avoided; too much protein and/or calcium can cause joint and skeletal problems. For more information on puppy nutrition, see page 141.

Modifying Diet

Suddenly switching a dog's food can lead to stomach upset and diarrhea. To avoid this, change the product gradually. On the first day, mix three parts of the current food with one part of the new food. On the next day, mix them evenly. On the third day, offer three-fourths new food. Then switch entirely to the new product.

TYPES OF FUEL: There are two broad categories of fuel: dry and canned.

DRY FUEL (front view)

Examine the nutritional purpose and ingredients carefully before selecting a brand.

DRY FUEL (side view)

CANNED FUEL (front view)

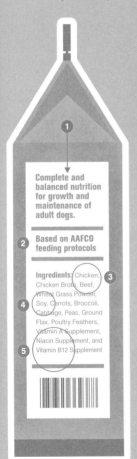

1 Complete and balanced nutrition for growth and maintenance of adult dogs.

2 Based on AAFCO feeding protocols

3 Ingredients: Chicken, Chicken Broth, Beef, Wheat Grass Powder, Soy, Carrots, Broccoli, Cabbage, Peas, Ground Flax, Poultry Feathers, Vitamin A Supplement, Niacin Supplement, and Vitamin B12 Supplement **4** **5**

1 Complete and balanced nutrition for growth and maintenance of overweight dogs.

2 Based on AAFCO feeding protocols

3 Ingredients: Beef, Lamb Broth, Liver, Wheat Grass Powder, Soy, Broccoli, Peas, Bonemeal, Vitamin A Supplement, and Niacin Supplement **4** **5**

CANNED FUEL (back view)

1 Nutritional purpose and adequacy statement

2 Indicates a high quality product was subjected to a feeding study instead of only a lab test

The order in which the ingredients are listed is determined by weight (heaviest is listed first)

3 Meat should be near the top of the list

4 Cereals and soy should be listed prominently

5 Vitamins, minerals, and preservatives should appear last, as they are used minutely

FUEL SUPPLEMENTS

NUTRITIOUS SNACKS

1. Low-calorie dog treats
2. Air-popped popcorn (no salt or butter)
3. Broccoli
4. Cooked green beans
5. Raw carrots

HAZARDOUS MATERIALS

1. Table scraps
2. Bones
3. Cat food
4. Chocolate
5. Onions
6. Milk

KITTY CHOW

CHOC

MILK

Fuel Supplements (Snacks)

Snacks should compose no more than 10 percent of a dog's daily caloric intake. Appropriate snacks include:

■ Commercial low-calorie dog treats

■ Air-popped popcorn without butter or salt

■ Broccoli

■ Cooked green beans

■ Raw carrots

The following snacks are unhealthy and possibly even fatal to dogs:

■ Table scraps (they are usually too fatty and not attuned to a dog's nutritional needs; if you must provide them, do so sparingly).

■ Bones (small ones can become caught in the airway; large ones may splinter and can cause any number of problems, from choking to intestinal blockage to internal punctures).

■ Cat food (dogs love it, but it is not formulated to meet their nutritional needs).

■ Chocolate (toxic to canines, small amounts of chocolate can make dogs sick; large amounts can be fatal).

■ Onions (consumption of too many onions will cause the dog's red blood cells to burst, triggering anemia).

■ Milk (dogs, like most adult mammals, often suffer from lactose intolerance; a large dose of milk can trigger intestinal distress and diarrhea).

Gas Emissions

Most canines will, from time to time, suffer from excess methane discharges. There are several ways to handle such exhaust problems.

■ Give the dog activated charcoal tablets, which will absorb the excess gas.

■ Overeating can cause gas, so try serving smaller portions in more feedings.

■ Dogs who eat too fast may swallow too much air. Ration their food more slowly or, if you have other dogs, allow them to eat in separate areas. Canines who eat in groups tend to bolt their food so others can't steal it.

■ Stop providing fatty, hard-to-digest table scraps and snacks.

■ Try elevated dog dishes, like those used for large breeds, to help prevent gas buildup.

Managing the Dog's Weight

Compare the weight of your dog with the weight of other dogs in its breed (see pages 26–38). If your dog is a mixed breed (or not described in this book), examine your model to see if it has a "waist"—a visible indentation behind the ribs. Overweight dogs lack this. Next, try to feel its ribs. If you can't, the dog is overweight. (If its ribs seem too pronounced, your dog may be underweight. Consider increasing its caloric intake.)

Weighing a Dog

[**1**] Weigh yourself on a bathroom scale (Fig. A).

[**2**] Pick up the dog and weigh again (Fig. B). If the dog is particularly large, be sure to exercise caution (Fig. C).

[**3**] Subtract the first weight from the second weight (Fig. D).

If your dog is too large to handle in this way, ask your veterinarian if you can periodically use the clinic's scale.

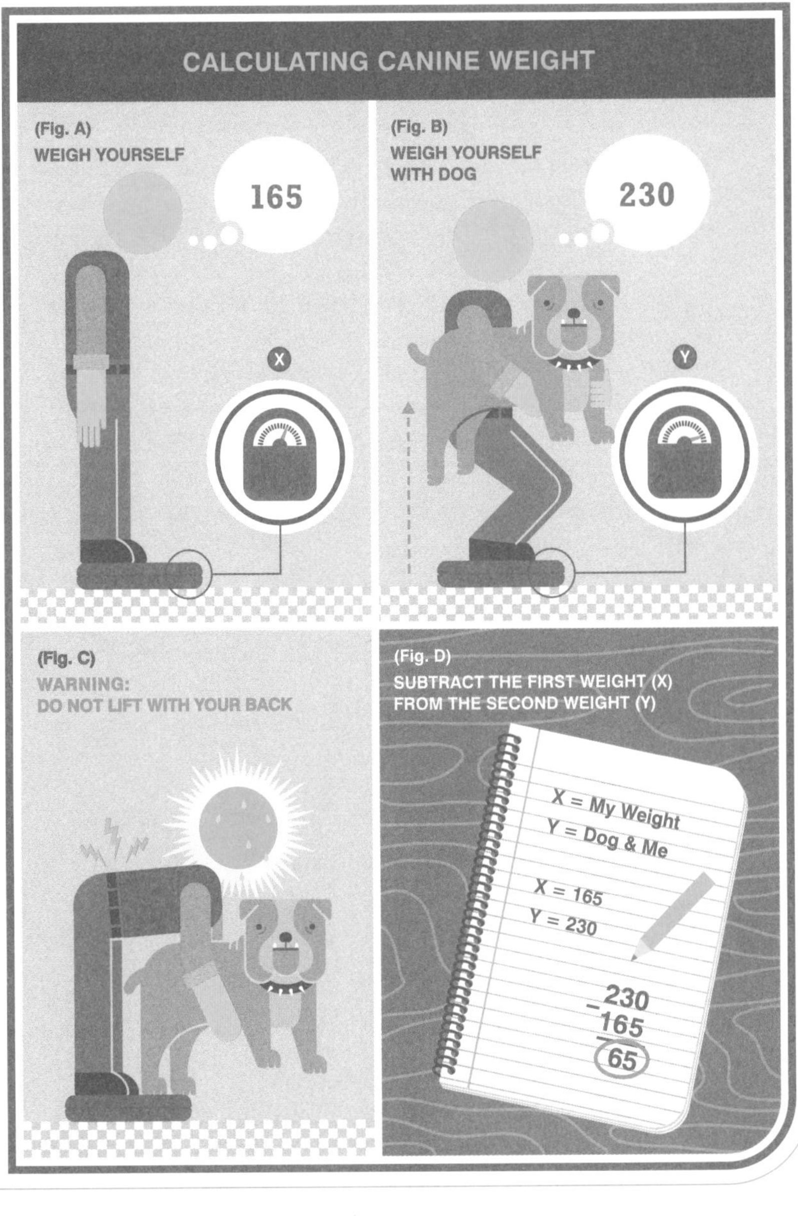
CALCULATING CANINE WEIGHT
(Fig. A)
WEIGH YOURSELF
165
X
(Fig. B)
WEIGH YOURSELF
WITH DOG
230
Y
(Fig. C)
WARNING:
DO NOT LIFT WITH YOUR BACK
(Fig. D)
SUBTRACT THE FIRST WEIGHT (X)
FROM THE SECOND WEIGHT (Y)
X = My Weight
Y = Dog & Me
X = 165
Y = 230
230
−165
65

Weight Reduction

Before changing your dog's diet, develop a plan of action with your veterinarian. Weight loss in canines is a slow process with several health risks. In some cases a special diet may be needed, or there may be other complicating concerns to consider, such as diabetes. Weight loss can be accomplished either by giving the dog less of its current food or switching it to a low-calorie "diet" product.

Keep the following tips in mind as you proceed with your program:

■ Weight loss should in most cases not exceed 8 ounces to 1 pound (225–450 g) per week.

■ During this time the dog should (if your vet concurs) also receive extra exercise.

■ Avoid fatty treats. Reward the canine with praise, or offer low-calorie tidbits such as broccoli, green beans, or carrots.

■ If the dog seems unsatisfied with the amount of food it receives, try serving it several, smaller meals a day.

■ If you have multiple canines, feed them in separate locations so the dieting dog does not receive extra food.

■ Be sure the dog has plenty of water at all times.

■ Be sure all family members understand the diet plan. One person providing unauthorized food can disrupt the program.

■ Weigh the dog weekly and keep track of its progress.

■ Remember: A dog loses roughly 1 pound (.5 kg) of weight for every 3,500 calories it expends.

Average Daily Water Intake Requirement*

BODY WEIGHT	WATER
■ 5 pounds/2 kg	■ 7 ounces/207 ml
■ 10 pounds/4.5 kg	■ 14 ounces/414 ml
■ 20 pounds/9 kg	■ 24 ounces/710 ml
■ 30 pounds/13.5 kg	■ 33 ounces/975 ml
■ 40 pounds/18 kg	■ 41 ounces/1.2 l
■ 50 pounds/22.5 kg	■ 48 ounces/1.4 l
■ 60 pounds/27 kg	■ 55 ounces/1.6 l
■ 70 pounds/31.5 kg	■ 62 ounces/1.8 l
■ 80 pounds/36 kg	■ 69 ounces/2 l
■ 90 pounds/41 kg	■ 75 ounces/2.2 l
■ 100 pounds/45.5 kg	■ 82 ounces/2.4 l

*Requirements include water absorbed from food and snacks.

Chapter 6

Exterior Maintenance

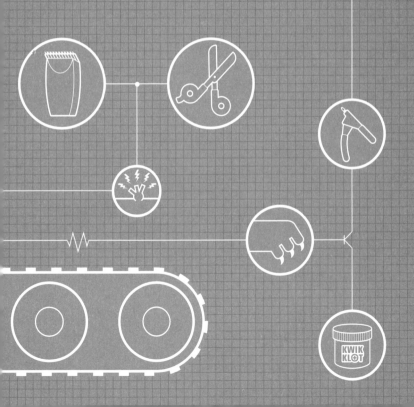

The amount of exterior detailing dogs require varies greatly from model to model. For instance, while the coats of shorthaired varieties are relatively easy to maintain, those with longer coats (collies, Old English sheepdogs) will almost certainly require regular professional attention. However, many issues are the same regardless of the breed, including nail upkeep and bathing protocols. Whatever your model, regular exterior maintenance will ensure that your canine functions in top operating condition.

Understanding the Coat

Most dog models include three kinds of hair—tactile hair, an outercoat, and an undercoat. The undercoat, also called the secondary coat, is made of dense, soft fur. It provides both insulation and support for the outercoat. The outercoat is composed of long, stiff guard hairs that protect the undercoat. The last type, tactile hair, includes the whiskers and other stiff facial hairs that provide sensory information about the outside world.

The heaviest shedders are dogs with well-developed double coats—a layer of long, coarse hair over short, dense hair. Double-coated dogs (including the Akita, Pomeranian, Newfoundland, and Siberian husky) will generally lose their undercoats twice each year and their outer-coats annually. The onset of shedding is linked to hormonal changes triggered by changes in the length of the day. A dog may also "drop its coat" (shed extensively) after a physically traumatic situation such as surgery or giving birth.

Dogs that lack double coats, or that live inside, may shed all year long instead of seasonally. Other models, including poodles and many terriers, do not shed at all.

Overview of Dog Hair Varieties

Your model will come with any of the following exterior finishes prein-stalled.

Long Hair: Found on such models as Old English sheepdogs, Newfound-lands, collies, golden retrievers, etc. Longhaired coats need daily brushing to prevent tangles and excessive shedding.

Short Hair: Found on such models as beagles and pointers. This type of coat calls for much less maintenance than other varieties, but it still requires combing and/or brushing on a regular basis.

Nonshedding Hair: As the name suggests, this hair is maintained by the unit year-round. However, it may still require regular clipping. This type of finish can be found on poodles and bichons frises.

Long and Silky Hair: Found on such models as Yorkshire terriers, Pekingese, and Afghan hounds. Without regular maintenance, these coats will quickly become matted.

Smooth Hair: These coats can be easily groomed with a brush. Smooth hair can be found on such breeds as Dobermans, greyhounds, and Lab-rador retrievers.

Wiry: Found on most terrier breeds, as well as schnauzers. Wirehaired dogs need regular combing and clipping to prevent matting. They can also be "hand stripped" (whereby loose hair is plucked from the coat), but this process can take hours, even for a small dog.

1 Nail Clippers
2 Styptic Powder
3 Comb
4 Scissors
5 Brush
6 Undercoat Rake
7 Shedding Tool
8 Grooming Glove
9 Currycomb

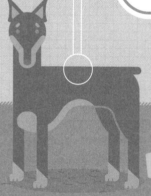

SMOOTH HAIR
Medium shedding

SHORT HAIR
Medium to heavy shedding

WIRY
Light to medium shedding

EXTERIOR FINISHES AND GROOMING ACCESSORIES:

ALL MODELS REQUIRE:

1 **2** **KWIK KLOT** **3**

4 **5**

6 **7**

NONSHEDDING HAIR

LONG HAIR
Heavy shedding

LONG & SILKY HAIR
Heavy shedding

HAIRLESS

Most models should be groomed on a daily basis.

Hairless: These models include such oddities as the Chinese Crested, but there are no true "hairless" breeds. All mammals have at least some hair. For these breeds skin care (particularly sunburn protection) is extremely important.

General Coat Maintenance

To minimize deposits of hair in the house, groom your dog regularly. It is advisable, if possible, to begin brushing a puppy at an early age. It will become used to, and may even enjoy, the process. Almost all dogs should be brushed thoroughly every day to remove dirt and loose hair, to prevent tangles and matting, and to disperse natural oils throughout the coat.

EXPERT TIP: Grooming is an excellent time to examine your dog for irritated skin, lumps, bumps, ticks, fleas, and any other problem that might require veterinary attention.

Grooming Tools

The following accessories will aid in the maintenance of the dog's exterior finish.

Brush: It is important to select a brush that is suitable for your dog's coat. The ideal tool is a soft wire brush that can remove tangles without irritating skin.

Comb: Usually made of steel and featuring both fine and coarse teeth, this tool can remove burrs and tangles and bring order to the coat of a longhaired dog.

Currycomb: Often made of rubber, this tool removes loose hair from short-haired breeds while also massaging the skin.

Grooming Glove: Covered with nubby, hair-catching material, the glove is useful for face grooming, and for brushing dogs with extremely short hair.

Nail Clippers: There are two basic types—guillotine-style clippers and standard scissors-style clippers. Both work well.

Scissors: Excellent for removing particularly stubborn tangles or burrs.

Shedding Tool: This bladelike device with serrated edges is ideal for removing excess fur from longhaired breeds.

Styptic Powder: This blood-clotting powder (available at most retailers) will quickly stop bleeding caused by trimming a dog's nails too closely.

Undercoat Rake: As the name implies, this tool removes loose hair from the dense undercoat of longhaired and thick-haired breeds, such as the husky and Irish setter.

Selecting a Professional Groomer

While owners can handle the day-to-day maintenance tasks described in this chapter, more extensive work should be left to experts. Most veterinarians keep lists of recommended groomers; a few even employ groomers on staff. Additional sources for recommendations include friends, reputable purebred breeders, and boarding kennels.

If your model has special needs (for instance, if it is geriatric or requires a medicinal shampoo regimen), make sure your choice is equipped to meet them. Also, be sure the groomer does not tranquilize dogs before handling them. Make a point of visiting the salon during business hours for a surprise inspection. Are the facilities clean? Are the dogs well-treated? What you pay will vary based on the breed, the amount of hair involved, and its condition. Depending on the model, grooming may be necessary once or twice a year, or as often as every 6 weeks.

⚠ *CAUTION: Before taking your dog to a groomer, make sure its vaccinations (especially for* bordetella, *or kennel cough) are current.*

Removing Mats

Mats are amalgams of tightly tangled hair usually pressed close to the dog's skin. When ignored, they can cause severe discomfort and skin irritation. Upon discovering a mat, use fingers and a comb to untangle as much as possible. If the mat, or a portion thereof, cannot be untangled, carefully cut it out by first placing a comb between the hair and the dog's skin, then trim out the clump with scissors. Since the mat is usually very close to the skin, the comb will act as a guard against cuts.

Bathing

To ensure a quality finish on the dog's exterior coating, you should bathe the animal on a regular basis. This experience can be an enjoyable one, especially if the dog is introduced to the process during puppyhood. For most breeds, a bath every few months should suffice, unless the animal tends to dirty itself more often. Brush the dog before bathing it to remove mats and tangles.

⚠ *CAUTION: Bathing the dog too frequently may lead to dry skin and/or skin irritation; if you must wash the dog often, or own a breed predisposed to dry skin, use a canine-formulated conditioning shampoo.*

[1] Place a rubber mat in the bathtub (Fig. A). This will give the dog a secure footing and will help it relax.

[2] Be sure all supplies are within your reach (Fig. B).

[3] Put a cotton ball in each of the dog's ears to keep out water (Fig. C).

[4] Place the dog in the tub. If the canine is a large model and you are unsure of your ability to lift it, seek help.

[5] Rinse the dog thoroughly with warm water, using a spray hose if available. Hold the nozzle as close to the dog's body as possible. Do not spray it in the face.

⚠ *EXPERT TIP: Throughout this process, it is important to stroke and reassure the dog frequently (especially if it is not used to bathing).*

(Fig. A)
INSTALL BATH MAT

(Fig. B)
GATHER SUPPLIES

1. Shampoo
2. Cotton balls
3. Spray hose
4. Mineral oil
5. Towel or blow-dryer

(Fig. C)
CANINE PREPARATION

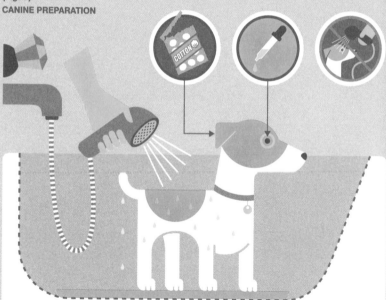

BATHING PROCEDURE: Bathing the model every few months will help

(Fig. D)
APPLY DOG-FORMULATED SHAMPOO

(Fig. E)
DON'T FORGET TO WASH

1. Waste port
2. Toes
3. Behind the ears
4. Under the chin

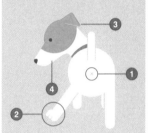

(Fig. F)
CHOOSE DRYING METHOD

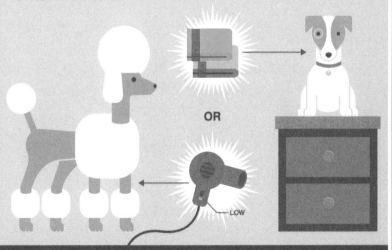

OR

LOW

to maintain a quality exterior finish. But washing it too often will dry the skin.

[6] Apply a dog-formulated shampoo, in small amounts, working from tail to head (Fig. D).

[7] Be sure the waste port, toes, and the areas behind the ears and under the chin are clean (Fig. E).

⚠ **CAUTION:** *Avoid getting shampoo in the dog's eyes. A drop of mineral oil in the corner of each eye immediately prior to bath time prevents irritation.*

[8] Rinse the dog thoroughly with warm water. Begin at the head. Squeeze excess water from the coat. Remove the cotton balls from its ears.

[9] Dry the dog with a towel or hair dryer (Fig. F). Dogs with kinky or long coats, including the Maltese, bichon frise, and poodle, look better blow-dried. Keep the dryer on its lowest setting, and never direct the air flow into the dog's face.

⚠ **CAUTION:** *Some breeds (including basset hounds and many members of the spaniel family) have excessively oily coats. If not bathed and properly groomed, the oil can become rancid and cause a dandruff-like condition called primary seborrhea. Medicinal shampoos can correct the problem. Consult your veterinarian for details.*

Ears

The ears should be checked weekly for signs of unpleasant odor, redness, and/or inflammation, all of which should be examined by a veterinarian. To remove excess dirt, use a baby oil- or alcohol-soaked cotton ball. Do not probe too deeply into the ear canal. Proper ear maintenance is particularly important in "droopy-eared" breeds (basset hounds, beagles, bloodhounds, etc.), because air may not circulate freely to their ear canals.

Eyes

A healthy dog's eyes should always be shiny and wide open. During grooming, gently wipe away any discharge that has accumulated around them (a warm washcloth may help). Consult your veterinarian if the discharge is green or yellow. White-haired dogs may develop discoloration in the fur around their eyes from excessive tearing. These stains can sometimes be reduced by applying commercial solutions available at all pet stores. Do not attempt this without consulting your veterinarian.

Teeth

A dog's teeth are subject to such problems as plaque buildup, periodontal disease, and occasional cavities. The teeth should be cleaned at least twice per week with a pet toothpaste and a toothbrush with soft bristles. Regular professional cleaning by a veterinarian is also a must.

EXPERT TIP: Never use human toothpaste, which can upset dogs' stomachs.

Anal Glands

Extremely unpleasant odors can result if the dog's anal sacs (two small glands bracketing the anus) become full and/or infected. If the dog frequently licks its rectal area, or if the dog frequently drags this area across the floor, be sure to mention this behavior to a veterinarian. Usually, the best way to address this problem is to regularly empty or "express" the anal glands. This procedure can be done by a professional groomer or at a veterinarian's office. With proper vet-guided instruction, dog owners can learn to execute the procedure themselves.

Nails

Nails should be trimmed approximately twice per month. Use a purpose-designed clipper (see page 123) and be sure to have cotton swabs and a bottle of styptic powder nearby. This commercially available blood-clotting powder can be used to stop bleeding if you accidentally trim a nail too closely.

[1] Instruct the dog to sit beside you and take one of its paws in your hand. A smaller dog can sit on your lap. Alternatively, have the dog roll onto its stomach on the floor.

[2] Clip the first nail in stages. Be careful not to trim the quick (the part of the nail containing nerves and blood vessels). If you cannot locate the quick, stop cutting at the spot where the nail begins to curve downward.

EXPERT TIP: If you have trouble spotting the quick, try trimming nails just after a bath, when it will be more visible. Applying baby oil to nails can also make the quick easier to see.

[3] If you accidentally clip the quick, comfort the dog and apply styptic powder to the nail using a moist cotton swab. Press firmly against the nail for 10 seconds.

TRIMMING THE NAILS

1. Trim nail at angle shown
2. Do not cut the quick (dark area)

If you cut the quick:

3. Dip cotton swab in water
4. Dip cotton swab in styptic powder and apply to the bleeding quick

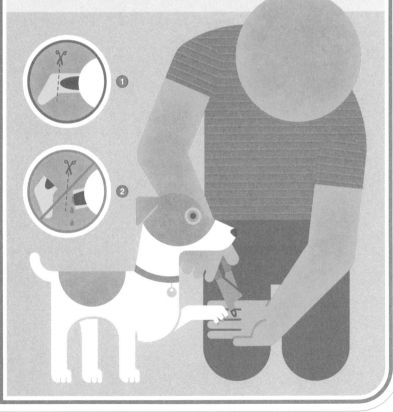

[4] Repeat the clipping process until all nails are trimmed. Each nail should be cut at a 45-degree angle away from the dog so the nail is flush with the floor when the dog is on its feet.

[5] Remember to trim the dewclaws, located on the inside of each leg.

Emergency Cleanups

Whenever you locate foreign or unidentified substances on your dog's coat, it is best to remove them immediately. Otherwise, the dog may ingest them via licking, which may lead to malfunction.

Burrs: Most can be removed with careful use of a metal comb. Deeply entangled burrs can often be released by working vegetable oil into the affected area. If this method fails to work, carefully remove the burrs with scissors.

Chewing Gum: Apply ice to the gum to reduce its stickiness, then clip from fur. Alternatively, there are several commercial products that facilitate gum removal without haircutting.

Paint: If it is a water-based paint, soak the affected area in water for 5 minutes or longer until it becomes pliant. Then rub the affected fur between your fingers to remove it. Any other type of paint will require careful clipping and trimming.

⚠ *CAUTION: Never use paint thinner, turpentine, gasoline, or any other such solvents on your dog.*

Skunk: If your dog is sprayed by a skunk, you can de-scent the model with a thorough bath in tomato juice. Place the dog in a basin filled with tomato juice; allow the exterior coat to soak in the juice for several minutes, then rinse and repeat. The dog may require several baths (over several days) before the scent disappears.

Tar: In many cases the tar-coated hair will have to be clipped away. However, petroleum jelly can sometimes remove the substance. Rub some into a small portion of the affected area, then wipe away the broken-up tar with a clean cloth. Repeat as many times as necessary. Bathe the dog with a degreasing shampoo afterward.

Chapter 7

Growth and Development

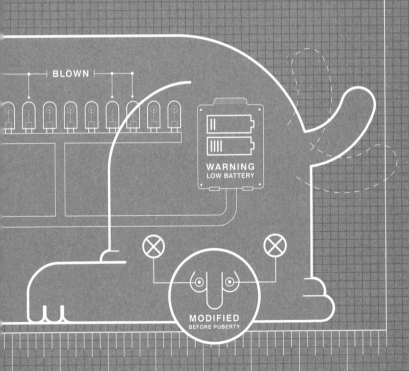

BLOWN

WARNING
LOW BATTERY

MODIFIED
BEFORE PUBERTY

Puppy Growth Stages

Unlike most consumer products, which can only be upgraded by purchasing and installing expensive peripherals, the dog has the ability to increase its cognitive and mechanical capacities on its own. This phenomenon is most obvious in puppies, who in a matter of months upgrade from fragile, highly dependent units into fully mature systems. This section offers an overview of that remarkable process.

Birth to 8 Weeks

The puppy is entirely dependent on its mother. Puppies are born with sealed eyes and ear canals. Walking begins at 16 days. Eyelids open at the age of 2 weeks, while ear canals open after approximately 17 days. Waste elimination without assistance from the mother (who licks the genital area to stimulate the process) begins at 23 days of age. At 25 days, puppies begin responding to sights and sounds. Baby teeth appear at 4 to 6 weeks; consumption of solid food begins at the same time.

Programming Milestones: Little true learning is possible at this time, though some rudimentary socialization can be accomplished. For instance, frequent, gentle handling will help the newborn become acclimated to people. Remember that the puppy must remain with its mother and littermates during this important period. Only they can help it download much of the programming necessary for proper dog behavior.

8 to 15 Weeks

Full weaning takes place at or before 8 weeks. Puppies can be supplied with small amounts of solid food (as a supplement to milk) as early as their fourth week, when their first set of teeth will begin to emerge. Choose a specially formulated puppy food that is thinned to the consistency of gruel. As the weeks pass, the amount of solid matter in the gruel should be increased.

Programming Milestones: This is the prime age for learning to interface with humans. Eight weeks is also the accepted time for a puppy to be removed from the litter and transferred to its adopted family. Crate training, leash training, and house-training instruction can begin.

16 Weeks to 11 Months

Puberty begins at 6 to 8 months of age. A female dog will reach sexual maturity between the ages of 9 and 15 months; males reach sexual maturity between 7 and 12 months. (See page 141 for more information.)

Programming Milestones: At 12 to 20 weeks, the puppy may become fearful if left alone or in new places. A puppy socialization class can mitigate the problem, which usually passes with time. Basic obedience-training downloads are best accomplished at this time.

12 Months

By the age of 1 year, puppies will have made the transformation into adult dogs. In most cases, you will want to switch the dog's fuel supply from a puppy-formulated mixture to a blend more suitable for adults.

Programming Milestones: The dog will ideally be fully socialized to humans at this point, and you may also notice an increased attention span. This is an excellent time to initiate advanced obedience training.

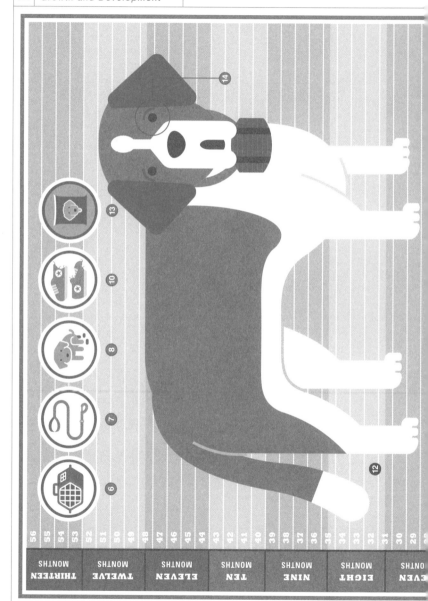

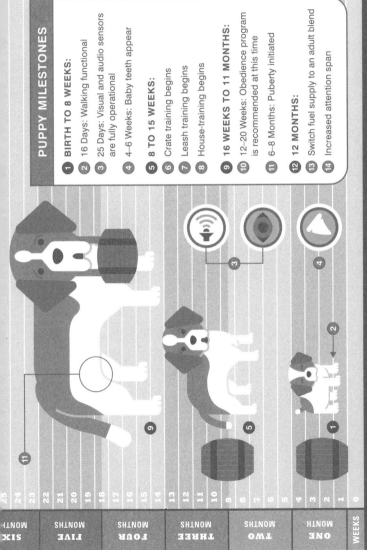

PUPPY MILESTONES

BIRTH TO 8 WEEKS:

1. 16 Days: Walking functional
2. 25 Days: Visual and audio sensors are fully operational
3. 4–6 Weeks: Baby teeth appear

8 TO 15 WEEKS:

5. Crate training begins
6. Leash training begins
7. House-training begins

16 WEEKS TO 11 MONTHS:

9. 12–20 Weeks: Obedience program is recommended at this time
10. 6–8 Months: Puberty initiated

12 MONTHS:

12. Switch fuel supply to an adult blend
13. Increased attention span

PUPPY GROWTH STAGES: During the first 12 months, your model will self-upgrade many times.

WEEKS
0
ONE MONTH — 1 2 3 4
TWO MONTHS — 5 6 7 8
THREE MONTHS — 9 10 11 12 13
FOUR MONTHS — 14 15 16 17
FIVE MONTHS — 18 19 20 21 22
SIX MONTHS — 23 24 25

Calculating Age in "Dog Years"

A popular misconception is that dogs age 7 years for each calendar year. In fact, canine aging is much more rapid during the first 2 years of a dog's life.

After the first 2 years the ratio settles down to 5 to 1 for small and medium breeds. For large breeds the rate is 6 to 1, and for giant breeds the rate is 7 to 1. Thus, at 10 years of age a Great Dane would be 80 years old while a pug would only be 64.

Teeth Development

The dog's first teeth will appear between 4 and 6 weeks of age, at approximately the same time the puppy is introduced to solid food. This first set is composed of baby teeth, as in humans. The front incisors

are replaced by permanent teeth at around 3 to 4 months. Permanent canines (incisors) appear during the sixth month; premolars arrive at 4 to 6 months and molars at 5 to 7 months. Once their permanent teeth come in, puppies develop an almost-overwhelming urge to chew, which helps set their teeth firmly in their jaws. To keep your canine from chewing furniture or other valuables, provide it with plenty of toys (and supervision).

Diet Requirements

Puppies should receive a high-quality diet specifically designed for their needs. Ask your veterinarian to recommend an appropriate commercial brand. In general, puppies should receive no more per feeding than they can consume in 5 to 10 minutes. Puppies 6 to 12 weeks old usually are fed three times a day; two times a day when aged 12 weeks to 6 months; and one or two times daily when older than 6 months.

⚠ *CAUTION: Puppies should never be given vitamins or dietary supplements of any kind unless recommended by a veterinarian.*

Sexual Maturity

The age of sexual maturity varies from breed to breed and from individual to individual. The range is as wide as 9 to 15 months for females and 7 to 12 months for males. Females typically go into heat (estrus) for 3-week periods twice yearly. While in estrus, the canine is receptive to the advances of males and is capable of breeding. It is important to keep the female confined or under close observation during these times, because she can attract male dogs from great distances.

Male dogs have no "cycle." They can breed year-round and will act whenever they encounter a receptive female. Male sexual maturity may also manifest itself in leg humping and in the lifting of the leg during urination. (See "Spaying and Neutering," below.)

EXPERT TIP: *As with human adolescents, dogs entering puberty often experience sometimes difficult personality changes. Extra exercise, plus spaying/neutering before puberty, can help mitigate such difficulties.*

Spaying and Neutering

It is the duty of every responsible pet owner to have his or her canine spayed or neutered. Unwanted litters contribute to a vast oversupply of dogs in the United States. Unless you plan to breed your dog (which is not recommended, except in the case of highly valued purebred models), it should be sterilized before reaching sexual maturity. For males this is called *neutering* (removal of the testicles); for females, *spaying* (removal of the ovaries and uterus). Neutered males are generally less aggressive, less prone to roam, and less excitable than their unaltered peers. They also suffer from fewer health problems such as prostate troubles and testicular cancer.

Likewise, females spayed before puberty have their chances of contracting mammary cancer (an extremely common malady) reduced to near zero. Also, the danger of ovarian cysts, uterine infections, and cancers of the reproductive tract (all very common malfunctions) are eliminated. Neutered and spayed dogs tend to gain weight more easily, but this can be countered by feeding 10 to 20 percent less food and increasing exercise. In most cases, neutering and spaying can be performed at any time past the age of 16 weeks.

ADVANTAGES OF SPAYING AND NEUTERING

NEUTERING THE MALE REDUCES THE RISK OF:

1. Aggression
2. Prostate troubles
3. Testicular cancer

SPAYING THE FEMALE REDUCES THE RISK OF:

4. Mammary cancer
5. Ovarian cysts
6. Uterine infections
7. Cancers of the reproductive tract
8. Unwanted puppies

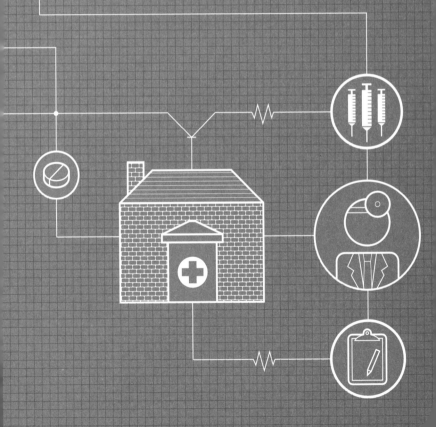

[Chapter 8]

Interior Maintenance

When dealing with mechanical or software glitches, dog owners can call on a vast, highly developed service and support infrastructure for assistance. This chapter explains how to locate and utilize a qualified service provider in your vicinity. It will also describe how to recognize and manage smaller problems that can be easily fixed in your own home.

Selecting a Service Provider

One of the first tasks a new dog owner must accomplish is selecting the right veterinarian. The ideal candidate will be available to service your pet for its entire lifespan. He or she can maintain long-term treatment and immunization records; chart reactions to specific medications; even develop an understanding of your dog's particular programming quirks. This extensive knowledge base is helpful during minor emergencies and can mean the difference between life and death during major ones. Here are some other guidelines to consider when selecting a service provider.

■ When considering candidates, consult friends who own dogs. Breed clubs can also provide lists of recommended doctors, including, in some cases, veterinarians with special knowledge of particular models.

■ Schedule an appointment with the veterinarians you are considering. Discuss your dog and its specific needs. Do you feel comfortable with the vet? What professional organizations does he or she belong to?

■ Examine the facility itself. Does it look and smell clean? What range of services does it provide? How are emergency after-hours calls handled?

■ Make sure your choice is a good fit logistically. Does the clinic keep business hours that are convenient for you? Is the office conveniently located? Patronizing a vet with odd hours and an out-of-the-way location is difficult at best, life-threatening at worst.

⚠ **EXPERT TIP:** *You might want to select a veterinarian before acquiring a dog. If you are unsure about which model to choose, a veterinarian can provide expert advice.*

Conducting a Home Maintenance Inspection

Dog owners should inspect their models regularly for potential health problems. The best time to do this is during the dog's regular grooming regimen. Here are some systems to review.

Mouth: Teeth should be white and gums should be pink (unless they are naturally pigmented black). There should be no lumps or bumps in the mouth. The model should not emit "doggy breath" (see page 154).

Eyes: A healthy dog should have clear eyes with no discharge, squinting, irritation, or cloudiness.

Ears: The interior of the ears should be pink, odorless, and free of dark-colored discharge. There should be no signs of tenderness, pain, or itching.

Weight: If you cannot feel the dog's ribs, the unit may be overweight. If the ribs are very pronounced, however, the canine could be underweight.

Paws: Check the feet for damage to the pads. Make sure the nails and dewclaws (if present) are trimmed and in good condition.

Waste Port: Make sure the anal area is clean, dry, and free of bumps and welts.

HOME MAINTENANCE INSPECTION

HEALTHY MODEL

1. Clean white teeth, pink gums (unless naturally pigmented black)
2. Clear eyes
3. Pink, no discharge
4. Proper weight
5. Trimmed nails
6. Clean waste port
7. Even, shiny coat without flea dirt or skin irritations

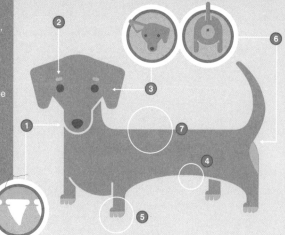

UNHEALTHY MODEL

1. Doggy breath
2. Discharge, squinting, irritation, or cloudiness
3. Discharge, tenderness, itching
4. Overweight or underweight
5. Damaged paws, untrimmed nails
6. Dirty waste port
7. Flea dirt
8. Bald spots
9. Excessive shedding

Skin: Use a comb to examine the skin. Look for "flea dirt" (excrement from fleas that resembles grains of pepper). Skin should be free of odor, grease, scabs, flakes, and other irritations.

Coat: Check the coat for bald spots, dullness, and/or excessive, unwarranted shedding.

Visiting Your Service Provider

Barring emergencies, most dogs will require a handful of veterinary visits during their first year of life and annual visits thereafter. Listed below is an approximate guideline of when you should expect to have the dog serviced and what you can expect a veterinarian to do.

Age 6–8 Weeks

- Physical examination
- DHPP immunization (a combination vaccination for distemper, hepatitis, parainfluenza, and parvovirus)
- Stool exam for parasites
- Deworming
- Begin heartworm preventative medication and (if seasonally appropriate) flea preventative

Age 10–12 Weeks

- Physical examination
- DHLPP immunization (DHPP plus vaccination for leptospirosis)
- Deworming

■ Kennel cough (Bordetella) vaccination

■ Administer heartworm preventative medication and (if seasonally appropriate) flea preventative

Age 14–16 Weeks

■ Physical examination

■ DHLPP immunization

■ Kennel cough (Bordetella) vaccination

■ Rabies vaccination

■ Administer heartworm preventative medication and (if seasonally appropriate) flea preventative

Annually

■ Physical examination

■ DHLPP booster immunization

■ Kennel cough (Bordetella) booster

■ Rabies booster (if state regulations mandate)

■ Deworming (if necessary)

■ Heartworm blood test

■ Wellness testing in mature dogs (initiated at 5 to 7 years to evaluate kidneys, liver, blood sugar, and other organ functions)

⚠ **CAUTION:** *In certain regions of the world, additional vaccinations, such as for Lyme disease, may be recommended or required. Currently, there is much debate about which immunizations to administer and how often they should be given. Consult your veterinarian for recommendations and the latest data.*

Potentially Major Hardware Glitches

Throughout its life, the average dog will display numerous mechanical "hiccups," most of which it will quickly resolve on its own. If the symptom(s) persist or worsen over a 24-hour period, however, you should consider seeking professional assistance.

Bleeding: A superficial cut or scrape can be treated at home. Deeper injuries or puncture wounds require immediate veterinary attention—as does persistent, uncontrolled bleeding from a wound or orifice. Occasional, slight bleeding during bowel movements is usually not a serious problem.

Breathing Difficulty: Prolonged respiratory distress (coughing, sneezing, labored breath, and so on) may signal anything from choking to heart failure. Consult your veterinarian immediately.

Collapse: If your dog has fallen and cannot stand up, contact your veterinarian immediately and prepare to take the dog to the clinic. Try to remember what transpired in the moments before the attack; knowledge of these events may be helpful in determining a cause.

Diarrhea: A brief bout can be triggered by something as minor as a change in diet. If the problem persists for 24 hours, consult your veterinarian. Prolonged bouts can lead to dehydration. The skin of dehydrated dogs loses its elasticity and will not immediately snap back when gently pulled.

Ear Discharge: If the normal, waxy discharge becomes excessive, takes on a new color, or develops a bad odor, consult your veterinarian.

Excessive Water Consumption: This can be an indicator, particularly in an older or overweight dog, of diabetes or kidney malfunction.

Eye Discharge: A certain amount of discharge from the eyes is normal. Excessive or green and/or yellow discharge should be reported to your veterinarian. Red and/or swollen eyes should also be checked.

Fever: A dog's normal core temperature is between 100.5 and 102.5°F (38–39°C). Any body temperature higher than 103°F (39.5°C) is considered a fever. Temperatures higher than 104.5°F (40.25°C) necessitate an immediate trip to the veterinarian. (See "Measuring the Dog's Core Temperature," page 159.)

Gum Discoloration: Pink gums indicate normal oxygenation of the gum tissue. Pale, white, blue, or yellow gums require veterinary attention. To assess your dog's circulation, briefly press on the gums and release. If it takes less than 1 second—or more than 3 seconds—for the area to return to its normal pink color, some sort of vascular disorder may be responsible.

Inappropriate Urination: In a house-trained adult dog, regular, unauthorized urination may signal problems such as kidney disorders, diabetes, a urinary tract infection, or even the onset of senility.

Limping (Persistent): Could indicate anything from a sprain to the onset of hip dysplasia or osteoarthritis. If the problem persists for more than an hour or two, consult a veterinarian.

Loss of Appetite: Can denote anything from the onset of an infectious disease to severe pain to a psychological imbalance. However, all dogs "go off their feed" occasionally, so there is no need to worry unless the problem persists for more than 24 hours.

Seizures: Could signal any number of malfunctions, from epilepsy to a severe head injury. Remain with the pet during the episode and, if possible, time how long it lasts. Once it passes, consult your veterinarian. If the seizure continues for longer than 5 minutes, transport the dog (if necessary, while still seizing) to the veterinary office. Keep hands clear of the dog's mouth.

Skin Irritation: A small patch of dry skin or a small hot spot (see page 154) can be dealt with at home. Any disruption that appears red and irritated, that is seeping, or that causes the canine obvious discomfort should be professionally assessed.

Tremors: Can indicate anything from neurological damage to poisoning. Consult your veterinarian immediately.

Vomiting: A dog who vomits once or twice in a 24-hour period should be monitored. In many cases, the problem will simply go away. However, persistent vomiting for 12 hours necessitates a trip to the vet. Vomiting blood necessitates immediate veterinary attention.

Weight Loss: Pronounced weight loss can indicate any number of disorders, including cancer. However, it could also simply mean that the dog isn't receiving enough calories. Consult your veterinarian.

Minor Hardware Glitches

Minor malfunctions can often be resolved using basic first-aid techniques. To gauge if the problem is indeed minor, ask what you would do if the same injury was sustained by a child. If you would take the child to a hospital, then take the dog to a veterinarian.

Damaged Dewclaws: Excessive nail growth, coupled with the dewclaws' lack of bony support, make them prone to lacerations if caught on carpeting, underbrush, or tall grass. If the tear is small, treat as a superficial cut (see next page). If severe, consult your veterinarian. Professional (surgical) removal of the dewclaw is often the best course of action.

Doggy Breath: May indicate gum disease, severe plaque buildup, or a number of other dental disorders. Sweet, fruity breath can indicate diabetes.

Hot Spots: These are localized allergic reactions that trigger severe itching and self-inflicted irritation (usually via licking). These moist skin lesions will cause a dog great discomfort and, if untreated, can worsen rapidly. If the area is small, clip away hair and clean with hydrogen peroxide. Clean the area daily with antibacterial and astringent products until it is completely healed. Antibiotics or hydrocortisone cream may be required. Consult your veterinarian about particularly large hot spots.

Minor Allergic Reaction: This often results from insect bites. Apply hydrocortisone cream two to three times daily.

Skin Irritation: Cleanse area, remove the causative agent, and apply hydrocortisone cream two to three times daily.

Superficial Cuts and Scrapes: Cleanse the area with mild soap and water. Baby wipes work well. Apply triple antibiotic ointment twice daily.

Torn and/or Bleeding Nail(s): If the torn portion is small and near the end of the nail, carefully remove it with a human nail trimmer (a tool ideal for trimming away small, jagged pieces). In all other instances, use a trimmer designed especially for canines. If the tear is close to the base of the nail, consult a veterinarian.

Creating a Home Repair Kit

While most medical issues should be taken to a veterinarian, some minor problems can be handled at home using the following equipment. Place all these items in one container (a small, plastic toolbox is ideal) and position it someplace easily accessible. Include the name and phone number of your veterinarian, along with the phone number of the nearest animal emergency clinic.

- Roll cotton and cotton balls
- Gauze pads and gauze tape
- Scissors
- Eyewash
- Oral syringes
- Large towel
- Exam gloves
- 1-inch surgical tape
- Ice pack
- Thermometer (preferably digital)
- Pill gun (see page 157)

You may also wish to keep a canine medical file near your home repair kit. This folder should contain all relevant information regarding your dog's medical history, including:

■ Information on all immunizations the dog has received (with dates)

■ A list of previously taken medications

■ Current medications, including heartworm and flea preventatives

■ Blood test dates and results

■ Owner copies of veterinary office invoices and examination sheets, if possible (these provide a useful "paper trail" of past conditions and treatments)

Medicinal Compounds

While most human medications can be ineffective or actually harmful for dogs, several can perform useful—perhaps lifesaving—service. However, you should never administer human medications, even the ones listed below, without first consulting your veterinarian. Even useful drugs may require an adjusted dosage.

Benadryl: An antihistamine useful for insect stings/bites, vaccination reaction, itchiness, etc. Ask your veterinarian about the proper dose.

Gas-X: Just as with humans, these pills stop gas pain and bloating in canines. Other popular brands will also accomplish this. Check with your veterinarian for the right dosage.

Hydrocortisone Ointment: For treating hot spots and allergic skin reactions.

Hydrogen Peroxide: A good general disinfectant.

Isopropyl Alcohol: An even mix of isopropyl (rubbing) alcohol and vinegar is useful for cleaning ears.

Pedialyte: Rehydrates and replaces electrolytes in dogs suffering from diarrhea.

Triple Antibiotic Ointment: For treating superficial cuts and abrasions.

Administering Pills

If you will be administering pills on a regular basis, you may wish to invest in a pill gun. This device consists of a long plastic tube with a plunger at one end, and is designed to "shoot" a pill directly into the dog's mouth port. If you do not have a pill gun, employ the following procedure instead.

[1] Using your nondominant hand, grasp the dog's head (Fig. A). Place your hand on top of muzzle, with thumb on one side and fingers on the other.

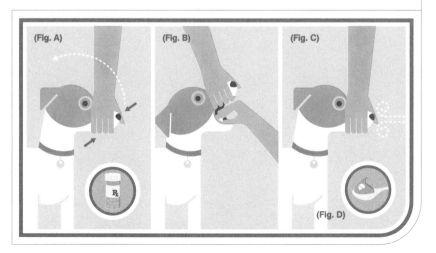

(Fig. A)   (Fig. B)   (Fig. C)   (Fig. D)

[2] Raise the dog's nose upward. Squeeze firmly behind the canine or "eye" teeth until the mouth opens (Fig. B).

[3] Place the pill between the thumb and forefinger of your dominant hand, then use the remaining three fingers of the same hand to open the lower jaw farther.

[4] Place the pill far back in the dog's mouth, close the mouth, and keep it closed (Fig. C).

⚠ **EXPERT TIP:** *Briefly blowing on its nose will stimulate the canine to swallow. Also, many dogs will take pills hidden in peanut butter or some other treat (Fig. D).*

[5] Offer a treat after the pill session, to make future encounters easier.

Measuring the Dog's Heart Rate

A normal, alert dog's pulse can range from 60 to 140 beats per minute. If it falls outside this range, contact your veterinarian immediately.

[1] Encourage the dog to lie down, then roll it onto its right side.

[2] Bend the front left leg, drawing the elbow back until it touches the chest.

[3] Place either your hand or a stethoscope over this spot.

[4] Count heartbeats while looking at the second hand of your watch. Count for 60 seconds. Alternately, count for 6 seconds and add a zero.

Measuring the Dog's Core Temperature

Use only a digital thermometer. Be aware that ear thermometers are incompatible with the structure of the canine ear canal.

[**1**] Have an assistant hold the head and front of the dog (Fig. E).

[**2**] Lubricate the thermometer with petroleum jelly or some other commercial lubricant (Fig. F).

[**3**] Lift the tail and insert the thermometer into the rectum (Fig. G) about 1 inch (2.5 cm). Hold it in place until the thermometer beeps.

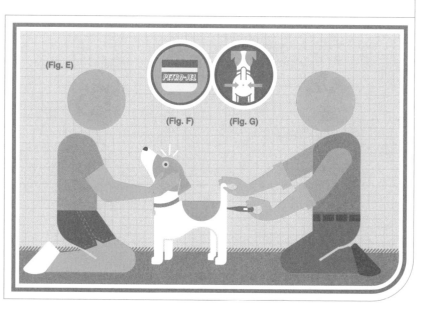

(Fig. E)

PETRO-JEL

(Fig. F)   (Fig. G)

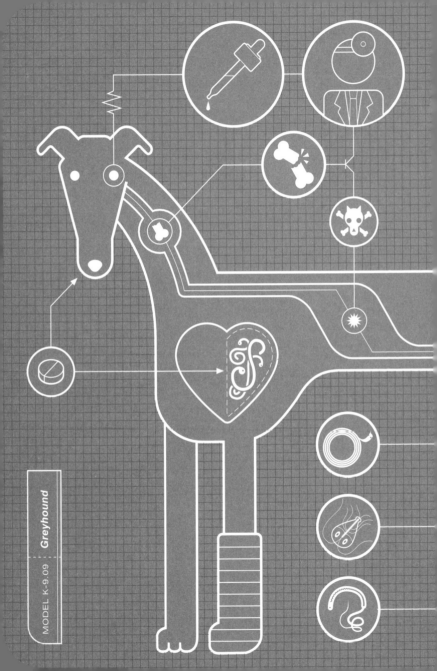

MODEL K-9.09   *Greyhound*

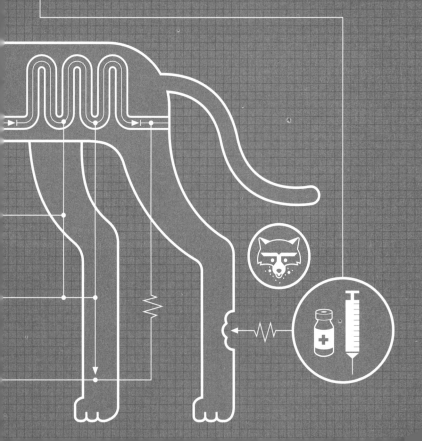

Chapter 9

Emergency
Maintenance

The following section offers a brief look at the most prominent—and dangerous—of canine-related malfunctions. Though the list is daunting, remember that proper maintenance and expert intervention can correct or mitigate most of these difficulties. For quick reference, disorders are flagged with a cross (✚) to indicate that immediate veterinary attention is required. A skull (☠) designates potentially lethal disorders.

Contagious Diseases

Vaccines are available for all of these disorders and should be administered on whatever schedule your veterinarian recommends.

✚ ☠ Rabies: A viral infection usually transmitted by the bite of an infected animal, rabies causes severe, fatal nervous system damage. State laws vary, but in some locales unvaccinated pets who encounter rabid animals are euthanized immediately.

✚ ☠ Canine Distemper: This virus is the most dangerous threat to the world's canine population. Among young dogs and puppies (the most susceptible population), the death rate for infected animals can reach 80 percent. Even dogs who survive often sustain severe, irreversible neurological damage. The disease is highly contagious.

✚ Canine Parainfluenza: This virus causes a mild respiratory tract infection not unlike the flu (hence the name).

✚ ☠ Canine Leptospirosis: A bacterial disease that can cause renal damage and even kidney failure. Exposure risk varies greatly, depending on location. Your veterinarian can provide an assessment of the risk your dog faces.

WARNING: Rabies will cause system malfunction and shutdown.

RABIES:

1. Spread by the bite of an infected animal
2. Prevented by vaccination
3. Spreads through the nervous system and attacks the brain and spinal cord
4. Always fatal to canines
5. Notify authorities IMMEDIATELY
6. **WARNING:** Leave rabid model alone

SYMPTOMS INCLUDE:
DILATED PUPILS
DRASTIC CHANGE IN DEMEANOR
CONSTANT GROWLING/BARKING
FOAMING AT THE MOUTH

 HAZARD: May be spread to humans; fatal if untreated

A standard treatment lasts 28 days.

If bitten, seek medical help immediately. Once symptoms appear, there is no cure.

✚ ☠ **Canine Parvovirus (Parvo):** A very contagious viral disease that surfaced in the late 1970s, parvo attacks the intestines, white blood cells, and heart. Dogs afflicted with parvo develop severe vomiting, followed by bloody diarrhea. Intensive medical treatment for 7 to 10 days can cure many adult canines, but in puppies the disorder is often fatal.

✚ **Canine Bordetella:** Also known as kennel cough, this bacterial infection causes severe, chronic cough that lasts 2 to 3 weeks.

✚ **Canine Coronavirus:** A virus that attacks the intestinal wall, causing gastroenteritis.

✚ **Lyme Disease:** A tick-borne disorder that can cause neuromuscular and joint disease, along with other problems. Lyme disease can also be contracted by humans and is most common in the Northeast and Upper Midwest regions of the United States.

Chronic Diseases

✚ ☠ **Cancer:** Dog and human cancer rates are roughly the same; approximately half the deaths of canines over the age of 10 are a consequence of this disease. Common forms of cancer in dogs include mammary, skin, mouth, neck, lymphomid, bone, and testicular. As with human cases, canine cancer is battled using surgery, drugs, and radiation, among other methods. Success rates depend on the form of cancer, aggressiveness of treatment, and how early the problem is discovered.

✚ **Heart Disease:** This can be either a genetic or an acquired malfunction. Approximately 3.2 million of the dogs examined in the United States each year have some form of acquired heart disease. Most commonly, the heart valves no longer close properly, interfering with blood flow; or the walls of the heart grow thin and weak. Either condition, if left untreated, can lead to heart failure. Symptoms include coughing, lethargy, heart enlargement, and difficulty breathing. Though there is no cure for heart disease, treatment can mitigate the symptoms and provide a longer, more comfortable life.

✚ ☠ **Kidney Disease:** The acute form of this disorder can attack suddenly and may be triggered by anything from a minor infection to physical trauma. Severe damage to, and loss of function in, the kidneys usually results. Though treatment options exist, a canine who survives the disorder will often have severely degraded renal function. Chronic kidney disease, usually seen in older dogs, advances much more gradually. Dietary changes can often slow its course. However, the disease is progressive, with many canines eventually succumbing to kidney failure.

✚ **Bladder Problems:** Canines can suffer from a variety of bladder-related difficulties, most of them familiar to humans, including kidney stones, cystitis (bladder infection), and bladder cancer.

✚ **Osteoarthritis:** This age-related malfunction is triggered when the cushion of cartilage between bones breaks down, causing inflammation. Pain medications, dietary supplements, and lifestyle changes can mitigate its effects to a degree. If a dog is overweight, a diet and mild exercise may result in significant improvement.

Hereditary Diseases

In many cases, specific dog breeds often suffer from genetic maladies. This doesn't mean you shouldn't acquire a particular model—only that you should be alert to its special needs. The following is a partial listing of possible maladies and some of the breeds they affect.

Back Problems: Often seen in beagles, cocker spaniels, dachshunds, and Pekingese.

Deafness: Sometimes seen in bull terriers (interestingly, only in the all-white models) and Dalmatians.

Diabetes: A fairly common problem for dachshunds.

Epilepsy: Sometimes seen in beagles, cocker spaniels, Labrador retrievers, and German shepherds.

Eye Problems: Difficulties can range from a predisposition to cataracts to corneal ulceration to extra eyelashes. Breeds prone to genetic eye conditions include (but are not confined to) Border collies, boxers, Chow Chows, cocker spaniels, Dobermans, Pekingese, poodles, Rottweilers, and schnauzers.

Heart Defects/Problems: Commonly seen in boxers, cavalier King Charles spaniels, and bulldogs. Difficulties can range from malformed heart valves to premature deterioration of the heart muscle.

Hip Dysplasia: A hip condition triggering sometimes severe lameness in the hindquarters. The disease is caused by an inherited "looseness" in the hip joint and is greatly aggravated in overweight dogs. It is seen in almost all large breeds, including German shepherds, Labrador retrievers, and Rottweilers. However, the disorder is rare in greyhounds.

Skin Conditions: Such problems manifest themselves in a wide variety of malfunctions across numerous breeds. For instance, boxers are prone to various "lumps and bumps," including dermoid cysts, gum tumors, skin tumors, and mast cell tumors, while West Highland white terriers, golden retrievers, bull terriers, and beagles can suffer from allergic dermatitis.

Allergies

Allergies are a malfunction of the canine's immune system that triggers an over-response to specific environmental factors (called allergens). They are as common among dogs as they are among people (and particularly troubling among purebreds, who may be genetically predisposed to react to specific allergens). Common triggers include everything from flea saliva and ordinary grass to a particular ingredient in a commercially produced dog food. Canine reactions to allergies can range from mild discomfort to life-threatening emergencies (including allergen-induced swelling and constriction of the airway).

In most cases, the symptoms will manifest themselves in the skin. Itchiness of the paws, ears, abdomen, face, and rectal area are most common. Other problems include hair loss, hives, and gastrointestinal distress. Allergic reactions triggered by insect bites can be very serious and may lead to a life-threatening condition called anaphylactic shock. If you suspect your dog is allergic to something in its environment, consult your veterinarian.

Poisons

Dogs are programmed to investigate new things, which means they can sometimes consume dangerous substances. If you see your dog consume such an item, immediately (if possible) flush its mouth with water to remove any remaining residue. Contact your veterinarian immediately for further instructions, or call the American Society for the Prevention of Cruelty to Animals (ASPCA) Animal Poison Control Center at (888) 426-4435 (4ANIHELP). If you are instructed to visit a clinic, try to bring the toxin's container with you; this may provide vital information about the substance your dog has ingested.

➕ ☠ Antifreeze: Dogs are attracted by the sweet taste of antifreeze. *Symptoms:* Convulsions, wobbling, vomiting, coma, and sudden death. *Treatment:* If you are absolutely certain the dog has consumed antifreeze, induce vomiting (see page 170) and seek immediate medical attention. Even with prompt medical intervention, antifreeze poisoning is often fatal.

➕ ☠ Aspirin: Aspirin can be toxic to dogs if improperly administered. *Symptoms:* Staggering, pale gums, blood-tinged vomit, bloody diarrhea, and collapse. *Treatment:* If recently consumed, induce vomiting (see page 170) and administer a solution of water and baking soda to neutralize the aspirin. It should consist of 1–2 teaspoons (5–10 ml) of baking soda mixed with approximately 2 tablespoons (30 ml) of water. Seek immediate veterinary attention.

➕ Chlorine: If you have a swimming pool on your property, remember to keep chlorine locked away at all times. *Symptoms:* Runny or irritated eyes, red mouth, vomiting, diarrhea, mouth and tongue ulcerations. **Treatment:** Rinse eyes and mouth with water, provide plenty of water to drink, and seek immediate veterinary attention.

✚ ☠ Lead: This toxin is often found in old paint chips. **Symptoms:** Poor appetite, weight loss, vomiting, escalating to convulsion, paralysis, blindness, coma. **Treatment:** Lead poisoning symptoms build slowly over time. If you suspect your dog has it, ask your veterinarian to run a blood or urine test.

✚ ☠ Turpentine: Dogs can be poisoned by turpentine if they get it on their fur and try to lick it off. Turpentine can also be absorbed directly into the skin. **Symptoms:** Inflamed and irritated skin, vomiting, diarrhea, unsteadiness, coma. **Treatment:** Wash the affected area thoroughly, then seek immediate veterinary care.

✚ ☠ Vermin Poisons: Canines can be harmed by ingesting rat poison, or even by ingesting rats that have ingested rat poison. **Symptoms:** Convulsions, stiffness, hemorrhage, collapse. A common toxin in these products is warfarin, which disrupts the dog's blood clotting ability. **Treatment:** The best approach depends on the active ingredient in the poison. If possible, obtain its original packaging and seek immediate veterinary care.

⚠ **CAUTION:** *Holiday poinsettias, which for decades were thought to be toxic to dogs, in fact pose no threat. However, mistletoe, holly, and Easter lilies can make canines violently ill.*

To Induce Vomiting

Administering $1/2$ to 1 teaspoon ($2^1/2$–5 ml) of syrup of ipecac (available in most drugstores) will cause the canine to vomit. Alternatively, a mixture consisting of 2 teaspoons (10 ml) of water and 2 teaspoons (10 ml) of 3 percent hydrogen peroxide should achieve the same effect.

Trauma

Canines are prone to numerous catastrophic malfunctions triggered by anything from inclement weather to unauthorized, uncontrolled interfaces with automobiles. In such situations, prompt, decisive action by the owner is the key first step toward full recovery.

✚ ☠ Bloat: A poorly understood condition usually seen in large, deep-chested breeds (Dobermans, Great Danes), bloat is seemingly associated with the rapid consumption of large amounts of dry food. Symptoms include nonproductive vomiting, severe discomfort, and swollen abdomen. Seek veterinary help immediately. Bloat is an extremely dangerous disorder that usually requires emergency surgery. If left untreated, it is fatal.

✚ ☠ Blocked Airway: Airway blockage (choking) can be triggered by traumatic injury, a foreign object in the throat, or a severe swelling or constriction (as from a too-tight collar) of the neck. Constriction injuries can also trigger pulmonary edema (buildup of fluid in the lungs). If a choking episode lasts for more than a few minutes, seek veterinary help. (See "The Heimlich Maneuver," page 183.)

✚ Broken Bone(s): Keep the dog calm. Do not try to apply a splint. If the bone has broken through the skin (a compound fracture), cover the injury with a bandage or clean cloth. Muzzle the dog (see page 181) so that it cannot inadvertently injure you during treatment or movement. Consult a veterinarian immediately.

✚ Dog Bites: All bites from another dog should be investigated by a veterinarian, because they can be more serious than they appear. Severe infection (becoming apparent after 24 hours) can accompany even a mild bite. Preliminary cleaning of the wound can be done with warm water and hydrogen peroxide. Be gentle and make sure the dog does not bite *you*.

✚ Eye Injury: If a foreign liquid is in the eye, flush with water or saline solution. Then seek professional help. Do not attempt to remove foreign objects (splinters, etc.) on your own. Virtually every eye problem merits immediate veterinary assistance.

✚ ☠ Frostbite: Remove the dog from the cold environment, then rewarm the affected tissues (usually the feet and/or ears) in warm water (approximately 104°F [40°C]). Do not rub or massage the tissue. Seek veterinary attention immediately.

✚ ☠ Heatstroke: Remove the dog from the heat. Place it in a cool bath, drench with cool water, or cover with a cool, water-soaked towel. Seek veterinary attention immediately.

✚ ☠ Severe Laceration with Uncontrolled Bleeding: Place a clean towel over the wound and then apply direct pressure to lessen loss of blood. Never attempt to apply a tourniquet. Seek veterinary care immediately.

✚ 💀 **Severe Trauma and/or HBC (Hit by Car):** Muzzle the dog to prevent it from injuring you (see page 181). Apply a clean cloth and pressure to any bleeding chest wounds. If breathing is severely labored, check mouth to make sure it is clear of obstructions. Lift into car using blanket or board as a stretcher. Seek veterinary care immediately.

✚ 💀 **Snakebite:** Do not apply a tourniquet or try to suck the venom out of the wound. To slow the circulation of the venom, limit your dog's activity as much as possible. Seek veterinary attention immediately. Snakebites are very painful, so handle the dog carefully.

Bugs in the System

A variety of internal and external parasites can invade your dog's systems, causing everything from acute discomfort to full system shutdown. Fortunately, most of these difficulties can be ended or avoided through careful maintenance and prompt medical attention.

Internal Parasites

✚ **Giardia:** This parasite causes mild enteritis and chronic diarrhea, particularly in puppies. Humans can also contract giardia (and suffer the same symptoms), though it is unclear whether the canine and human varieties of this parasite are the same. The right medication (administered by a veterinarian) will eliminate the problem.

✚ 💀 **Heartworms:** These mosquito-borne parasites can grow into foot-long worms that lodge in the right ventricle of the heart, causing significant damage to it and the lungs. Heartworms are deadly if untreated. Your vet-

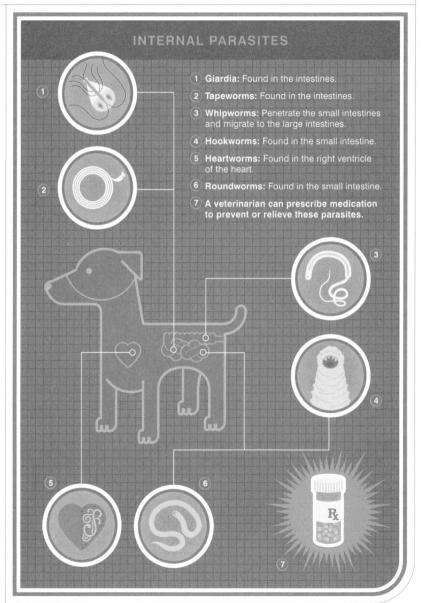

INTERNAL PARASITES

1. **Giardia:** Found in the intestines.
2. **Tapeworms:** Found in the intestines.
3. **Whipworms:** Penetrate the small intestines and migrate to the large intestines.
4. **Hookworms:** Found in the small intestine.
5. **Heartworms:** Found in the right ventricle of the heart.
6. **Roundworms:** Found in the small intestine.
7. **A veterinarian can prescribe medication to prevent or relieve these parasites.**

erinarian can prescribe a heartworm preventative, which may also prevent hookworms, roundworms, and whipworms.

✚ Hookworms: These small, blood-sucking parasites attach themselves to the walls of the small intestine. Signs include diarrhea, weakness, and anemia. They can be removed with a deworming medication. Prevention is easily accomplished by most heartworm medications.

✚ Roundworms: These intestinal parasites primarily afflict puppies less than 3 months old. Mature dogs may develop an immunity that prevents roundworm eggs from maturing into adults. However, the eggs will remain dormant in their bodies, waiting to infect the next generation. Puppy deworming medication destroys them, and standard heartworm medications stop initial infections. This parasite is potentially transmissible to humans.

✚ ☠ Tapeworms: The eggs of these parasites are most commonly transmitted via fleas, feces, and uncooked animal carcasses. There are several varieties, a few of which cause their canine hosts no lasting harm, but all should be promptly destroyed with deworming treatments. A few varieties produce eggs that may be transferred to humans and can lead to life-threatening cysts.

✚ Whipworms: These worms penetrate the small intestine as larvae, then migrate to the large intestine where they mature into adults. Signs include diarrhea, weight loss, and bloody stool. Whipworms can be eradicated with deworming compounds. Prevention is easily accomplished with many heartworm preventatives.

External Parasites

✚ **Fleas:** Though usually only an annoyance for most canines, these blood-sucking parasites can cause life-threatening blood loss in puppies and severely infested adults. Various shampoos, medicines, and topical applications can eliminate small-to-medium infestations (consult your veterinarian about the proper course of action). In some cases, fleas can cause an allergic reaction, transmit disease, and/or cause anemia.

⚠ **CAUTION:** *Never use a topical flea treatment formulated for dogs on cats. Such products are highly toxic to felines.*

✚ **Flies/Fly-strike:** Flies are a bigger problem than most people realize, particularly for dogs forced to live outside. Fly-strike is caused when numerous biting flies afflict the edges of the dog's ears, causing rawness, scabs, and, if no action is taken, infection. The area should be cleaned carefully with warm water and peroxide. Veterinary care may be necessary in advanced cases. Prevention is accomplished by daily application of a fly repellant. The surest cure for fly-strike is to bring the dog indoors.

✚ **Lice:** Lice can infest a dog by the thousands, causing severe itching. Eliminating them requires veterinary intervention.

✚ **Mites:** This parasite is responsible for an illness called mange. Demodectic or "red" mange produces small, hairless, irritated patches on the dog's coat. Sarcoptic mange or "scabies" triggers severe itching along with hair loss. Mites can also enter the ears, where they cause great discomfort and inevitably trigger bacterial infections. Mites should be treated by a veterinarian as soon as possible.

EXTERNAL PARASITES: These parasites can invade your canine's

1. **Fleas:** Usually an annoyance, may be fatal to puppies.
2. **Flies:** Bites may cause infection.
3. **Lice:** Cause severe itching.
4. **Mites:** Cause mange.
5. **Ticks:** Can transmit Lyme disease.
6. **Use shampoos, medicines, and topical applications for fleas.**
7. **A veterinarian is needed for flies, lice, and mites.**
8. **Remove ticks with tweezers, then immerse in alcohol.**

64x

32x 128x

16x 256x

8x ZOOM 512x

4x 2x

PARASMITE!

6   7   8

system, causing acute discomfort.

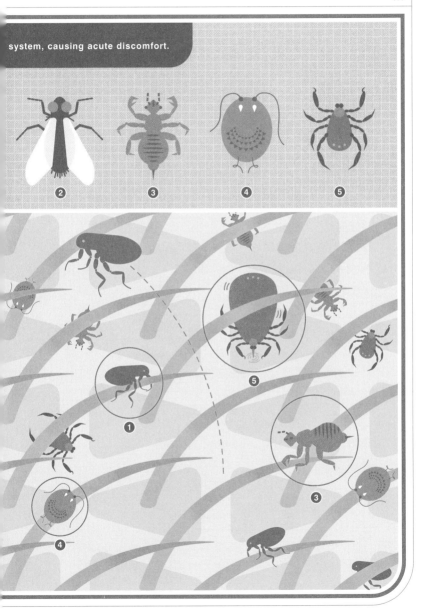

②   ③   ④   ⑤

✚ Ticks: Remove them using tweezers. Try not to touch the ticks, as they can transmit disease to humans. Kill them by immersing them in alcohol. It is a good idea to inspect your dog for ticks after walking in the woods. Deer ticks can carry and transmit Lyme disease, which can lead to neurological and cardiac malfunction. (See "Contagious Diseases," page 162.)

Behavioral/Psychological Disorders

Not all malfunctions are hardware issues. Some dogs may develop software glitches that can only be resolved by specialists. Here are some of the most common.

Obsessive-Compulsive Behaviors: Obsessive behavior in dogs often mirrors the same disorder in humans. Affected canines will engage in repetitive behaviors (licking of the lower legs, tail chasing, pacing, fence running) that seem to serve no useful function and can even be harmful. In some cases, these may be triggered by separation anxiety, boredom, or other stress factors. Treatment by an animal behaviorist may help. Also, research suggests that the same antidepressants sometimes prescribed for humans with obsessive-compulsive disorder may alleviate dog symptoms as well. Consult your veterinarian before attempting such a course of treatment.

Phobias: Dogs, just like humans, can develop extreme, irrational fears of common objects and routine sensory stimuli—anything from the odor of a particular food to open flames to vacuum cleaners. The most common is a fear of thunderstorms or other loud noises. While many dogs are, to some degree, afraid of loud sounds, a few become so panic-stricken that they may burst through windows in an attempt to escape. In these extreme cases, an animal behaviorist (and a great deal of time) is needed to alleviate the problem.

Rage Syndrome: A fit that is similar to epilepsy, except that the dog involved displays uncontrollable aggression instead of seizing. This hereditary defect is seen in dogs of questionable or poorly managed genetic heritage and is in most cases untreatable. The only way to fully avoid this problem (which appears occasionally in such models as the springer spaniel and cocker spaniel) is to acquire your dog from a reputable breeder or other high-quality source.

Separation Anxiety: Dogs were designed for communal living, so spending long periods of time alone is, to some degree, always stressful for them. However, some canines take their discomfort to phobic levels, doing extensive damage to their owners' homes whenever they are left by themselves. Separation anxiety can also trigger other difficulties, such as obsessive-compulsive behaviors. Consult your veterinarian and/or an animal behaviorist about treatment options.

Emergency Transport Techniques

In the event that you need to transfer a canine that has been severely injured, use the following techniques to insure the safety of both the dog and the owner.

[1] Assess the scene. If the injured dog was hit by a car, be sure that the road is clear before attempting to help the animal.

[2] Approach the injured dog slowly. If it is growling, baring its teeth, or showing other signs of fear and/or aggression, be very careful. Remember, even a trusted family pet can lash out if suffering from severe pain.

[3] If the dog appears agitated, muzzle it using a commercial muzzle or a piece of fabric (panty hose work well) wound around the jaws and then tied behind the neck (Fig. A). A towel may be placed over the dog's head, in lieu of or in addition to a muzzle, to help calm the animal.

[4] If the dog is bleeding severely, place a bandage or clean cloth over the wound and apply pressure.

[5] Transport the dog to a vehicle using either a flat board, blanket, tarp, or other piece of sturdy cloth (Fig. B). Pull the dog carefully onto the transport vehicle (this is usually a two-person job). Smaller dogs may be moved in a box or crate.

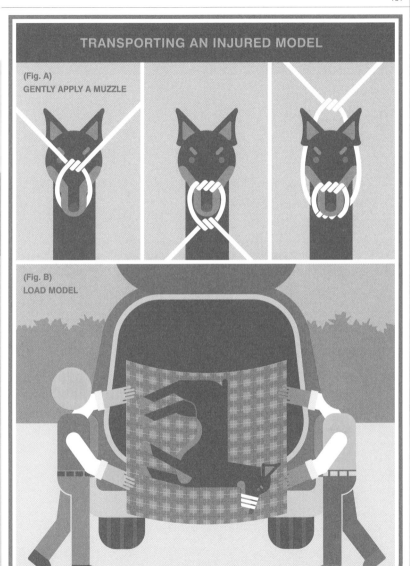

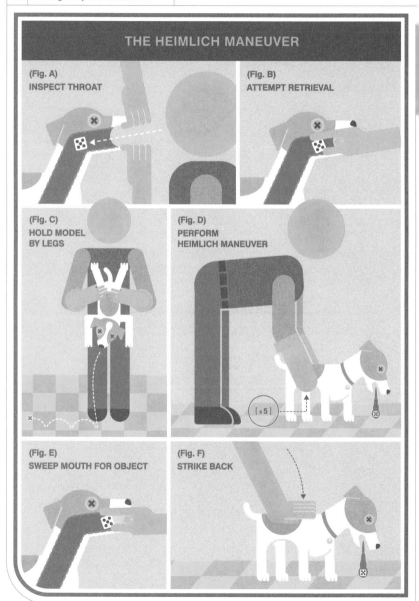

THE HEIMLICH MANEUVER

(Fig. A)
INSPECT THROAT

(Fig. B)
ATTEMPT RETRIEVAL

(Fig. C)
HOLD MODEL
BY LEGS

(Fig. D)
PERFORM
HEIMLICH MANEUVER

[x5]

(Fig. E)
SWEEP MOUTH FOR OBJECT

(Fig. F)
STRIKE BACK

The Heimlich Maneuver

If a dog starts choking or appears to have difficulty breathing, it may have an obstruction in its throat. Employ the following maneuver to repair the problem.

[1] Open the dog's mouth and look at the back of its throat (Fig. A). If you can see the object causing the choking, remove it (Fig. B). If the dog is unconscious, pulling its tongue forward will give a better view and perhaps dislodge the object.

⚠ *CAUTION: Even an unconscious dog may bite on instinct. Be careful.*

[2] If the dog is small enough, pick it up and hold it by the hips with its head hanging down (Fig. C). For larger dogs, hold the hind legs in the air so its head hangs down. These techniques may cause the object to simply drop out. If not, you must perform the Heimlich maneuver.

[3] With the dog either standing or lying down, place your arms around its waist with hands clasped around its stomach. Close your hands into one fist and place it just behind the last rib.

[4] Compress the stomach by pushing up five times rapidly (Fig. D).

[5] Sweep your finger through the dog's mouth to see if the object has dislodged (Fig. E).

[6] If it hasn't, strike the dog sharply between the shoulder blades with the flat side of one hand (Fig. F), then repeat abdominal compressions. Alternate these procedures until the object is dislodged.

[7] If the object is dislodged but the dog no longer appears to be breathing, continue to the next section on artificial respiration and CPR.

Artificial Respiration and CPR

As with humans, dogs whose respiration and/or heart has stopped can be assisted with artificial respiration and cardiopulmonary resuscitation (CPR). However, these are last-ditch procedures that should only be attempted if you are absolutely sure the dog has stopped breathing. Place your hand on the left side of the chest to feel for a heartbeat (if you find one, the dog is still breathing). Alternatively, hold a mirror in front of the dog's nose and watch for condensation (if you see it, the dog is still breathing). Still another method is to place a cotton ball before the dog's nose and watch for even the slightest movement in the filaments.

⚠ *CAUTION: A dog's pulse cannot be taken at the neck. For additional instructions about monitoring the dog's heart rate, see page 158.*

[1] Inspect the airway for obstructions. Lay the dog on its side, tilt its head slightly back, pull the tongue out of the way, and use your fingers to feel for and remove obstructions. Perform the Heimlich maneuver if necessary (see previous page). If clearing the obstruction does not reinstate normal respiration, proceed to the next step.

[2] Be sure the dog's neck is straight. For medium to large dogs, place your hand around the muzzle, hold it closed, and place your mouth around its nose. For smaller dogs (under 30 pounds), your mouth should cover the dog's nose and lips (Fig. A).

CARDIOPULMONARY RESUSCITATION (CPR)

(Fig. A)
ADMINISTER MOUTH-TO-MOUTH

(Fig. B)
CHEST COMPRESSIONS

[3] Give four or five quick, forceful breaths.

[4] Check for response. If normal breathing resumes, stop. If not, or if breathing is shallow, resume CPR. Give 20 breaths per minute for small dogs, or 20 to 30 breaths per minute for medium and large dogs.

[5] Check for heartbeat by placing your hand on the left side of the dog's chest. If none is detected, begin compressions along with rescue breathing.

[6] For most dogs, compressions can be performed while the animal lies on its side (Fig. B). The back is better for barrel-chested canines such as bulldogs. Whatever the approach, be sure the dog is on firm ground. Compressions will not be effective on a soft surface.

[7] For small dogs, place your palm and fingertips over the ribs at the point where the elbow meets the chest. Kneel down next to the dog, then compress the chest approximately 1 inch, twice per second. Alternate every five compressions with one breath. After 1 minute, check for heartbeat. If none is found, continue.

[8] For medium to large dogs, kneel down next to the canine, extend your elbows, and cup your hands on top of each other. Place hands over the ribs at the point where the dog's elbows meet the chest, then compress it 2 to 3 inches, one-and-a-half to two times per second. Alternate every five compressions with one breath. After 1 minute, check for heartbeat. If you find none, continue.

[9] For very large dogs (over 100 pounds or 45 kg), compress the chest 2 to 3 inches once per second, alternating every 10 compressions with breath. After 1 minute, check for heartbeat. If you find none, continue.

⚠ **CAUTION:** *The chances of reviving a canine with CPR are minimal. After 20 minutes of CPR, it is unlikely that the animal will be revived, even with professional intervention.*

Pet Insurance

Repairing a severely ill canine can be quite costly. In some cases, owners will choose to euthanize the dog rather than shoulder the expense. Pet insurance can help reduce the impact of unexpected maintenance costs. Just as with human health policies, owners pay a regular premium in exchange for help that ranges from coverage of annual checkups and immunizations to medical emergencies. Some companies offer annual preset spending limits, while others use deductibles. Premium payments, which are based on services offered and the condition/age of the canine, can range from $100 a year to more than $500.

Be advised that pet insurance is still a relatively rare phenomenon in the United States, with less than 500,000 American pet owners holding policies. Consult your veterinarian for information about reputable companies offering this service.

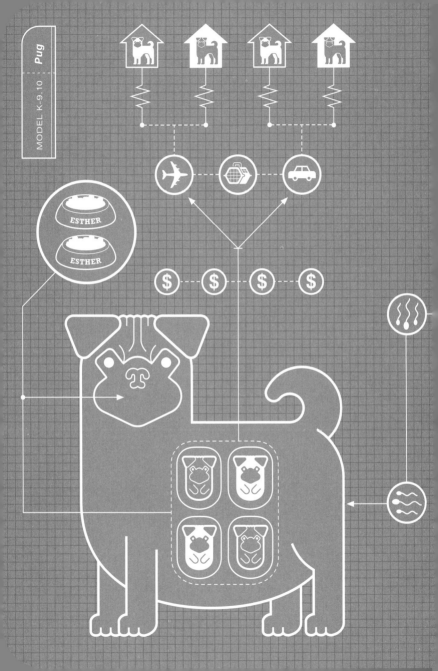

Chapter 10

Advanced Functions

If you have followed the information in the previous chapters, you now possess a healthy, well-behaved, semi-autonomous dog with all the programming necessary for a lifetime of companionship. However, home enthusiasts interested in even more add-ons can consult the following survey of options.

Home and Personal Defense

Training a dog to defend your home can be problematic. Though professional guard dog programs are available (ask your veterinarian and/or local breed club for references), in many cases this level of indoctrination is not necessary. Models created for defense (Rottweilers, German shepherds, Doberman pinschers, etc.) are in most cases hardwired to be suspicious of strangers, warn off trespassers, guard their home territory, and attack determined aggressors. Given the proper stimuli, these "killer aps" will self-activate. For many owners, in fact, the biggest challenge will be *controlling* such instincts, not developing them.

Owners of guard models would be better served by investing in extensive obedience training. This will provide the sorts of downloads needed in the real world: the ability to control the canine in public situations; to have it come promptly when called; and, perhaps most importantly, to make it instantly stop whatever it might be doing.

EXPERT TIP: The dog's most useful intruder repellant is its bark. In many cases, small and nervous dogs make the best home defense systems because they will raise the alarm at the slightest external stimulus.

Insurance Issues

Be advised that some insurance companies refuse to write homeowners policies for clients who own certain dog models deemed to be "dangerous." The list varies from company to company, but usually includes all the common guarding varieties such as pit bulls, Rottweilers, mastiffs, Doberman pinschers, and German shepherds. Owning a mixed breed that contains these particular bloodlines may also cause an insurance company to refuse coverage. A potential client's particular dog need not have been involved in any incidents; the mere fact that it belongs to a particular breed can make obtaining insurance difficult. At present, there is no legislation in the United States outlawing or regulating this practice.

Contests

If you would like to test the performance of your model against those of other enthusiasts, there are plenty of events in which you and your canine can participate.

Agility Competitions (Fig. A): In this test of training, intelligence, and canine stamina, owner-guided dogs race the clock as they tackle complex obstacle courses filled with hurdles, tunnels, and jumps. Models ranging from purebreds to mutts can participate, and there are separate divisions for different dog sizes. However, the canines must be young and fit, because agility events can be very demanding.

Dog Shows (Fig. B): Hundreds of dog shows, big and small, are held in the United States throughout the year. The best-known are conducted under the auspices of the American Kennel Club and open only to AKC-registered pure-

(Fig. A)
AGILITY COMPETITIONS

(Fig. C)
FLY BALL COMPETITIONS

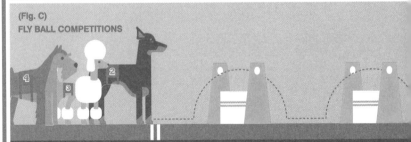

CONTESTS: One way to test the performance of your model is to enter it in various

(Fig. B)
DOG SHOWS

competitions. Judges evaluate agility, obedience, beauty, and other desirable traits.

breds. Dogs are judged on their conformation to their "breed standard" (a multipage set of technical specs outlining a model's appropriate physical makeup). Enthusiasts can attend or participate in specialty shows (encompassing only a single breed), all-breed shows (large events at which almost any AKC-recognized model can participate), and matches (essentially practice gatherings popular with novice owners and young dogs). Dog show competitors are judged on how well they adhere to their breed standard and little else.

Fly Ball Competitions (Fig. C): This most exciting of all canine sports is essentially a relay race in which teams of four dogs compete against each other and the clock. Each dog runs a course of hurdles to reach a "fly ball box." The dog presses a lever at the bottom of the box, which shoots a tennis ball into the air. The dog grabs the ball and dashes back to the start/finish line, sending the next dog on his team down the course. Dogs compete in different size divisions, though, of course, canines built for speed (Border collies, Jack Russell terriers) have a distinct advantage.

Obedience Competitions: These events test both the intelligence of the dogs and the training ability of their owners. Contests include distance control (getting canines to unfailingly obey commands, even when the person giving them is far away), scent discrimination (selecting one differently scented object from among many), heel work, and other even more complicated maneuvers.

Breed-specific Gatherings: Organizations dedicated to individual breeds often hold their own local, regional, and national rallies, many with events geared to the strengths of their particular model. For instance, retrieving competitions for Labrador and other retrievers; simulated underground prey pursuits for West Highland terriers; and races for Jack Russell terriers.

Hardware Modifications

Purebred owners sometimes amputate (dock) the tails and trim (crop) portions of the ears of various breeds so that they conform to a particular aesthetic standard. For instance, the ears of Doberman pinschers, American Staffordshire terriers, and boxers are, in their natural state, disarmingly floppy. Surgery must be performed to give them their intimidating points. Likewise, boxers, Doberman Pinschers, and other breeds often have most of their tails docked. This is usually accomplished between 3 and 5 days of age.

Neither of these procedures is necessary for the health and happiness of the animal. Indeed, in recent years a backlash against such "cosmetic surgery" has developed, with some even charging that it amounts to animal cruelty. As of now the decision remains a personal one—though, of course, any such procedure should be done only under a veterinarian's care.

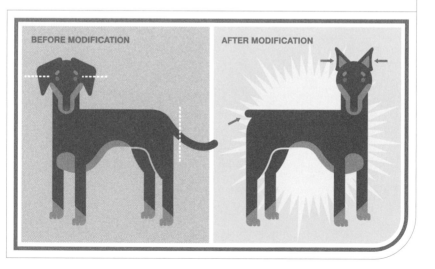

BEFORE MODIFICATION

AFTER MODIFICATION

There is one form of elective surgery that can actually *improve* the health and safety of your dog. Canines have an extra, rudimentary nail, called a dewclaw, located on each foot. It performs no function and on the hind limbs often isn't even connected to supporting bone. Dewclaws can pose a problem for dogs who spend any amount of time outdoors. They can snag on underbrush, causing painful, bloody injuries. They can be surgically removed from puppies at 3 to 5 days of age, and from older dogs during spaying/neutering or anytime thereafter. The procedure is minor and recovery rapid.

Reproduction

For a number of reasons, chief among them pet overpopulation, the breeding of dogs is not recommended by most veterinarians and trainers. However, if you own a purebred (some of whom are sold on condition that they be bred at least once), here is a brief overview of what to expect during the mating and reproduction process.

Selecting a Mate

Puppies are strongly influenced by the mental and physical strengths—and shortcomings—of their parents. For this reason, it is important to pick a strong breeding partner for your dog. Here are some of the most important factors to consider.

■ Choose a mate from a reputable, experienced breeder.

■ Make sure the mate is AKC-registered, or registered with another reputable breed association.

■ Carefully investigate the genetic heritage of the potential mate. Be extremely wary if information about the canine's lineage isn't available.

■ Check the potential mate carefully for genetic abnormalities. If there are any questions, a veterinary checkup may be in order.

■ Be wary of any personality foibles, which may be reflected in the puppies. Be particularly skeptical of potential mates that show undue aggression.

Mating

A dog should be at least 20 months old before it begins to mate. Most female dogs go into heat (estrus) twice each year. During the middle portion of estrus, the female will become receptive to male dogs. She will indicate her preparedness by standing still among male dogs and "flagging" her tail (moving it to one side).

When this occurs, the female dog should be introduced to a male dog (the mating will be more successful if it takes place on the male's territory). If the dogs appear compatible and the female is receptive, mating can be allowed to proceed. Though ejaculation usually takes

less than a minute after coupling, the dogs may remain connected or "tied" for as long as 40 minutes. Shortly after ejaculation, the male will dismount and, still connected to the female, may turn so that he is facing away from her. This uncomfortable-looking maneuver is natural and to be expected. The mating can be repeated every second day, until the female rejects the male.

EXPERT TIP: *Female dogs can be impregnated by more than one dog. In theory, a single litter could contain puppies with several different fathers.*

Pregnancy

On average, canine pregnancies last 63 days, though the duration can vary from 59 to 66 days. At 5 weeks, the mother's nipples will become enlarged and her abdomen will swell. At 7 weeks, her mammary glands will enlarge. In the days before the birth, these glands may also secrete watery milk. During pregnancy the mother's body weight may increase as much as 50 percent (a little over 30 percent is more typical).

Prenatal Monitoring

Your veterinarian can detect a pregnancy at 3 to 4 weeks via ultrasound, X-ray, or abdominal palpitation. Though a well-balanced diet for the mother is important, the volume of food need not be increased during the first 6 weeks. After that time, however, food intake should increase until, by week 8 or 9, the mother eats as much as double her usual amount (provided in small, multiple meals). Special vitamin supplements may also be prescribed. Mild exercise can be maintained to help keep the dog physically fit.

Preparing for Birth

Though in most cases birthing can be accomplished at home, it is wise to discuss the situation with your vet in advance. Also, certain breeds, such as bulldogs, have such difficult vaginal births that cesarean section deliveries are recommended.

Approximately 10 days before the birth, provide the mother with a "whelping box" where she can deliver her litter. It should have walls high enough to corral the puppies, but low enough so the mother can leave easily. It should also be large enough for the mother to lie down in during nursing. Cover the bottom with soft towels and place the box in a quiet area.

Birth

During the first stage of labor, the female may pant, whimper, lick herself energetically, and repeatedly get up and lie down in her whelping box. As the situation progresses, she may lie down on her side with her head up, looking at her hindquarters. Visible straining will be evident. Puppies will usually appear head first (though tail first is not uncommon), enclosed in a bluish membrane. Once birth is accomplished, the mother will tear open the membrane, chew through the umbilical cord, and vigorously lick the puppy to stimulate respiration. Shortly after the birth of each puppy, its individual placenta will also pass. Births can occur from 30 minutes to 2 hours apart.

⚠️ *CAUTION: Inexperienced mothers may not chew open the membrane or cut the umbilical cord, so be prepared to help her. In general, the larger the dog breed, the bigger the litter. Toy breeds often have one to four puppies, while larger breeds can have eight, twelve, or more.*

Canine Travel

It is not uncommon for users to transport their dogs via automobile or plane to various destinations. When traveling with your dog, use the following handling guidelines to minimize damage to your model.

Automobile Travel

It is acceptable for larger dogs to ride in a seat, like a human passenger (Fig. A). If your dog has never done this before, consider making one or two short "practice" excursions to be sure the canine keeps its place and does not try to roam around the car. Smaller dogs may prefer to be transported in their sleeping crates, as this provides a secure refuge from a strange situation (Fig. B). Be aware that all dogs are fascinated by the smells they encounter when they stick their noses out the window of a moving car. It is acceptable to indulge this desire, but never leave the window open so far that the dog can jump or fall out (Fig. C).

During long car trips, allow the dog to make regular rest and exercise stops (always leash it before opening the car door). Bring along food, water, and treats in a separate container. If your dog is prone to getting carsick, your veterinarian may recommend medication (bringing the dog on a few short "practice" trips may prevent the problem altogether).

⚠ *CAUTION: Never, for any reason, leave your dog alone in a car. Changes in outdoor temperatures are unpredictable and can lead to stress, hypothermia, heat exhaustion, and worse.*

AUTOMOBILE TRANSPORT

(Fig. A)
LARGER MODELS CAN SIT UP FRONT

(Fig. B)
USE CARRIER FOR SMALLER MODELS

(Fig. C)
KEEP WINDOW OPEN PARTIALLY

Air Travel

If possible, avoid traveling with your dog by airplane. The only exception to this rule is if the dog is very small and permitted to fly in the cabin, secured inside a travel carrier that can fit under your seat (an industry-wide airline regulation). Larger dogs must travel in the aircraft's hold—a rough, frightening, and potentially dangerous practice. The environment is extremely uncomfortable, and the dog could die of overheating in the event of a long flight delay. There is also the ever-present danger of its carrier being misrouted to the wrong destination.

If you have no choice but to travel by air, familiarize yourself with the airline's pet transportation protocols well in advance of the flight. Procure an airline-approved shipping kennel and make sure all necessary paperwork is completed. Try to select a nonstop flight and, if possible, do not fly during the hottest (or coldest) part of the day. Travel on the same flight as your dog, if possible, and inform at least one flight attendant and the pilot that your canine is in the hold.

⚠️ *CAUTION: Veterinarians can prescribe tranquilizers during travel, but this will place your dog under the influence of an unfamiliar drug while stowed in the hold, far from help should something go wrong. Discuss the risks and benefits with your veterinarian before proceeding.*

Old Age

The age at which a dog can be considered elderly varies widely among models. In general, the larger the dog, the more quickly it declines. For instance, a Great Dane could be considered "senior" at age 5, while a smaller toy poodle would still be spry at twice that age. Remember, however, that just because a dog is chronologically old doesn't mean that an endless series of malfunctions is in store. In many cases an elderly dog can enjoy many healthy, active, pain-free years.

One of the best ways to prolong the life and improve the functions of an elderly dog is to carefully regulate its fuel intake. Older dogs exercise less and thus need fewer calories. And since age reduces their ability to digest and absorb nutrients, high-quality food specifically formulated for their needs is a necessity. Excessive amounts of protein, phosphorus, and sodium can aggravate kidney and heart problems, so most such foods contain smaller amounts of higher-quality protein, along with reduced quantities of other elements. Levels of vitamins, zinc, fatty acids, and fiber, however, are increased.

Common Age-Related Malfunctions

■ Gradual decline of auditory sensors

■ Degradation of visual sensors caused primarily by lens deterioration or cataracts

■ Gastrointestinal distress caused by lack of tolerance for dietary changes

■ Loss of muscle and bone mass, cartilage deterioration, and arthritis

■ Hair whitening and loss

■ Heart murmurs triggered by scarred or poorly functioning heart valves

■ Incontinence triggered by loss of kidney function and bladder control; decreasing mental function may also cause the dog to "forget" its house-training

Obsolescence and Deactivation

When compared to other consumer items, the service lifetime of a dog is quite impressive. Larger models can function for a decade, while compact units may approach twice that. But even though your dog will almost certainly outlast your car, television, and computer, its time with you may still seem startlingly, even heartbreakingly, brief.

This is because while many people profess to "love" their car, television, or computer, with dogs they truly mean it. While canines can be programmed to do many useful things, their most important application is as a companion and friend. When the time approaches to part with that friend, owners may feel great trepidation. Yet this is also the time when they can render their greatest service to a loyal canine companion.

No two situations are alike, but in most cases an elderly dog should be maintained for as long as it remains in relatively good health and free of severe, chronic pain. Though the animal may be a shadow of its former self, rest assured that this is more troubling to its human companions than to the animal. Nothing in the dog's vast programming base corresponds to the human emotions of regret and painful nostalgia. In other words, an elderly dog does not fret over days gone by and days to come. It lives solely for the here and now.

That fact is very important when considering how to handle a canine's final days. In some cases an elderly dog will deactivate at a time and place of its own choosing. But in situations where declining health incapacitates the dog or causes it to suffer, the owner must act on its behalf. When the pain and disability in a dog's life seems to outweigh the pleasure, and when there is no reasonable hope of recovery, euthanasia should be considered. This procedure is painless and can be performed at the veterinarian's office. At the appropriate time the dog receives an overdose of anesthetic that causes almost immediate unconsciousness, followed rapidly by death.

Coping with the deactivation of a canine companion can be difficult. In some cases, the mourning period may be as long as that for the loss of a human. There is nothing unnatural about such feelings. National and local grief counseling groups are available to help bereaved dog owners through this period.

Rest assured that, given enough time, the pain of loss will pass. It will be replaced by many happy memories, the warranty for which can never expire.

[Appendix]

Troubleshooting

For easy access, this section contains answers to frequently asked questions about common canine behavior issues, malfunctions, and quirks. When problems arise with your model, this should be the first place you look.

SYMPTOM:	EXPLANATION:
Dog has consumed an unauthorized, indigestible item.	If the item is fairly small (say, the size of a marble), non-toxic, and smooth, watch the dog's stool for the next few days to see if it passes. If it doesn't, contact your veterinarian. An X-ray may be necessary to find the object and decide on a course of action. However, if the object poses a threat of internal injury (jagged edges, potentially toxic, uncomfortably large), contact your veterinarian immediately. Emergency surgery may be required to remove it. ⚠ **CAUTION:** *If your dog consumes string, tinsel, or a similar substance, and you notice it protruding from the rectum, do not attempt to pull it out. This risks internal damage. Contact your veterinarian immediately.*
Dog hates men in hats, little girls in dresses, women with high-pitched voices, or some other odd subset of the human race.	Some dogs are genetically predisposed to fearful behavior. However, others can acquire such fear if they undergo a traumatic experience during their early puppyhood. For instance, if a puppy has a frightening encounter with a man in a hat, that experience may ingrain itself so deeply that it forevermore fears and hates men in hats. This reaction can also be more general; an afflicted dog may simply despise all men. The usual treatment method is desensitization: gradual exposure to the thing the dog fears. This can be a rather lengthy, involved process, so consult a trainer, veterinarian, or animal behaviorist before attempting it.

SYMPTOM:	EXPLANATION:
Dog destroys furnishings or other household items when left alone.	This common (albeit expensive) problem can be caused by several things. The dog may be suffering from severe separation anxiety and taking out its angst on the home furnishings. It may suffer from barrier frustration, attacking doors and/or windows in an attempt to get outside. Or the dog may simply be bored. In such cases, the destructive activity has no particular focus. The canine may assault a chair on Monday and a piano leg on Tuesday. Mild cases of separation anxiety can sometimes be treated by giving the dog more exercise (a tired canine is infinitely less destructive) or providing it with interesting toys. However, in some cases this fear approaches phobic proportions. Medication and/or intervention by an animal behaviorist may be required.
Dog is terrified of thunderstorms.	The first step to alleviating this very common problem is to speak to the dog in an upbeat and sympathetic voice. Your reassuring tone will suggest that there is nothing to be afraid of. Distract the dog from the storm by playing with it or offering it a treat. In some cases this works, but in others (extreme cases in which the dog may break furniture or vomit from fear) the services of an animal behaviorist may be required.
Dog barks whenever someone talks on the phone.	This common behavior is usually triggered by a simple misunderstanding. The dog does not realize the person on the phone is talking to someone else. Since there is no one else in the room, the dog thinks the person must be talking to it—and it is responding.

SYMPTOM:	EXPLANATION:
Dog loathes the mail carrier and greets him with violent barking.	Highly territorial dogs seem to despise these civil servants with a special vigor. The reason is because they arrive at more or less the same time every day, come right up to the front door, and sometimes actually slide objects through it. This puts a dog's territorial defense programming into overdrive. Even worse, the mail carrier inevitably departs soon after the dog begins barking, leading it to conclude that it "repelled" the invader. Thus, what looks to humans like pointless aggression can be effective strategy to a canine.
Crate-trained puppy barks incessantly while confined.	First, make sure the puppy is receiving a proper amount of exercise before being crated, that its sleeping arrangements are comfortable, and that it has at least one chew toy. Then, do something that many owners find very hard—ignore the barking. It is natural for puppies who find themselves alone to call out, and it takes time for a dog to learn that this is unacceptable behavior. If you go to the crated puppy when it barks, it learns that such behavior brings attention. And if you hold out for a while, then go to the dog, you teach that prolonged, relentless barking brings results. Never go to the crated dog while it barks. Wait until it stops, then go.
Dog is extremely shy around strangers and/or other dogs.	Some dogs are simply shy by nature. Others were made that way by a bad experience during puppyhood. To improve the situation, one can stage low-key encounters with strangers (strangers to the dog, not to the owner). The visitor should be very friendly and nonthreatening. Treats should be offered. The dog should be praised for showing even the slightest bit of self-confidence. Repeating this exercise may reinforce the idea that meeting new people and animals is not something to be feared—or feared as much.

SYMPTOM:	EXPLANATION:
Dog displays a great deal of aggression toward other canines.	Some breeds are genetically predisposed to canine aggression. Most of the guarding breeds do not play well with others, and terriers are legendary for their lack of social skills. If your dog is thrust into situations where it encounters other canines, it is your responsibility to keep the unit under control through careful obedience training and leashing.

If the dog only becomes aggressive with canines walking near its home or, perhaps, encroaching on its yard, then the source of its belligerence may be a strongly developed sense of territoriality. Such a dog may be able to consort with other dogs on neutral territory (the sidewalk, a dog park) with no difficulty at all. |
| Dog digs up the yard. | A common problem among bored outdoor dogs, excessive digging can be stopped simply by making the canine an *indoor* pet. Another approach is to designate a particular part of the yard as okay for digging and try to confine the activity there. Seed the area with toys and treats, then actively praise the canine when it begins turning that section of earth. To prevent digging altogether, pick up feces from around the yard, deposit them in canine-excavated holes, and cover them with a small amount of dirt. They will make an unpleasant (and, perhaps, behavior-changing) surprise for the dog when it attempts to resume its excavation work.

Supervision will always be necessary to make sure a digging dog does not return to free-range excavation. This behavior can be particularly strong among terriers and terrier mixes, who were created to dig small animals out of their underground lairs (the name terrier means, literally, "earth dog.") |

SYMPTOM:	EXPLANATION:
After meals, dog wipes its muzzle on the carpet.	This programmed behavior is another remnant of the wolf operating system. After dining on a kill, wolves routinely rub their faces on the ground to remove blood and offal from their faces. Domestic canines, even though their mealtimes are usually much less messy, do the same thing.
Dog jumps on owner, family members, and/or visitors.	In most cases, this is simply an overexuberant greeting. Correct the problem not by shouting at the dog or "kneeing" (using a knee to deliver a blow to the dog's chest), but by ignoring the behavior. Make no reaction at all, for good or ill. Just move away from the dog so that it cannot continue. In most cases, the dog will eventually stop. Another alternative is to command the dog to sit when it seems about to jump.
Dog greets visitors with a bizarre, snarl-like expression.	Most canines are capable of a "smile"—a combination greeting/submission gesture. In some cases, dogs who are particularly excited about greeting someone will overdo it, producing a ghastly, all-teeth-bared expression that can be intimidating to anyone who does not understand what the dog is feeling. ⚠ *CAUTION: If you encounter a strange dog wearing this expression, assume it is hostile until it proves otherwise.*
Dog humps people and inanimate objects.	In many cases mounting is done to display dominance, not necessarily for sexual reasons. Should your dog initiate such behavior, push him down immediately. The mounting of inanimate objects may be performed by young canines—both male and female models—to relieve sexual frustration.

SYMPTOM:

EXPLANATION:

Dog attempts to chase cars, joggers, bikers, and any other fast-moving object.	The sight of any speeding object will activate remnants of the wolf operating system associated with the pursuit of prey. The best way to stop this behavior is to keep the dog indoors, in a securely fenced yard, or on a leash. All dogs possess this pursuit protocol, but in some models the urge can be almost overwhelming. Greyhounds and cairn terriers, among others, are so keen to chase that they cannot be trusted off their leads in public for any reason.

EXPERT TIP: If you ever find yourself pursued by a dog, the best tactic is to stop, turn, and then face it. Most such dogs have been overwhelmed by their chase programming. Removing the stimuli can cause the units to automatically reset.

Dog eats grass.	This behavior is as normal as the human consumption of lettuce. Canines seem to need the roughage, though they derive little nutrient value from it. In rare circumstances, nauseated dogs will consume large amounts of grass to induce vomiting.

Dog eats its own feces.	This behavior, known as pica, is most commonly seen in puppies and dogs on diets, both of whom may seek more nutrient or caloric value from undigested particles in the stool. Commercial products can be placed on the dog's food that will impart a bitter taste to its feces. Alternatively, lace feces left in the yard with jalapeño sauce. This is best done under cover of darkness, to prevent queries from neighbors.

SYMPTOM:	EXPLANATION:
Dog drags its hindquarters across the ground.	This is usually due to irritation of the rectal area, often caused by anal gland problems. (See "Exterior Maintenance," page 129.) Other triggers include allergic skin diseases and, in some cases, tapeworms.
Dog drools excessively.	Though it is rarely mentioned in breed guides, many canine models drool. Indeed, Saint Bernards and mastiffs are famous—or, rather, infamous—for their expectoratory excess. The phenomenon can be particularly pronounced after exercise. Nothing can be done to stop it, although some owners carry paper towels to keep their models presentable during long walks. ⚠ *CAUTION: If a dog who normally does not drool suddenly starts, watch the behavior carefully and contact your veterinarian if it does not end quickly. It could indicate dental problems, sickness, or ingestion of a toxin.*
Dog greets visitors and even members of its immediate family by urinating.	Releasing a small (or not-so-small) amount of urine is a common submission gesture among canines. Also, dogs with relatively weak bladders who become over-stimulated (often when guests visit) may lose urinary tract integrity. Barring a medical problem, the best approach is to keep comings and goings as low-key as possible. For instance, when arriving home from work, avoid making a huge fuss, vigorously petting the dog, and speaking to it in an excited voice. Give a perfunctory initial greeting and allow the dog time to adjust to the new situation before providing a warmer response. Instruct all visitors to do the same.

SYMPTOM: | EXPLANATION:

Dog lifts its leg to urinate.

This common behavior can perplex the novice dog owner. Male canines, as they reach sexual maturity, often begin to use sprays of urine to mark the boundaries of what they perceive as their territory. (See "House-Training," page 84.) In order to make themselves appear large and intimidating, they hike their legs to place the stream as high as possible. The higher the mark—or so its creator wants others to think—the bigger the dog. Females will occasionally engage in this behavior. Some males neutered before sexual maturity never do.

Adult, house-trained dog begins urinating in the home.

Healthy canines, particularly males, mark the boundaries of their territory with urine. Unfortunately, they sometimes do this indoors. Once a dog "marks" an indoor spot, it may return to it again and again, guided and stimulated by the smell of previous visits. It is important to clean such areas with an odor-cutting compound (available at pet stores). If your dog has not been neutered, have a veterinarian perform this procedure immediately. Then observe the dog carefully as it makes its rounds through the house. It you catch the dog trying to urinate in its favorite spot, immediately escort it outside. Repeat until it understands the new protocol.

⚠ **CAUTION:** *Accidental indoor urination can also be a symptom of physical ailments. See page 165.*

SYMPTOM:	EXPLANATION:
Dog's coat seems dull.	If the dog has no apparent medical problems, an improper diet may be to blame. Some foods, particularly homemade ones, may lack a proper balance of vitamins, minerals, and/or essential fats. Changing to a higher quality, more readily digestible food may be the solution.
Dog makes an alarming series of gagging/snorting sounds that last for 30 to 60 seconds.	This phenomenon is called reverse sneezing—a series of rapid, spasmodic inhalations caused by irritation of the pharynx. Severe cases can be treated with drugs, but in most instances it is no more dangerous than a sneezing fit.
Dog shows no interest in you or your family, refuses to perform any useful tasks, and displays subpar intelligence.	Consult your veterinarian. You may have accidentally acquired a cat.

Technical Support

The following organizations offer valuable information and/or services to dog owners.

 Animal Poison Control Center **(888) 426-4435**

Run by the American Society for the Prevention of Cruelty to Animals (ASPCA), the Animal Poison Control Center is staffed 24 hours a day, 7 days a week by veterinarians. They can advise during poison emergencies, provide treatment protocols, and even consult with clients' personal veterinarians. There may be a $45 charge for the service, depending on the circumstances, so have your credit card ready.

1-800-Save-A-Pet.com
(800) 728-3273
A national, nonprofit clearinghouse for mixed and purebred dogs in need of homes. Web-based search service allows for the easy location of rescue groups in particular areas.

American Animal Hospital Association
Member Service Center
(800) 883-6301
Can provide information on AAHA-approved veterinary hospitals in your area. For more information, visit www.healthypet.com.

AMERICAN KENNEL CLUB:
AKC Breeder Referral Service
(900) 407-7877
For a free Dog Buyer's Educational Packet, call AKC Customer Service at (919) 233-9767. For information on breed rescue organizations throughout the United States, visit www.akc.org/breeds/rescue.cfm.

AKC Canine Legislation Department
(919) 816-3720
E-mail contact: doglaw@akc.org
Monitors federal, state, and local legislation relating to dog ownership.

AKC Companion Animal Recovery
(800) 252-7894
E-mail contact: found@akc.org
A 24-hour hotline to which owners of dogs with microchip identification can report their lost canines and/or receive information about their whereabouts.

American Society for the Prevention of Cruelty to Animals
(212) 876-7700
www.aspca.org
Founded in 1866, the ASPCA is the oldest humane organization in the Western Hemisphere. Among many other things, it provides humane education, advice on obtaining medical services, and support for animal shelters.

American Veterinary Medical
Association
(847) 925-8070
www.avma.org
A not-for-profit association of roughly
70,000 veterinarians that can provide
information on AVMA-accredited
facilities in your area.

Humane Society of the
United States
(202) 452-1100
www.hsus.org
Animal advocacy and information clearinghouse covering such topics as pet
adoption, care, and rights.

National Pesticide Information
Center
(800) 858-7378
Offers free information about the toxicity
of common compounds such as lawn
care and gardening products.

Petswelcome.com
Extensive Internet site offering
comprehensive information on traveling
with dogs, including listings of hotels
that take pets; kennels; amusement
park pet facilities; and how to cope with
emergencies on the road.

Glossary of Terms

■ Allergen: A substance that can induce an allergic reaction.

■ Allergy: A hypersensitivity in the immune response system. Symptoms may vary from minor skin irritation and gastrointestinal disturbances to a violent, sometimes life-threatening reaction called anaphylactic shock.

■ Anal sacs: Glands bracketing the anus that secrete a pungent fluid during bowel movements. Used by dogs to identify each other.

■ Anestrus: The sexually inactive period for female dogs between estrus cycles.

■ Breed: Group of dogs who exhibit a particular set of physical/mental characteristics developed through selective mating.

■ Conformation: The primary judging criteria at dog shows. Winning dogs "conform" most closely to the physical standard of their breeds.

■ Cropping: Trimming the ears to conform to an artificial aesthetic standard.

■ Dewclaws: A vestigial nail located on the inside of each canine leg. Often surgically removed.

■ Docking: The surgical removal of most of the tail.

■ Dysplasia: Abnormal bone or tissue development. Most commonly seen as hip dysplasia, a hereditary condition in which the hip joint fails to develop properly.

■ Estrus: Period in which a female dog is in heat.

■ Hackles: Neck and back hair.

■ Heat: Period in which a female dog is receptive to mating. See *Estrus*.

■ Lipoma: A benign fat tumor extremely common in older canines.

■ Mutts: Dogs of no specific "pure" breed; also known as mongrels or mixed breeds.

■ Muzzle: The projecting portion of the canine face, including the mouth, nose, and jaws. Also a fastening or covering for this part of the dog, used to prevent biting and/or eating.

■ Neutering: Sterilization of a male dog via removal of the testicles.

■ Parasites: Internal and external life forms that use other animals (in this case, dogs) as hosts. Includes, but is not confined to, heartworms, fleas, tapeworms, and mites.

■ Proestrus: The period just before a female dog enters estrus (heat).

■ Purebreds: Dogs belonging to a specific breed produced through selective mating.

■ Sight Hounds: Hunting dogs such as borzois and greyhounds that track prey primarily by sight.

■ Spaying: Sterilization of a female dog via hysterectomy.

■ Stripping: The removal of dead hairs from a dog's coat.

■ Tricolor: A canine coat with three colors.

■ Whelping: The act of giving birth.

■ Withers: The point just behind the neck from which a dog's height is determined.

Index

1-800-Save-A-Pet.com, 216

accessories, 53–56
adult dogs
    advantages and disadvantages, 42–43
    interfacing with children, 57, 59–60
    pre-acquisition inspection checklist, 48–49
age in "dog years," 140
age-related malfunctions, 203
aggression toward other canines, 210
agility competitions, 191
air travel, 202
airway, blocked, 170
Akita Inus, 26–27
alcohol, isopropyl, 157
allergic reactions, minor, 154
allergies, 167
American Animal Hospital Association, 216
American Kennel Club, 216
American Staffordshire terriers, 27
American Veterinary Medical Association, 217
anal glands
    as body part, 14
    inspection, 147
    maintenance, 129–30
Animal Poison Control Center, 216
animal shelters, as vendor, 43–44
antibiotic ointment, triple, 157
antifreeze, 168
appetite loss, 152–53
artificial respiration and CPR, 184–87
aspirin, 168
audio cues, 70
auditory sensors (hearing), 18
automobile travel, 200–201

back problems, 166
barking
    as audio cue, 70
    in crate, 209
    at mail carriers, 209
    whenever someone talks on phone, 208
basset hounds, 27
bathing, 125–28
beagles, 27–28, 144–45
beds, 53
behavioral/psychological disorders, 178–79
Benadryl, 156
birth, 199
bites, from other dogs, 171
bladder problems, 165
bleeding, 151
bloat (condition), 170
bloating, 156
body, 14–15
body language, 71

bones, broken, 170–71
Boston terriers, 86–87
bowls, water/food, 56
boxers, 28
breath, 154
breathing difficulty, 151
breeders, as vendors, 44
breed rescue groups, as vendors, 45
breeds
    breed-specific gatherings, 194
    nonstandard, off-brand, 38–39
    selecting, 40–49
    top-selling, 26–38
    types, 24–26
brushes, 53, 120–21, 122
burrs, 132

cancer, 164
canine bordetella, 164
canine coronavirus, 164
canine distemper, 162
canine leptospirosis, 162
canine parainfluenza, 162
canine parvovirus, 164
cardiopulmonary resuscitation (CPR), 184–87
car travel, 200–201
cats
    acquiring by mistake, 215
    interfacing with, 63–66
chains, 77, 78
chasing fast-moving objects, 212
chewing gum, 132
chihuahuas, 28
children, interfacing with, 57–60
chlorine, 168–69
cleanups, emergency, 132–33
clippers, 120–21
coat
    as body part, 14
    dull, 215
    inspection, 149
    maintenance, 122–23
    parts, 118
    types, 40, 119–22
collapse, 151
collars, 56, 73
collies, 29, 68–69
combs, 53, 120–21, 122
come command, 98–100
commands, voice-activated
    come, 98–100
    heel, 96, 97
    sit, 94, 95
    stay, 94, 95, 97
conditioning, physical, 75
consumption of indigestible item, 207

contests, 191–94
coronavirus, canine, 164
CPR (cardiopulmonary resuscitation), 184–87
crates, 56
crate training, 81–84, 209
currycombs, 120–21, 122
cuts, superficial, 155

dachshunds, 29, 102–3
deafness, 166
defense of home and people, 190–91
destruction of furnishings or other items, 208
dewclaws, damaged, 154
diabetes, 166
diagram and parts list, 13–18
diarrhea, 151
diet, modifying, 107
    See also food
diseases
    chronic, 164–65
    contagious, 162–64
    heart, 164–65
    hereditary, 166–67
    kidney, 165
distemper, 162
Doberman pinschers, 29, 32
doggie breath, 154
doghouses, 80
dog ownership, advantages of, 41–42
dog runs, 77, 79
dogs, other
    aggression toward, 210
    bites from, 171
    interfacing with, 60–63
    shyness around, 209
dog shows, 191, 193, 194
"dog years," 140
dominance, 88
    establishing, 89, 92
dragging hind quarters across ground, 213
drool, excessive, 213

ears
    discharge from, 151
    hearing, 18
    inspection, 126, 147
    maintenance, 128–29
    styles, 13
eating own feces, 212
emergency cleanups, 132–33
emergency maintenance, 160–87
emergency transport techniques, 180–81
epilepsy, 166
euthanasia, 204–5
exercise and fitness, 74–77
exterior maintenance, 116–33
eyes
    discharge from, 152
    injury to, 171
    inspection, 129, 147
    maintenance, 129
    problems, 166

sight, 15, 18
styles, 13

familial considerations, 41
fears, 178–79
feces, eating own, 212
feeding, 107
    See also food
fencing, 77, 78
fetching, 75–77
fever, 152
financial obligations, 41
first aid kit, 155–56
first night at home, 66–67
fleas, 175
flies, 175
fly ball competitions, 194
fly-strike, 175
food, 102–15
    brand selection, 106–7
    daily requirements, 105
    puppies, 141
    supplements (snacks), 110–12
    types, 104–5, 108–9
    unhealthy or fatal, 111
frostbite, 171
furnishings, destruction of, 208

gagging/snorting sounds, 215
gas emissions, 111–12
Gas-X, 156
gatherings, breed-specific, 194
gender selection, 43
genitals, 15
German shepherds, 32
giardia, 172
golden retrievers, 32
grass eating, 212
greyhounds, 32–33, 160–61
groomers, professional, 123–24
grooming gloves, 120–21, 123
grooming tools, 120–21, 122–23
growling, 70
growth and development, 134–43
grunting, 70
guard dogs, 190–91
gum discoloration, 152

hairless, 121, 122
hair varieties, 119–22
hardware glitches
    minor, 154–56
    potentially major, 151–53
hardware modifications, 195–96
hatred for subset of human race, 207
HBC (hit by car), 171–72
head, 13–14
hearing, 18
heart defects/problems, 166
heart disease, 164–65
heart rate measurement, 158
heartworms, 172

heatstroke, 171
heel command, 96, 97
height, 15
Heimlich maneuver, 182–84
herding dogs, 26
hip dysplasia, 166–67
history of dogs, 22–23
hit by car (HBC), 171–72
home
    defense of, 190–91
    first night at, 66–67
    installation of dog, 50–67
    preparing for dog, 52–53
hookworms, 174
hot spots, 154
hounds, 25
house-training, 84, 85
howling, 70
Humane Society of the United States, 217
human speech, 72
humping people and inanimate objects, 211
hunting, 88
hydrocortisone ointment, 156
hydrogen peroxide, 156

identification methods, 73
immunizations, 149–50
insurance
    homeowners, 191
    pet, 187
introduction, initial, 56–66
invisible fences, 77, 79

Jack Russell terriers, 33, 50–51
jumping on people, 211

kennel cough, 164
kidney disease, 165

Labrador retrievers, 33–34
laceration with uncontrolled bleeding, 171
lead, as poison, 169
leashes, 56
leash training, 92–100
leptospirosis, canine, 162
lice, 175
life span, 19
limping, persistent, 152
long and silky hair, 119, 121
long hair, 119, 120
Lyme disease, 164

mail carriers, 209
maintenance
    emergency, 160–87
    exterior, 116–33
    inspection at home, 147–49
mate selection, 196–97
mating, 197–98
mat removal, 124
medicinal compounds, 156–57
memory capacity, 19

microchip, for identification, 73
mites, 175
mouth
    inspection, 147
    taste sensors, 18
muzzle, wiping on carpet, 211

nail clippers, 120–21, 123
nails
    torn or bleeding, 155
    trimming, 130–32
name selection, 67
National Pesticide Information Center, 217
neutering, 142–43
Newfoundlands, 34
nipples, 15
nonshedding hair, 119, 120
nonsporting dogs, 25–26
nose, 14, 18

obedience competitions, 194
obedience programs, 101
obsessive-compulsive behaviors, 178
ointment, triple antibiotic, 157
old age, 203
olfactory sensors (smell), 18
organizations, 216–17
osteoarthritis, 165
outdoor storage, 80
outercoat, 118

paint, 132
parainfluenza, canine, 162
parasites
    external, 175–78
    internal, 172–74
parts list, 13–15, 18
parvo, 164
paws, 15, 147
Pedialyte, 157
Pekingese, 34
personal defense, 190–91
pet stores, as vendors, 44
Petswelcome.com, 217
phobias, 178–79
physical conditioning, 75
physical makeup, 74
physical requirements, 40–41
physical stamina, 74
pills, administering, 157–58
poisons, 168–69
poodles, 34–35
pregnancy, 198
prenatal monitoring, 198
private individuals, as vendors, 45
psychological disorders, 178–79
pugs, 35, 188–89
puppies
    advantages and disadvantages, 42
    food, 141
    growth stages, 136–39
    interfacing with children, 57, 58

milestones, 139
pre-acquisition inspection checklist, 46–47

rabies, 162, 163
rage syndrome, 179
reproduction, 196–99
roundworms, 174

schedule demands, 41
scissors, 120–21, 123
scrapes, superficial, 155
secondary coat, 118
seizures, 153
sensor specifications, 15–18
separation anxiety, 179
sexual maturity, 141–43
shedding tools, 120–21, 123
Shih Tzus, 35, 116–17
short hair, 119, 120
shyness, 209
sight, 15, 18
sit command, 94, 95
size, 40, 74
skin
    conditions, 167
    inspection, 149
    irritation of, 153, 154
skunks, 133
sleep mode, 72
smell, sense of, 18
smooth hair, 119, 121
snacks, 110–12
snakebites, 172
snarl-like expression, 211
snorting sounds, 215
socialization, 88, 92
sounds, 70
spaying, 142–43
speech, human, 72
sporting dogs, 24
stamina, 74
stay command, 94, 95, 97
strangers, shyness around, 209
styptic powder, 120–21, 123

tactile hair, 118
tactile sensors, 18
tags, identification, 56, 73
tail, 15
tapeworms, 174
tar, 133
taste sensors, 18
teeth
    as body part, 14
    development, 140–41
    maintenance, 129
temperament, 40
temperature measurement, 159
terriers, 25, 86–87
territoriality, 88
territorial marking, 89
thunderstorms, fear of, 208

ticks, 178
tongue, 14, 18
toys (breed), 24–25
toys (for play), 53
training, 92–100
    coming when called, 98–100
    crate training, 81–84, 209
    heeling, 96, 97
    house-training, 84, 85
    leash training, 92–93
    sitting, 94, 95
    socialization, 92
    staying, 94, 95, 97
    tips, 100
transport techniques, emergency, 180–81
trauma, 170–72
travel, 200–202
tremors, 153
triple antibiotic ointment, 157
troubleshooting, 207–15
    dominance issues, 89, 92
turpentine, 169

undercoat, 118
undercoat rakes, 120–21, 123
urination
    in the home, 84, 214
    inappropriate, 152
    troubleshooting, 213

vendor selection, 43–45
vermin poisons, 169
veterinarians
    selecting, 146–47
    visits to, 149–50
visual sensors (sight), 15, 18
vomiting
    inducing, 170
    as symptom, 153

waste disposal protocols, 81–85
waste port, 147
water
    average daily requirement, 115
    excessive consumption, 152
weather conditions, 74–75
weight
    calculating, 112–13, 147
    range, 15
    reducing, 114
weight loss, as symptom, 153
whining, 70
whipworms, 174
wiry hair, 119, 121
working dogs, 24

yard
    containment protocol, 77–80
    digging up, 210
Yorkshire terriers, 35, 38

OWNER'S CERTIFICATE

Congratulations! Now that you've studied all the instructions in this manual, you are fully prepared to maintain your new dog. With the proper care and attention, your model will provide you with many years of fun and happiness. Enjoy!

Owner's name

_____

Model's name

_____

Model's date of acquisition

_____

Model's breed, if any

_____

Model's gender

_____

Model's coat color

_____

About the Authors:

A veterinarian for 25 years and operator of Indianapolis's Broad Ripple Animal Clinic for 22 years, DR. DAVID BRUNNER specializes in treating small animals—cats and dogs. He has two daughters, Molly and Kendell, and two black Labrador retrievers, Lucy and Noel, both of whom come to work with him every day.

SAM STALL is the coauthor of *As Seen on TV: 50 Amazing Products and the Commercials That Made Them Famous* and *Dirty Words of Wisdom*. He resides in Indianapolis with his three terrier mixed-breeds, Tippy, Katie, and Gracie, as well as his wife, Jami (who has no terrier blood whatsoever), and their cat, Ted.

About the Illustrators:

PAUL KEPPLE and JUDE BUFFUM are better known as the Philadelphia-based studio HEADCASE DESIGN. Their work has been featured in many design and illustration publications, such as *American Illustration, Communication Arts,* and *Print*. Paul worked at Running Press Book Publishers for several years before opening Headcase in 1998. Both graduated from the Tyler School of Art, where they now teach. While illustrating this book, Jude acquired a Boston terrier named Huxley, which he has since programmed to sit, stay, roll over, and mix cocktails. Paul's dog, an imaginary Jack Russell named Crackers, was last seen romancing a pair of running shoes.

JAKE MA...

GRAPHIC NO...

FAST-PITCH
FEUD

STONE ARCH BOOKS
a capstone imprint

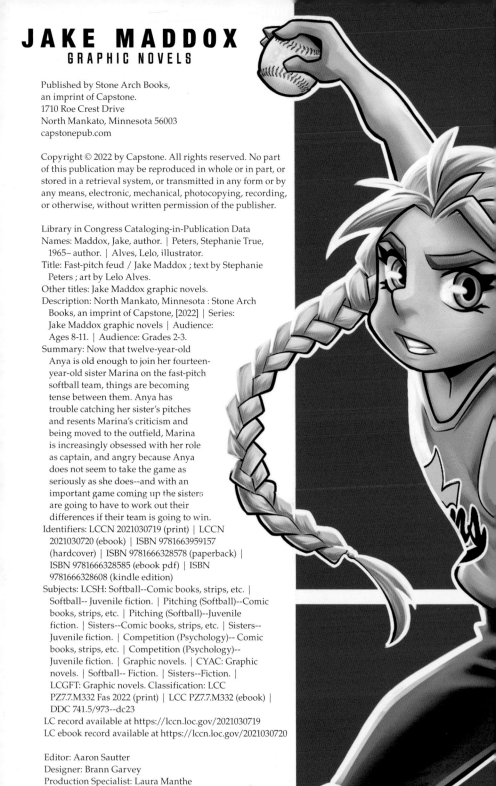

JAKE MADDOX
GRAPHIC NOVELS

Published by Stone Arch Books,
an imprint of Capstone.
1710 Roe Crest Drive
North Mankato, Minnesota 56003
capstonepub.com

Library in Congress Cataloging-in-Publication Data
Names: Maddox, Jake, author. | Peters, Stephanie True,
    1965– author. | Alves, Lelo, illustrator.
Title: Fast-pitch feud / Jake Maddox ; text by Stephanie
    Peters ; art by Lelo Alves.
Other titles: Jake Maddox graphic novels.
Description: North Mankato, Minnesota : Stone Arch
    Books, an imprint of Capstone, [2022] | Series:
    Jake Maddox graphic novels | Audience:
    Ages 8-11. | Audience: Grades 2-3.
Summary: Now that twelve-year-old
    Anya is old enough to join her fourteen-
    year-old sister Marina on the fast-pitch
    softball team, things are becoming
    tense between them. Anya has
    trouble catching her sister's pitches
    and resents Marina's criticism and
    being moved to the outfield, Marina
    is increasingly obsessed with her role
    as captain, and angry because Anya
    does not seem to take the game as
    seriously as she does--and with an
    important game coming up the sisters
    are going to have to work out their
    differences if their team is going to win.
Identifiers: LCCN 2021030719 (print) | LCCN
    2021030720 (ebook) | ISBN 9781663959157
    (hardcover) | ISBN 9781666328578 (paperback) |
    ISBN 9781666328585 (ebook pdf) | ISBN
    9781666328608 (kindle edition)
Subjects: LCSH: Softball--Comic books, strips, etc. |
    Softball-- Juvenile fiction. | Pitching (Softball)--Comic
    books, strips, etc. | Pitching (Softball)--Juvenile
    fiction. | Sisters--Comic books, strips, etc. | Sisters--
    Juvenile fiction. | Competition (Psychology)-- Comic
    books, strips, etc. | Competition (Psychology)--
    Juvenile fiction. | Graphic novels. | CYAC: Graphic
    novels. | Softball-- Fiction. | Sisters--Fiction. |
    LCGFT: Graphic novels. Classification: LCC
    PZ7.7.M332 Fas 2022 (print) | LCC PZ7.7.M332 (ebook) |
    DDC 741.5/973--dc23
LC record available at https://lccn.loc.gov/2021030719
LC ebook record available at https://lccn.loc.gov/2021030720

Editor: Aaron Sautter
Designer: Brann Garvey
Production Specialist: Laura Manthe

Printed and bound in the USA. PO4608

FAST-PITCH FEUD

Text by Stephanie True Peters
Art by Lelo Alves
Cover art by Berenice Muñiz
Lettering by Jaymes Reed

from left to right:

Reese, Coach Watkins, Christie, Stacy,
Anya, Marina, Teagan, Lisa, Iris
Ellie - not pictured

Two summers ago, I played catcher for the Geckos, a slow-pitch softball team.

My sister Marina was the pitcher.

PING!

Playing catcher was fun, even when I didn't have much to do

I got it!

Go, Na-na, go!

Out!

Yes!

WHAP!

And I always had the best view of the action!

The next season, Marina earned a spot on the Dragons. They were one of the best fast-pitch teams for older girls.

Thanks for helping me practice my new windup.

No problem!

At first, catching for her was easy.

But after a few weeks, her pitches were way too hot for me to handle!

Yikes!

Sorry!

FWISH!

I stuck to catching slow pitches for my team after that.

Gotcha!

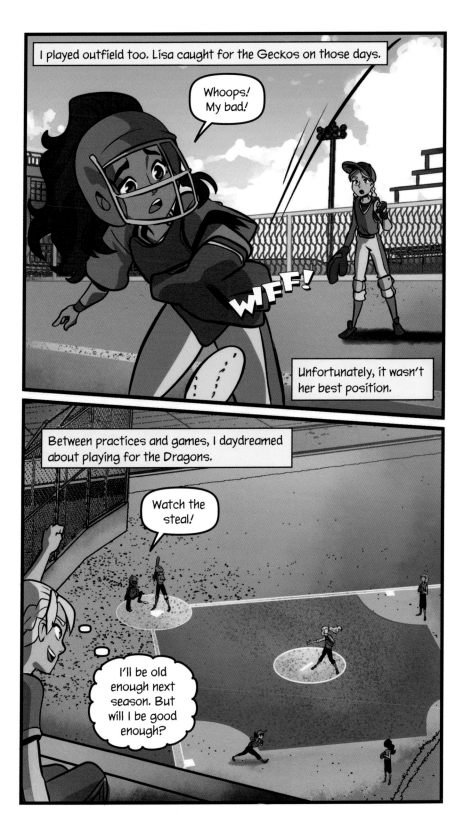

12

13

14

15

Tryouts ended with position play.

I wasn't sure about catcher, but Stacy told me to go for it.

She did?

Yep!

Umph! I feel like a turtle with its shell on backwards.

Stacy said to put on the chest protector last.

Otherwise, it gets in the way!

Lisa looks good.

Stacy had taught Lisa more than how to put on pads.

I need to bring it when it's my turn!

WHAP!

But when my turn came, I wasn't too graceful on my way to the plate.

TRIP!

Agh!

My tryout for catcher went downhill from there.

Oof!

Sorry!

WHAP!

It's not your fault, Christie!

I hated that Marina was right. Luckily, I'd done enough to make the team.

I think we both know who *really* messed up, don't we?

Lisa
I made catcher! How about you?

Anya
I got left out. 😭

Lisa
?????

Anya
Left outfielder, that is! 😂

Lisa
Phew! 😂 C U tomorrow!

17

Play is to first or second! Watch for the sacrifice!

Thanks to Stacy, we all knew what to do when the batter bunted.

TINK!

Bunt! Heads up at first!

Out!

Woo-hoo!

25

As I watched my sister, things were getting serious.

Iris, you have to be louder, or we're going to collide for real!

Yeah. Got it.

Marina is taking the fun out of playing for everyone.

So I decided to put the fun back in.

Aye, aye, Captain Na-na!

Captain Na-na?

Anya, set up those cones for a fielding drill.

SMASH!

Hey, everyone, we'll be playing the Phoenix on—

That ball is going, going, GONE!

Did you see their hitters? We'll have to work extra hard if we want to beat the Phoenix.

HA HA HA HA HA!

Say, if we're the Dragons, we should really *scorch* the other teams, right?

My joking around seemed to help my teammates.

Can you throw me that ball, Anya?

Why, I'd *glove* to!

Unfortunately, not everyone on the team appreciated my sense of humor.

You need to take tomorrow's game seriously. Got it?

Got it . . . Captain Na-na!

27

It didn't take a genius to see that Lisa blamed herself for our shrinking lead.

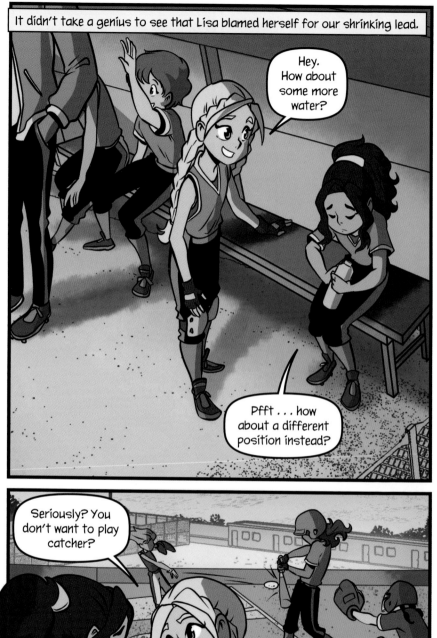

That evening, my mind was whirling.

We finally beat the Rocs by two runs.

I'm sorry we missed it, but we'll be at your next games.

Is Stacy really going to play for the Fireballs?

Will Lisa quit if she has to catch for Marina?

Earth to Anya! Hey, Anya, can you change the channel?

THUD! THUD!

Hurry up in there, bathroom hog!

If Lisa quits, where will Coach Watkins get another catcher?

Would Coach consider me to be catcher?

I wanted the position more than anything. But wanting it wasn't enough.

33

The old ballfield hadn't been used for years.

This seems like a good place if you want to keep your private lessons private.

I hope I don't trip like I did at tryouts!

Yeah, that was memorable! But you'll get used to the pads in time.

We started by working on the basics.

You'll be off-balance if your stance isn't wide enough.

Right. I'd fall backward . . . again.

35

The catcher is the captain of the defense.

So, if you have a runner on first with no outs, what do you tell your teammates?

Watch for a steal or a bunt. Play is to first or second.

Good. But be louder, so everyone can hear you!

WATCH FOR A STEAL OR A BUNT! PLAY IS TO FIRST OR SECOND!

Now, that's what I'm talking about!

Speaking of talking, what did you say to Marina during the Griffins' game?

Hey, you got this! Now send in some sizzlers, okay?

That worked?

She ended the inning with a strikeout, didn't she?

I didn't see Marina until practice.

Good news! Coach Watkins says you should suit up!

Awesome! What did Marina say when you told her?

Me? I didn't tell her. I thought you were going to yesterday!

Uh, oh.

Hey!

What's this about you playing catcher?

Back-up catcher.

And only while I'm playing for the Fireballs.

41

There was a lot riding on how I did behind the plate.

Stacy needs me to do well so she can play for the Fireballs.

Good throw, Anya!

Lisa hopes I'll do well so I can catch for Marina.

Marina, go in for Christie.

As for me, I don't care who's pitching.

I just want to be catcher.

Marina wasn't kidding about starting early. The next day the sun was barely up before we hit the field.

Hurry up and get your gear on. We've got work to do.

Shouldn't we wait for Stacy?

Stacy is meeting with the Fireballs today. It's just you and me.

I hadn't caught for my sister for more than a year. Her pitches were even harder and faster than I remembered.

I'll start with a few easy ones.

That was an easy one?

WHAP!

But her throws weren't always accurate.

Why did you move?

Um, so I could catch the ball?

Or should I have let it blow by me?

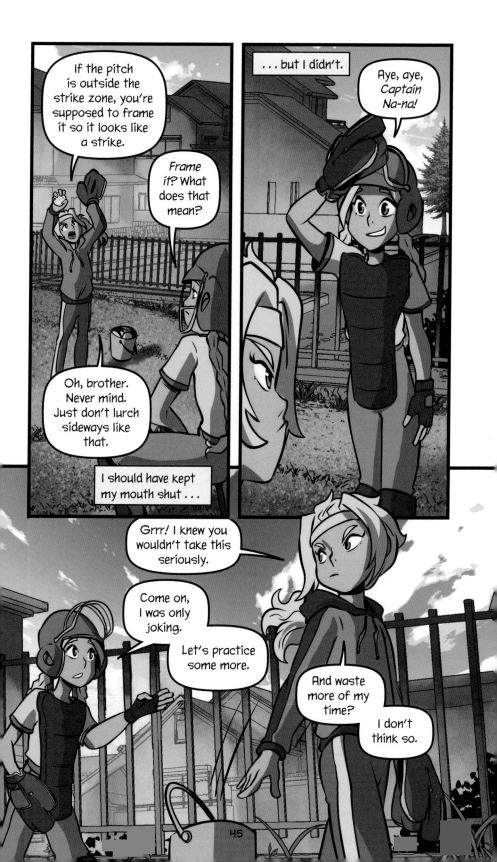

With the Phoenix game looming, I spent the morning watching how-to videos to get some catching tips.

Ugh, enough. I need to move!

What is Marina doing here? Pitchers hardly ever bat.

Well, that was terrible.

Ha! And that's why!

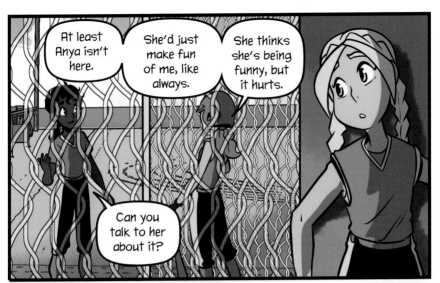

At least Anya isn't here.

She'd just make fun of me, like always.

She thinks she's being funny, but it hurts.

Can you talk to her about it?

She'd just make more jokes.

Then I'd get mad at her.

And then things would be even worse.

I don't know how we're going to play together as pitcher and catcher against the Phoenix.

That bike ride home was the longest ever.

I thought hard about what Marina said.

THMP!

She'd just make fun of me, like always.

I couldn't have become a catcher without the team's support, especially Stacy.

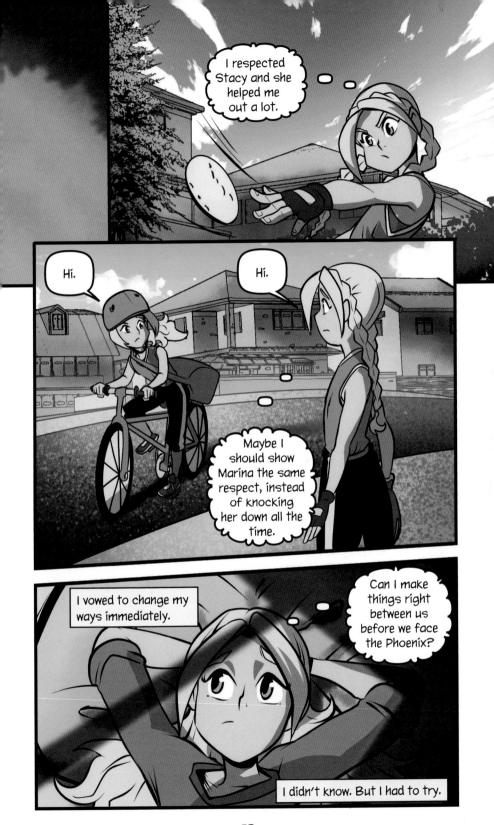

54

I slept like a baby that night and woke up to sunshine.

It's a perfect softball kind of day!

Still, I was kind of nervous about the game.

Marina was on edge too. But for once, I didn't make it worse by teasing her.

Let's get going so we have plenty of time to warm up.

Okay!

Coach is starting me in left field, and it's all thanks to you!

That's awesome! But you earned that position on your own.

57

60

For one long moment, I thought Marina had forgotten our old secret sister signal.

But she remembered.

Love you, Ya-ya!

63

VISUAL DISCUSSION QUESTIONS

1. A high, wide view of a location helps to establish where a story takes place or what kind of story it will be. Can you tell what type of story will be told just by looking at this panel?

2. A sequence of panels can help to quickly show the action of a scene. Can you tell what's happening in this group of panels?

Well, that was terrible.

Ha! And that's why!

3. Facial expressions and hand gestures can often show what a character is thinking or feeling more than words. What feelings do you think Marina is showing in this scene?

4. A split panel can show something that happens in different places at the same time. Can you think of another way the artist could have shown these characters speaking on the phone?

5. Dramatic lighting is often used to show the mood of a scene in a story. Look at the lighting in the above panel. Can you tell what Anya is thinking or feeling?

MORE ABOUT SOFTBALL

Slow-Pitch vs. Fast-Pitch Softball

There are some different rules between slow-pitch and fast-pitch softball. Here are a few of the differences between the two versions.

1. The Pitch

In slow-pitch softball, a pitcher uses a half-windmill windup. She swings her arm back until it's parallel to the ground. Then she swings it forward and releases the ball so it arcs up in the air as it heads toward home plate.

In fast pitch, the pitcher holds the ball in front of her. With a super-fast motion, she rotates her arm backward in a full circle while taking a big stride forward. She releases the ball as it passes her hip to throw it like a rocket toward home plate. Top-notch pitchers can throw at speeds up to 60 miles (96.6 kilometers) per hour!

2. Number of Players

Slow, arcing pitches allow batters to hit a lot of long fly balls and home runs. Unlike baseball and fast-pitch teams, slow-pitch teams have four outfielders instead of three. The extra outfield position gives younger players the chance to make catches and throw out runners.

3. Catcher's Equipment

Catchers in fast-pitch softball squat directly behind home plate and handle pitches coming at them at full speed. They need to wear complete protective gear including a catcher's mask, a padded chest protector, and shin guards. Catchers in slow pitch are less likely to be injured by a pitch. They aren't required to wear any equipment. But many catchers still choose to wear a mask to protect their faces.

4. Stealing

Stealing bases is allowed in fast-pitch softball but not in slow pitch. However, leading, or taking a few steps away from the base before the ball is pitched, is not permitted. A runner can only leave her base when the ball leaves the pitcher's hand.

A catcher is always watching for runners to steal. When she thinks a runner might try it, she rises up out of her crouch just a little bit. When the pitch hits her glove, she's ready to throw sooner—and hopefully beat the runner to get an out.

5. Bunting

Bunting isn't allowed in slow pitch. But the play is an important and exciting part of the fast-pitch game. Bunting can help a runner steal or advance safely to the next base. A bunt is a short hit directed toward the ground near home plate. In the time it takes the catcher or another player to get the ball, a base runner can often reach the next base. Sometimes the batter can get to first base too. But bunting can be risky. If the catcher throws the ball quickly, she can get the batter or the runner out. Sometimes defenses can even get both of them out to get a thrilling double play!

GLOSSARY

chest protector (CHEST pruh-TEK-ter)—a protective pad worn over the chest by a catcher or an umpire to shield the body

infield (IN-feeld)—the area of a softball field that includes first, second, and third bases, and home plate

inning (IN-ing)—a period of time during a softball game in which each team gets a turn at bat until they get three outs

intense (in-TENS)—having strong feelings about or showing a strong reaction to something

league (LEEG)—a group of sports teams that play against each other

outfield (OUT-feeld)—the grassy area behind first, second, and third bases

pointer (POIN-tur)—a piece of advice on how to succeed at something

postpone (pohst-POHN)—to delay something until a later time

sacrifice (SAK-ruh-fise)—to hit a ball in a way that results in an out, but allows a runner to advance to the next base

strike zone (STRIKE ZOHN)—the area above home plate between a batter's knees and shoulders

tryout (TRAHY-out)—a trial or test to determine if someone is skilled enough to join a team

ABOUT THE AUTHOR

 **Stephanie True Peters** has been writing books for young readers for more than 25 years. Among her most recent titles are *Catch Soccer's Beats* and *Skateboard Summer* for Capstone's Jake Maddox Graphic Novels series. An avid reader, workout enthusiast, and beach wanderer, Stephanie enjoys spending time with her children, Jackson and Chloe, her husband Dan, and the family's two cats and two rabbits. She lives and works in Mansfield, Massachusetts.

ABOUT THE ARTISTS

Lelo Alves is an illustrator, animator, graphic designer, game designer, and musician in João Pessoa, Brazil. **Lelo has loved drawing since childhood. His friends and coworkers encouraged Lelo to pursue an education and career in illustration and design. Lelo currently works for publishers in Brazil, Portugal, and the United States.**

Berenice Muñiz is a graphic designer and illustrator from Monterrey, Mexico. She has done work for publicity agencies, art exhibitions, and even created her own webcomic. These days, Berenice is devoted to illustrating comics as part of the Graphikslava crew.

Jaymes Reed has operated the company Digital-CAPS: Comic Book Lettering since 2003. He has done lettering for many publishers, most notably Avatar Press. He's also the only letterer working with Inception Strategies, an Aboriginal-Australian publisher that develops social comics with public service messages for the Australian government. Jaymes is a 2012 and 2013 Shel Dorf Award Nominee.

READ THEM ALL!

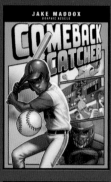